Marie A. Westlick,
Mantua,
Ohio.

1897.

MRS. SIDDONS AS THE TRAGIC MUSE (SIR J. REYNOLDS).

SHAKESPEARE'S

TRAGEDY OF

MACBETH.

EDITED, WITH NOTES,

BY

WILLIAM J. ROLFE, LITT. D.,

FORMERLY HEAD MASTER OF THE HIGH SCHOOL, CAMBRIDGE, MASS.

WITH ENGRAVINGS.

NEW YORK:

HARPER & BROTHERS, PUBLISHERS,

FRANKLIN SQUARE.

1895.

PREFACE.

In this edition of *Macbeth* the text is the result of a careful collation of the Folio of 1623 with all the modern editions that are of any critical value.

In the notes I have been under special obligations to Mr. Horace Howard Furness, who has kindly allowed me to make free use of his "New Variorum" edition of the play (Philadelphia, 1873), in which much of my work was already done to my hand, and who has given me other help which I could hardly have got elsewhere. My indebtedness to him is acknowledged on almost every page, but I do not know how to state it in full.

So much has been written on *Macbeth* that the main difficulty has been in selecting and condensing from it; but, as in former volumes of the series, I have preferred to give too much rather than too little, bearing in mind that the great majority of readers and students have not access to a full Shakespearian library. The *teacher*, whether he have that privilege or not, will find Mr. Furness's edition invaluable for reference. It is a complete *apparatus criticus* compressed into a single volume, presenting in the most convenient form what one would else have to "turn o'er many books" to find, some of them so rare and costly as to be within the reach of only a favored few.

THE HARMUIR, OR HEATH.

CONTENTS.

THE VILLAGE OF GLAMIS.

GLAMIS CASTLE.

INTRODUCTION TO MACBETH.

I. THE HISTORY OF THE PLAY.

Macbeth was first printed in the folio of 1623, where it occupies pages 131 to 151 inclusive, in the division of "Tragedies." It was registered in the books of the Stationers' Company, on the 8th of November, 1623, by Blount and Jaggard, the publishers of the folio, as one of the plays "not formerly entered to other men." It was written between 1604 and 1610; the former limit being fixed by the allusion to the union of England and Scotland under James I. (iv. 1. 120), and the latter by the MS. Diary of Dr. Simon Forman, who saw the play performed "at the Globe, 1610, the 20th of April, Saturday."* It may then have been a

* This MS. is preserved in the Bodleian Library at Oxford. The passage referring to *Macbeth* is as follows, the spelling being modernized:

"In Macbeth, at the Globe, 1610, the 20th of April, Saturday, there was to be observed first how Macbeth and Banquo, two noblemen of

new play,* but it is more probable, as nearly all the critics agree, that it was written in 1605 or 1606. The accession

Scotland, riding through a wood, there stood before them three women, fairies or nymphs, and saluted Macbeth, saying three times unto him, Hail, Macbeth, king of Codor, for thou shall be a king, but shall beget no kings, etc. Then said Banquo, What, all to Macbeth and nothing to me? Yes, said the nymphs, Hail, to thee, Banquo; thou shall beget kings, yet be no king. And so they departed, and came to the Court of Scotland, to Duncan king of Scots, and it was in the days of Edward the Confessor. And Duncan bade them both kindly welcome, and made Macbeth [*sic*] forthwith Prince of Northumberland, and sent him home to his own castle, and appointed Macbeth to provide for him, for he would sup with him the next day at night, and did so. And Macbeth contrived to kill Duncan, and through the persuasion of his wife did that night murder the king in his own castle, being his guest. And there were many prodigies seen that night and the day before. And when Macbeth had murdered the king, the blood on his hands could not be washed off by any means, nor from his wife's hands, which handled the bloody daggers in hiding them, by which means they became both much amazed and affronted. The murder being known, Duncan's two sons fled, the one to England, the [other to] Wales, to save themselves; they being fled, they were supposed guilty of the murder of their father, which was nothing so. Then was Macbeth crowned king, and then he for fear of Banquo, his old companion, that he should beget kings but be no king himself, he contrived the death of Banquo, and caused him to be murdered on the way as he rode. The next night, being at supper with his noblemen, whom he had bid to a feast, to the which also Banquo should have come, he began to speak of noble Banquo, and to wish that he were there. And as he thus did, standing up to drink a carouse to him, the ghost of Banquo came and sat down in his chair behind him. And he, turning about to sit down again, saw the ghost of Banquo, which fronted him so that he fell in a great passion of fear and fury, uttering many words about his murder, by which, when they heard that Banquo was murdered, they suspected Macbeth. Then Macduff fled to England to the king's son, and so they raised an army and came into Scotland, and at Dunscenanyse overthrew Macbeth. In the mean time, while Macduff was in England, Macbeth slew Macduff's wife and children, and after, in the battle, Macduff slew Macbeth. Observe also how Macbeth's queen did rise in the night in her sleep, and walked, and talked and confessed all, and the Doctor noted her words."

* The Clarendon Press editors think it was, since otherwise Forman

of James made Scottish subjects popular in England, and the tale of *Macbeth and Banquo* would be one of the first to be brought forward, as Banquo was held to be an ancestor of the new king. A Latin "interlude" on this subject was performed at Oxford in 1605, on the occasion of the king's visit to the city; but there is no reason for supposing, as Farmer did, that Shakespeare got the hint of his tragedy from that source.

It is barely possible that there was an earlier play on the subject of Macbeth. Collier finds in the Registers of the Stationers' Company, under date of August 27, 1596, the entry of a "Ballad of Makdobeth," which he gives plausible reasons for supposing to have been a drama, and not a "ballad" properly so called. There appears to be a reference to the same piece in Kemp's *Nine Days' Wonder*, printed in 1600, where it is called a "miserable stolne story," the work of "a penny Poet."

Steevens maintained that Shakespeare was indebted, in the supernatural parts of *Macbeth*, to *The Witch*, a play by Thomas Middleton, which was discovered in manuscript towards the close of the last century. Malone at first took the same view of the subject, but afterwards came to the conclusion

"would scarcely have been at the pains to make an elaborate summary of the plot." But that merely shows that the play was new to *him*, and that the story made a deep impression upon him.

The same editors find "an obvious allusion to the ghost of Banquo" in Beaumont and Fletcher's *Knight of the Burning Pestle*, produced in 1611:

> "When thou art at the table with thy friends,
> Merry in heart and fill'd with swelling wine,
> I'll come in midst of all thy pride and mirth,
> Invisible to all men but thyself;"

and they think that "this supports the inference that *Macbeth* was in 1611 a new play, and fresh in the recollection of the audience." But Mr. Halliwell finds quite as obvious an allusion to Banquo's ghost in the *Puritan*, printed in 1607: "we'll ha' the ghost i' th' white sheet sit at upper end o' th' table."

that Middleton's play was the later production, and that he must therefore be the plagiarist. The Clarendon Press editors take the ground that there are portions of Macbeth which Shakespeare did not write; that these were interpolated after the poet's death, or at least after he had ceased to be connected with the theatre; and that "the interpolator was, not improbably, Thomas Middleton." Mr. F. G. Fleay also, in a paper read before the New Shakspere Society, June 26, 1874, makes this statement: "*Macbeth* in its present state is an altered copy of the original drama, and the alterations were made by Middleton."*

These views have found little favour with other Shakespearian critics. A more satisfactory explanation of the imperfections of the play ascribes them to the haste with which it was written.† White, who refers its composition to "the period between October, 1604, and August, 1605," remarks: "I am the more inclined to this opinion from the indications which the play itself affords that it was produced upon an emergency. It exhibits throughout the hasty execution of a grand and clearly conceived design. But the haste is that

* The Clarendon Press editors and Mr. Fleay agree quite closely in regard to the portions of the play which they assign to Middleton. Their criticisms on most of these passages are mentioned in our notes. We may refer those who are interested in the literature of the subject to the C. P. ed. of *Macbeth*, p. viii. fol., Furness's "New Variorum" ed. of *Macbeth*, p. 388 fol., *Transactions of New Shakspere Society*, 1874, p. 339 fol. and 498 fol., and Fleay's *Shakespeare Manual*, part ii., chap. x.

† Mr. F. J. Furnivall, in his introduction to Gervinus's *Commentaries on Shakespeare*, translated by Miss Bunnett (London: 1874), referring to Mr. Fleay's criticisms, says: "Mr. Hales thinks that the change to the trochaic metre* in Hecate's speeches, and their inferior quality, point to a different hand, perhaps Middleton's; but that is all of the play that he or I (who still hesitate) can yet surrender. The wonderful pace at which the play was plainly written—a feverish haste drives it on—will account for many weaknesses in detail."

* This is evidently a slip of the pen. Mr. Furnivall meant to write "to the *iambic* metre." The witches, as Mr. Hales remarks, always speak in trochaics, and Hecate always in iambics (*Trans. of New Shaksp. Soc.* 1874, p. 507).

of a master of his art, who, with conscious command of its resources, and in the frenzy of a grand inspiration, works out his composition to its minutest detail of essential form, leaving the work of surface finish for the occupation of cooler leisure. What the Sistine Madonna was to Raphael, it seems that *Macbeth* was to Shakespeare—a magnificent impromptu; that kind of impromptu which results from the application of well-disciplined powers and rich stores of thought to a subject suggested by occasion. I am inclined to regard *Macbeth* as, for the most part, a specimen of Shakespeare's unelaborated, if not unfinished, writing, in the maturity and highest vitality of his genius. It abounds in instances of extremest compression and most daring ellipsis, while it exhibits in every scene a union of supreme dramatic and poetic power, and in almost every line an imperially irresponsible control of language. Hence, I think, its lack of completeness of versification in certain passages, and also some of the imperfection of the text, the thought in which the compositors were not always able to follow and apprehend."

II. THE HISTORICAL SOURCES OF THE PLAY.

Shakespeare drew the materials for the plot of *Macbeth* from Holinshed's "Chronicles of Englande, Scotlande, and Ireland," the first edition of which was published in 1577, and the second (which was doubtless the one the poet used) in 1586–87.* The extracts from Holinshed in our notes will show that the main incidents are taken from his account of

* Rev. C. E. Moberly, in his edition of *Macbeth* (London: 1872), says that the whole story is told "in *Albion's England*, published just before Elizabeth's death." The first edition of *Albion's England*, containing thirteen "books" of the poem, appeared in 1586, but the story of Macbeth is in the "Fifteenth Book," which forms part of the "Continuance," first published in 1606.

As Shakespeare used the second edition of Holinshed in writing *Richard II.* (see our edition of that play, p. 14), there can be no doubt that he used it for *Macbeth*, which was written later.

two separate events—the murder of Duncan by Macbeth, and that of King Duffe, the great-grandfather of Lady Macbeth, by Donwald. It will be seen, too, that Shakespeare has deviated in other respects from the chronicle, especially in the character of Banquo.

Although, as Knight remarks, "the interest of *Macbeth* is not an *historical* interest," so that it matters little whether the action is true or has been related as true, we may add, for the benefit of our younger readers, that the story of the drama is almost wholly apocryphal. The more authentic history is thus summarized by Sir Walter Scott:

"Duncan, by his mother Beatrice a grandson of Malcolm II., succeeded to the throne on his grandfather's death, in 1033: he reigned only six years. Macbeth, his near relation, also a grandchild of Malcolm II., though by the mother's side, was stirred up by ambition to contest the throne with the possessor. The Lady of Macbeth also, whose real name was Graoch, had deadly injuries to avenge on the reigning prince. She was the granddaughter of Kenneth IV., killed 1003, fighting against Malcolm II.; and other causes for revenge animated the mind of her who has been since painted as the sternest of women. The old annalists add some instigations of a supernatural kind to the influence of a vindictive woman over an ambitious husband. Three women, of more than human stature and beauty, appeared to Macbeth in a dream or vision, and hailed him successively by the titles of Thane of Cromarty, Thane of Moray, which the king afterwards bestowed on him, and finally by that of King of Scots; this dream, it is said, inspired him with the seductive hopes so well expressed in the drama.

"Macbeth broke no law of hospitality in his attempt on Duncan's life. He attacked and slew the king at a place called Bothgowan, or the Smith's House, near Elgin, in 1039, and not, as has been supposed, in his own castle of Inverness. The act was bloody, as was the complexion of the times;

but, in very truth, the claim of Macbeth to the throne, according to the rule of Scottish succession, was better than that of Duncan. As a king, the tyrant so much exclaimed against was, in reality, a firm, just, and equitable prince.* Apprehensions of danger from a party which Malcolm, the eldest son of the slaughtered Duncan, had set on foot in Northumberland, and still maintained in Scotland, seem, in process of time, to have soured the temper of Macbeth, and rendered him formidable to his nobility. Against Macduff, in particular, the powerful Maormor of Fife, he had uttered some threats which occasioned that chief to fly from the court of Scotland. Urged by this new counsellor, Siward, the Danish Earl of Northumberland, invaded Scotland in the year 1054, displaying his banner in behalf of the banished Malcolm. Macbeth engaged the foe in the neighbourhood of his celebrated castle of Dunsinane. He was defeated, but escaped from the battle, and was slain at Lumphanan in 1056."

Whether Shakespeare was ever in Scotland is a question that has been much discussed. Knight (*Biography*, ed. 1865, p. 420 fol.) endeavours to prove that the poet visited that country in 1589, but most of the editors agree that there is no satisfactory evidence of his having ever been there.†

III. CRITICAL COMMENTS ON THE PLAY.

[*From Hazlitt's "Characters of Shakespeare's Plays."*‡]

Macbeth (generally speaking) is done upon a stronger and more systematic principle of contrast than any other of

* As Rev. Mr. Moberly remarks, this view is confirmed by Mr. E. A. Freeman (*Norman Conquest*, ii. p. 55): "All genuine Scottish tradition points to the reign of Macbeth as a period of unusual peace and prosperity in that disturbed land."

† For a good summary of the discussion see Furness's *Macbeth*, p. 407 fol.

‡ *Characters of Shakespeare's Plays*, by William Hazlitt, edited by W. Carew Hazlitt (London, 1869), p. 17.

Shakespeare's plays. It moves upon the verge of an abyss, and is a constant struggle between life and death. The action is desperate and the reaction is dreadful. It is a huddling together of fierce extremes, a war of opposite natures which of them shall destroy the other. There is nothing but what has a violent end or violent beginnings. The lights and shades are laid on with a determined hand; the transitions from triumph to despair, from the height of terror to the repose of death, are sudden and startling; every passion brings in its fellow-contrary, and the thoughts pitch and jostle against each other as in the dark. The whole play is an unruly chaos of strange and forbidden things, where the ground rocks under our feet. Shakespeare's genius here took its full swing, and trod upon the farthest bounds of nature and passion. This circumstance will account for the abruptness and violent antitheses of the style, the throes and labour which run through the expression, and from defects will turn them into beauties. "So fair and foul a day," etc. "Such welcome and unwelcome news together." "Men's lives are like the flowers in their caps, dying or ere they sicken." "Look like the innocent flower, but be the serpent under it." The scene before the castle-gate follows the appearance of the witches on the heath, and is followed by a midnight murder. Duncan is cut off betimes by treason leagued with witchcraft, and Macduff is ripped untimely from his mother's womb to avenge his death. Macbeth, after the death of Banquo, wishes for his presence in extravagant terms, "To all, and him, we thirst," and when his ghost appears, cries out, "Avaunt and quit my sight," and being gone, he is "himself again." . . . In Lady Macbeth's speech, "Had he not resembled my father as he slept, I had done't," there is murder and filial piety together, and in urging him to fulfil his vengeance against the defenceless king, her thoughts spare the blood neither of infants nor old age. The description of the witches is full of the same contradictory principle;

they "rejoice when good kings bleed,"* they are neither of the earth nor the air, but both; "they should be women, but their beards forbid it;" they take all the pains possible to lead Macbeth on to the height of his ambition, only to betray him "in deeper consequence," and after showing him all the pomp of their art, discover their malignant delight in his disappointed hopes by that bitter taunt, "Why stands Macbeth thus amazedly?" We might multiply such instances everywhere. . . .

[*From Mrs. Jameson's "Characteristics of Women."* †]

In the mind of Lady Macbeth, ambition is represented as the ruling motive, an intense overmastering passion, which is gratified at the expense of every just and generous principle, and every feminine feeling. In the pursuit of her object, she is cruel, treacherous, and daring. She is doubly, trebly dyed in guilt and blood; for the murder she instigates is rendered more frightful by disloyalty and ingratitude, and by the violation of all the most sacred claims of kindred and hospitality. When her husband's more kindly nature shrinks from the perpetration of the deed of horror, she, like an evil genius, whispers him on to his damnation. The full measure of her wickedness is never disguised, the magnitude and atrocity of her crime is never extenuated, forgotten, or forgiven, in the whole course of the play. . . . Lady Macbeth's amazing power of intellect, her inexorable determination of purpose, her superhuman strength of nerve, render her as fearful in herself as her deeds are hateful; yet she is not a mere monster of depravity, with whom we have nothing in common, nor a meteor whose destroying path we watch in ignorant affright and amaze. She is a terrible impersonation of evil

* Mr. Furness, quoting this in his edition of *Macbeth* (p. 415), asks: "Is it not passing strange that Hazlitt should have forgotten that this line is none of Shakespeare's?"

† American ed. (Boston: 1857), p. 443 fol.

passions and mighty powers, never so far removed from our own nature as to be cast beyond the pale of our sympathies; for the woman herself remains a woman to the last—still linked with her sex and with humanity.

We must bear in mind that the first idea of murdering Duncan is not suggested by Lady Macbeth to her husband: it springs within *his* mind, and is revealed to us [i. 3. 130–137] before his first interview with his wife—before she is introduced or even alluded to.

It will be said that the same "horrid suggestion" presents itself spontaneously to her, on the reception of his letter; or, rather, that the letter acts upon her mind as a prophecy of the Weird Sisters on the mind of her husband, kindling the latent passion for empire into a quenchless flame. We are prepared to see the train of evil, first lighted by hellish agency, extend itself to *her* through the medium of her husband; but we are spared the more revolting idea that it originated with her. The guilt is thus more equally divided than we should suppose, when we hear people pitying "the noble nature of Macbeth," bewildered and goaded on to crime, solely or chiefly by the instigation of his wife.

It is true that she afterwards appears the more active agent of the two; but it is less through her preëminence in wickedness than through her superiority of intellect. The eloquence—the fierce, fervid eloquence with which she bears down the relenting and reluctant spirit of her husband, the dexterous sophistry with which she wards off his objections, her artful and affected doubts of his courage—the sarcastic manner in which she lets fall the word coward—a word which no man can endure from another, still less from a woman, and least of all from a woman he loves—and the bold address with which she removes all obstacles, silences all arguments, overpowers all scruples, and marshals the way before him, absolutely make us shrink before the commanding intellect of the woman, with a terror in which interest and admiration are strangely mingled.

Again, in the murdering scene, the obdurate inflexibility of purpose with which she drives on Macbeth to the execution of their project, and her masculine indifference to blood and death, would inspire unmitigated disgust and horror, but for the involuntary consciousness that it is produced rather by the exertion of a strong power over herself than by absolute depravity of disposition and ferocity of temper. This impression of her character is brought home at once to our very hearts with the most profound knowledge of the springs of nature within us, the most subtle mastery over their various operations, and a feeling of dramatic effect not less wonderful. The very passages in which Lady Macbeth displays the most savage and relentless determination are so worded as to fill the mind with the idea of sex, and place the *woman* before us in all her dearest attributes, at once softening and refining the horror and rendering it more intense. Thus when she reproaches her husband for his weakness—"From this time such I account thy love." Again, "Come to my woman's breasts And take my milk for gall," etc. "I have given suck, and know how tender 'tis To love the babe that milks me," etc. And lastly, in the moment of extremest terror comes that unexpected touch of feeling, so startling, yet so wonderfully true to nature—"Had he not resembled my father," etc. Thus in one of Weber's or Beethoven's grand symphonies, some unexpected soft minor chord or passage will steal on the ear, heard amid the magnificent crash of harmony, making the blood pause and filling the eyes with unbidden tears.

It is particularly observable that in Lady Macbeth's concentrated, strong-nerved ambition, the ruling passion of her mind, there is yet a touch of womanhood: she is ambitious less for herself than for her husband. It is fair to think this, because we have no reason to draw any other inference either from her words or her actions. In her famous soliloquy, after reading her husband's letter, she does not once refer to herself. It is of him she thinks: she wishes to see her husband on the throne, and to place the sceptre within *his* grasp. The strength of her affection adds strength to her ambition. Although in the old story of Boethius we are told that the wife of Macbeth "burned with unquenchable desire to bear the name of queen," yet in the aspect under which Shakespeare has represented the character to us the selfish part of this ambition is kept out of sight. We must remark also, that in Lady Macbeth's reflections on her husband's character, and on that milkiness of nature which she fears "may impede him from the golden round," there is no indication of female scorn: there is exceeding pride, but no egotism, in the sentiment or the expression; no want of wifely or womanly respect and love for *him*, but, on the contrary, a sort of unconsciousness of her own mental superiority, which she betrays rather than asserts, as interesting in itself as it is most admirably conceived and delineated. Nor is there any thing vulgar in her ambition; as the strength of her affections lends to it something profound and concentrated, so her splendid imagination invests the object of her desire with its own radiance. We cannot trace in her grand and capacious mind that it is the mere baubles and trappings of royalty which dazzle and allure her: hers is the sin of the "star-bright apostate," and she plunges with her husband into the abyss of guilt to procure for "all their days and nights sole sovereign sway and masterdom." She revels, she luxuriates, in her dream of power. She reaches at the golden diadem which is to sear her brain; she perils life and soul for its attainment, with an enthusiasm as perfect, a faith as settled, as that of the martyr who sees at the stake heaven and its crowns of glory opening upon him. . . .

Lady Macbeth having proposed the object to herself, and arrayed it with an ideal glory, fixes her eye steadily upon it, soars far above all womanish feelings and scruples to attain it, and stoops upon her victim with the strength and velocity of a vulture; but having committed unflinchingly the crime necessary for the attainment of her purpose, she stops there. After the murder of Duncan, we see Lady Macbeth, during the rest of the play, occupied in supporting the nervous weakness and sustaining the fortitude of her husband. . . . But she is nowhere represented as urging him on to new crimes; so far from it, that when Macbeth darkly hints his purposed assassination of Banquo, and she inquires his meaning, he replies, "Be innocent of the knowledge, dearest chuck, Till thou approve the deed." The same may be said of the destruction of Macduff's family. Every one must perceive how our detestation of the woman had been increased, if she had been placed before us as suggesting and abetting those additional cruelties into which Macbeth is hurried by his mental cowardice.

If my feeling of Lady Macbeth's character be just to the conception of the poet, then she is one who could steel herself to the commission of a crime from necessity and expediency, and be daringly wicked for a great end, but not likely to perpetrate gratuitous murders from any vague or selfish fears. I do not mean to say that the perfect confidence existing between herself and Macbeth could possibly leave her in ignorance of his actions or designs: that heart-broken and shuddering allusion to the murder of Lady Macduff (in the sleeping scene) proves the contrary. But she is nowhere brought before us in immediate connection with these horrors, and we are spared any flagrant proof of her participation in them. . . .

Another thing has always struck me. During the supper scene, . . . her indignant rebuke [to her husband], her low whispered remonstrance, the sarcastic emphasis with which she combats his sick fancies, and endeavours to recall him to himself, have an intenseness, a severity, a bitterness, which makes the blood creep. Yet, when the guests are dismissed, and they are left alone, she says no more, and not a syllable of reproach or scorn escapes her: a few words in submissive reply to his questions, and an entreaty to seek repose, are all she permits herself to utter. There is a touch of pathos and of tenderness in this silence which has always affected me beyond expression: it is one of the most masterly and most beautiful traits of character in the whole play.

Lastly, it is clear that in a mind constituted like that of Lady Macbeth conscience must wake some time or other, and bring with it remorse closed by despair, and despair by death. This great moral retribution was to be displayed to us—but how? Lady Macbeth is not a woman to start at shadows; she mocks at air-drawn daggers; she sees no imagined spectres rise from the tomb to appal or accuse her. The towering bravery of *her* mind disdains the visionary terrors which haunt her weaker husband. We know, or rather feel, that she who could give a voice to the most direful intent, and call on the spirits that wait on mortal thoughts to "unsex her," and "stop up all access and passage of remorse"—to that remorse would have given nor tongue nor sound; and that rather than have uttered a complaint, she would have held her breath and died. To have given her a confidant, though in the partner of her guilt, would have been a degrading resource, and have disappointed and enfeebled all our previous impressions of her character; yet justice is to be done, and we are to be made acquainted with that which the woman herself would have suffered a thousand deaths rather than have betrayed. In the sleeping scene we have a glimpse into that inward hell: the seared brain and broken heart are laid bare before us in the helplessness of slumber. By a judgment the most sublime ever imagined, yet the most unforced, natural, and inevitable, the sleep of her who murdered sleep is no longer repose, but a condensation of resistless horrors which the prostrate intellect and the powerless will can neither baffle nor repel. We shudder and are satisfied; yet our human sympathies are again touched; we rather sigh over the ruin than exult in it; and after watching her through this wonderful scene with a sort of fascination, we dismiss the unconscious, helpless, despair-stricken murderess with a feeling which Lady Macbeth, in her waking strength, with all her awe-commanding powers about her, could never have excited.

It is here especially we perceive that sweetness of nature which in Shakespeare went hand in hand with his astonishing powers. He never confounds that line of demarcation which eternally separates good from evil, yet he never places evil before us without exciting in some way a consciousness of the opposite good which shall balance and relieve it. . . .

What would not the firmness, the self-command, the enthusiasm, the intellect, the ardent affections of this woman have performed, if properly directed? but the object being unworthy of the effort, the end is disappointment, despair, and death.

The power of religion could alone have controlled such a mind; but it is the misery of a very proud, strong, and gifted spirit, without sense of religion, that instead of looking upward to find a superior, it looks around and sees all things as subject to itself. Lady Macbeth is placed in a dark, ignorant, iron age; her powerful intellect is slightly tinged with its credulity and superstitions, but she has no religious feeling to restrain the force of will. She is a stern fatalist in principle and action—"What is done, is done," and would be done over again under the same circumstances; her remorse is without repentance or any reference to an offended Deity; it arises from the pang of a wounded conscience, the recoil of the violated feelings of nature; it is the horror of the past, not the terror of the future; the torture of self-condemnation, not the fear of judgment; it is strong as her soul, deep as her guilt, fatal as her resolve, and terrible as her crime.

If it should be objected to this view of Lady Macbeth's character, that it engages our sympathies in behalf of a perverted being, and that to leave her so strong a power upon our feelings in the midst of such supreme wickedness involves a moral wrong, I can only reply in the words of Dr. Channing, that "in this and the like cases our interest fastens on what is *not* evil in the character—that there is something kindling and ennobling in the consciousness, however awakened, of the energy which resides in mind: and many a virtuous man has borrowed new strength from the force, constancy, aud dauntless courage of evil agents."

This is true; and might he not have added that many a powerful and gifted spirit has learned humility and self-government from beholding how far the energy which resides in mind may be degraded and perverted?

[*From Fletcher's "Studies of Shakespeare."**]

Macbeth seems inspired by the very genius of the tempest. This drama shows us the gathering, the discharge, and the dispelling of a domestic and political storm, which takes its peculiar hue from the individual character of the hero. It is not in the spirit of mischief that animates the "weird sisters," nor in the passionate and strong-willed ambition of Lady Macbeth, that we find the mainspring of this tragedy, but in the disproportioned though poetically tempered soul of Macbeth himself. A character like this, of extreme selfishness, with a most irritable fancy, must produce, even in ordinary circumstances, an excess of morbid apprehensiveness; which, however, as we see in him, is not inconsistent with the greatest physical courage, but generates of necessity the most entire moral cowardice. When, therefore, a man

* *Studies of Shakespeare, etc.*, by George Fletcher (London, 1847), p. 109 fol.

like this, ill enough qualified even for the honest and straightforward transactions of life, has brought himself to snatch at an ambitious object by the commission of one great sanguinary crime, the new and false position in which he finds himself by his very success will but startle and exasperate him to escape, as Macbeth says, from "horrible imaginings" by the perpetration of greater and greater actual horrors, till inevitable destruction comes upon us amidst universal execration. Such, briefly, are the story and the moral of *Macbeth*. The passionate ambition and indomitable will of his lady, though agents indispensable to urge such a man to the one decisive act which is to compromise him in his own opinion and that of the world, are by no means primary springs of the dramatic action. Nor do the "weird sisters" themselves do more than aid collaterally in impelling a man, the inherent evil of whose nature and purpose has predisposed him to take their equivocal suggestions in the most mischievous sense. And, finally, the very thunder-cloud which, from the beginning almost to the ending, wraps this fearful tragedy in physical darkness and lurid glare, does but reflect and harmonize with the moral blackness of the piece. . . .

The very starting-point for an inquiry into the real, inherent, and habitual nature of Macbeth, independent of those particular circumstances which form the action of the play, lies manifestly, though the critics have commonly overlooked it, in the question, With whom does the scheme of usurping the Scottish crown by the murder of Duncan actually originate? We sometimes find Lady Macbeth talked of as if she were the first contriver of the plot, and suggester of the assassination; but this notion is refuted, not only by implication, in the whole tenor of the piece, but most explicitly in i. 7. 48–52. Most commonly, however, the *witches* (as we find the "weird sisters" pertinaciously miscalled by all sorts of players and of critics) have borne the imputation of being the first to put this piece of mischief in the hero's mind. Yet the prophetic words in which the attainment of royalty is promised him contain not the remotest hint as to the means by which he is to arrive at it. They are simply "All hail, Macbeth! that shalt be king hereafter"—an announcement which, it is plain, should have rather inclined a man who was *not* already harbouring a scheme of guilty ambition to wait quietly the course of events. According to Macbeth's own admission, the words of the weird sisters on this occasion convey any thing rather than an incitement to murder to the mind of a man who is not meditating it already. This supernatural soliciting is only made such to the mind of Macbeth by the fact that he is already occupied with a purpose of assassination. This is the true answer to the question which he puts to himself in i. 3. 132–142. . . .

The first thing that strikes us in such a character is the intense selfishness—the total absence both of sympathetic feeling and moral principle—and the consequent incapability of remorse in the proper sense of the term. So far from finding any check to his design in the fact that the king bestows on him the forfeited title of the traitorous thane of Cawdor as an especial mark of confidence in his loyalty, this only serves to whet his own villainous purpose. The dramatist has brought this forcibly home to us in i. 4. 10–58. It is from no "compunctious visiting of nature," but from sheer *moral cowardice*—from fear of *retribution in this life*—that we find Macbeth shrinking, at the last moment, from the commission of his enormous crime. This will be seen the more attentively we consider i. 7. 1–25, and 31–35. In all this we trace a most clear consciousness of the impossibility that he should find of masking his guilt from the public eye—the odium which must consequently fall upon him in the opinions of men — and the retribution it would probably bring upon him. But here is no evidence of true *moral* repugnance, and as little of any religious scruple — "We'd jump the life to come." The dramatist, by this brief but significant parenthesis, has taken care to leave us in no doubt on a point so momentous towards forming a due estimate of the conduct of his hero. However, he feels, as we see, the dissuading motives of worldly prudence in all their force. But one devouring passion urges him on—the master-passion of his life—the lust of power, i. 7. 26. Still, it should seem that the considerations of policy and safety regarding this life might even have withheld him from the actual commission of the murder, had not the spirit of his wife come in to fortify his failing purpose. At all events, in the action of the drama it is her intervention, most decidedly, that terminates his irresolution, and urges him to the final perpetration of the crime which he himself had been the first to meditate.

It is most important that we should not mistake the nature of Macbeth's nervous perturbation while in the very act of consummating his first great crime. The more closely we examine it, the more we shall find it to be devoid of all genuine compunction. This character is one of intense selfishness, and is therefore incapable of any true moral repugnance to inflicting injury upon others; it shrinks only from encountering public odium, and the retribution which that may produce. Once persuaded that these will be avoided, Macbeth falters not in proceeding to apply the dagger to the throat of his sleeping guest. But here comes the display of the other part of his character—that extreme nervous irritability which, combined with an active intellect, produces in him so much highly poetical rumination—and at the same time, being unaccompanied with the slightest portion of self-command, subjects him to such signal moral cowardice. We feel bound the more earnestly to solicit the reader's attention to this distinction, since, though so clearly evident when once pointed out, it has escaped the penetration of some even of the most eminent critics. The poetry delivered by Macbeth, let us repeat, is not the poetry inspired by a glowing or even a feeling heart—it springs exclusively from a morbidly irritable fancy. We hesitate not to say that his wife mistakes, when she apprehends that the "milk of human kindness" will prevent him from "catching the nearest way." The fact is that, until after the banquet scene, she mistakes his character throughout. She judges of it too much from her own. Possessing generous feeling herself, she is susceptible of remorse. Full of self-control, and afflicted with no feverish imagination, she is dismayed by no vague apprehensions, no fantastic fears. Consequently, when her husband is withheld from his crime simply by that dread of contingent consequences which his fancy so infinitely exaggerates, she, little able to conceive of this, naturally ascribes some part of his repugnance to that "milk of human kindness," those "compunctious visitings of nature," of which she *can* conceive. . . . The perturbation which seizes Macbeth the instant he has struck the fatal blow, springs not, we repeat, from the slightest consideration for his victim. It is but the necessary recoil in the mind of every moral coward, upon the final performance of any decisive act from which accumulating selfish apprehensions have long withheld him — heightened and exaggerated by that excessive morbid irritability which, after his extreme selfishness, forms the next great moral characteristic of Macbeth. It is the sense of *all* the *possible* consequences to *himself*, and that alone, which rushes instantly and overwhelmingly upon his excitable fancy, so as to thunder its denunciations in his very ears.

The following scene shows us Macbeth, when his paroxysm ensuing upon the act of murder has quite spent itself, and he is become quite himself again — that is, the cold-blooded, cowardly, and treacherous assassin. Let any one who may have been disposed, with most of the critics, to believe that Shakespeare has delineated Macbeth as a character originally remorseful, well consider that speech of most elaborate, refined, and cold-blooded hypocrisy, in which, so speedily after his poetical whinings over his own *misfortune* in murdering Duncan, he alleges his motives for killing the two sleeping attendants. Assuredly, too, the dramatist had his reasons for causing Macbeth's hypocritically pathetic description of the scene of the murder to be thus publicly delivered in the presence of her whose hands have had so large a share in giving it that particular aspect. It lends double force to this most characteristic trait of Macbeth's deportment, that he should not be moved even by his lady's presence from delivering his affectedly indignant description of that bloody spectacle, in terms which must so vividly recall to her mind's eye the sickening objects which his own moral cowardice had compelled her to gaze upon. His words draw from Lady Macbeth the instant exclamation, "Help me hence, ho!" And shortly after she is carried out, still in a fainting state. . . . Even her indomitable resolution may well sink for the moment under a stroke so withering, for which, being totally unexpected, she came so utterly unprepared. It is remarkable that, upon her exclamation of distress, Macduff, and shortly after Banquo, cries out, "Look to the lady;" but that we find not the smallest sign of attention paid to her situation by Macbeth himself, who, arguing from his own character to hers, might regard it merely as a dexterous feigning on her part. A character like this, we cannot too often repeat, is one of the most cowardly selfishness, and most remorseless treachery, which all its poetical excitability does but exasperate into the perpetration of more and more extravagant enormities. . . .

"But in them nature's copy 's not eterne" has been interpreted by some critics as a deliberate suggesting, on Lady Macbeth's part, of the murder of Banquo and his son. . . . The natural and unstrained meaning of the words is, at most, nothing more than this, that Banquo and his son are not immortal. It is not she, but her husband, that draws a practical inference from this harmless proposition. That "they are assailable" may be "comfort," indeed, to him; but it is evidently none to her, and he proceeds to tell her that "there shall be done A deed of dreadful note." Still provokingly unapprehensive of his meaning, she asks him anxiously, "What 's to be done?" But he, after trying the ground so far, finding her utterly indisposed to concur in his present scheme, *does not dare* to communicate it to her in plain terms, lest she should chide the fears that prompt him to this new and gratuitous enormity, by virtue of the very same spirit that had made her combat those which had withheld him from the one great crime which she had deemed necessary to his elevation. It is only through a misapprehension, which unjustly lowers the generosity of her character and unduly exalts that of her husband, that so many critics have represented this passage ("Be innocent of the knowledge," etc.) as spoken by Macbeth out of a magnanimous desire to spare his wife all guilty participation in an act which at the same time, they tell us, he believes will give her satisfaction. It is, in fact, but a new and signal instance of his moral cowardice. . . . It is most important, in order to judge aright of Shakespeare's metaphysical, moral, and religious meaning in this great composition, that we should not mistake him as having represented that spirits of darkness are here permitted absolutely and gratuitously to seduce his hero from a state of perfectly innocent intention. It is plain that such an error at the outset vitiates and debases the moral to be drawn from the whole piece. Macbeth does not project the murder of Duncan because of his encounter with the weird sisters; the weird sisters encounter him because he has projected the murder—because they know him better than his royal master does, who tells us, "There is no art to find the mind's construction in the face." But these ministers of evil are privileged to see "the mind's construction" where human eye cannot penetrate—in the mind itself. They repair to the blasted heath because, as one of them says afterwards of Macbeth, "something wicked this way comes." In the next two lines—"I come, Graymalkin!—Paddock calls"—we perceive the connection of these beings with the world invisible and inaudible to mortal senses. It is only through these mysterious answers of theirs that we know any thing of the other beings whom they name thus grotesquely, sufficiently indicating spirits of deformity akin to themselves, and like themselves rejoicing in that elemental disturbance into which they mingle as they vanish from our view. . . .

In v. 3. 22–28, we have mere *poetical whining* over his own most merited situation. Yet Hazlitt, among others, talks of him as "calling back all our sympathy" by this reflection. Sympathy indeed! for the exquisitely refined selfishness of this most odious personage! This passage is exactly of a piece with that in which he envies the fate of his royal victim, and seems to think himself hardly used that Duncan, after all, should be better off than himself. Such exclamations, from such a character, are but an additional title to our detestation; the man who sets at naught all human ties should at least be prepared to abide in quiet the inevitable consequences. But the moral cowardice of Macbeth is consummate. . . .

There is no want of physical courage implied in Macbeth's declining the combat with Macduff. He may well believe that now, more than ever, it is time to "beware Macduff." He is at length convinced that "fate and metaphysical aid" are against him; and, consistent to the last in his hardened and whining selfishness, no thought of the intense blackness of his own perfidy interferes to prevent him from complaining of falsehood in those evil beings from whose very nature he should have expected nothing else. There is no cowardice, we say, in his declining the combat under such a conviction. Neither is there any courage in his renewing it; for there is no room for courage in opposing evident fate. But the last word and action of Macbeth are an expression of the *moral* cowardice which we trace so conspicuously throughout his career; he surrenders his life that he may not be "baited with the rabble's curse." So dies Macbeth, shrinking from deserved opprobrium; but he dies, as he has lived, *remorseless.* . . .

[*From Hunter's "New Illustrations of Shakespeare."**]

Beside the main subject of the midnight murder of a king sleeping in the house of one of his nobles, and surrounded by his guards, the death and appearance of the ghost of Banquo, and the whole machinery and prophecy of the wayward sisters, with the interior view of a castle in which is a conscience-stricken monarch reduced to the extremity of a siege, the poet seems to have intended to concentrate in this play many of the more thrilling incidents of physical and metaphysical action. The midnight shriek of women; sleep, with its stranger accidents, such as laughing, talking, walking, as produced by potions, as disturbed by dreams, as full of wicked thoughts; the hard beating of the heart; the parched state of the mouth in an hour of desperate guilt; the rousing of the hair at a dismal treatise; physiognomy; men of manly hearts moved to tears; the wild thoughts which haunt the mind of guilt, as in the air-drawn dagger, and the fancy that sleep was slain and the slayer should know its comforts no more; death in some of its stranger varieties—the soldier dying of wounds not bound up, the spent swimmer, the *pilot* wrecked on his way *home*, the horrible mode of Macdonnel's death, the massacre of a mother and her children, the hired assassins perpetrating their work on the belated travellers—these are but a portion of the terrible circumstances attendant on the main events of this tragic tale.

* *New Illustrations of the Life, Studies, and Writings of Shakespeare*, by Joseph Hunter (London, 1845), vol. ii. p. 160.

He goes for similar circumstances to the elements, and to the habits of animals about which superstitions had gathered —the flitting of the bat, the flight of the crow to the rooky wood, the fights of the owl and the falcon, and of the owl and the wren, the scream of the owl, the chirping of the cricket, the croak of the prophetic raven, and bark of the wolf, the horses devouring one another; the pitchy darkness of night, the murky darkness of a lurid day, a storm rattling in the battlements of an ancient fortress—we have all this before we have passed the bounds of nature and entered the regions of metaphysical agency.

There we have the spirits which tend on mortal thoughts, the revelations by magot-pies, the moving of stones, the speaking of trees, and lamentings heard in the air, and almost the whole of the mythology of the wayward sisters—their withered and wild attire, their intercourse with their queen, their congregating in the hour of storms on heaths which the lightning has scathed, the strange instruments employed by them, the mode of their operations, and their compelling the world invisible to disclose the secrets of futurity.

[*From Bucknill's* " *The Mad Folk of Shakespeare.*"*]

Evidently Macbeth is a man of sanguine nervous temperament, of large capacity and ready susceptibility. The high energy and courage which guide his sword in the battles of his country are qualities of nerve-force which future circumstances will direct to good or evil purposes. Circumstances arise soliciting to evil; "supernatural soliciting," the force of which, in these anti-spiritualist days, it requires an almost unattainable flight of the imagination to get a glimpse of. It must be remembered that the drama brings Macbeth face to face with the supernatural. What would be the effect upon a man of nervous sensibility of such appearances as the

* *The Mad Folk of Shakespeare*, by J. C. Bucknill, M. D. (London, 1867), pp. 7, 10, 44.

weird sisters? Surely most profound. We may disbelieve in any manifestations of the supernatural, but we cannot but believe that were their occurrence possible they would profoundly affect the mind. Humboldt says that the effect of the first earthquake shock is most bewildering, upsetting one of the strongest articles of material faith, namely, the fixedness of the earth. Any supernatural appearance must have this effect of shaking the foundations of the mind in an infinitely greater degree. Indeed, we so fully feel that any glimpse into the spirit-world would effect in ourselves a profound mental revulsion, that we readily extend to Macbeth a more indulgent opinion of his great crimes than we should have been able to do had he been led on to their commission by the temptations of earthly incident alone. . . .

To the Christian moralist Macbeth's guilt is so dark that its degree cannot be estimated, as there are no shades in black. But to the mental physiologist to whom nerve rather than conscience, the function of the brain rather than the power of the will, is an object of study, it is impossible to omit from calculation the influences of the supernatural event, which is not only the starting-point of the action, but the remote cause of the mental phenomena. . . .

What was Lady Macbeth's form and temperament? In Maclise's great painting of the banquet scene she is represented as a woman of large and coarse development: a Scandinavian Amazon, the muscles of whose brawny arms could only have been developed to their great size by hard and frequent use; a woman of whose fists her husband might well be afraid. . . . Was Lady Macbeth such a being? Did the fierce fire of her soul animate the epicene bulk of a virago? Never! Lady Macbeth was a lady, beautiful and delicate, whose one vivid passion proves that her organization was instinct with nerve-force, unoppressed by weight of flesh. Probably she was small; for it is the smaller sort of women whose emotional fire is the most fierce, and she herself bears unconscious testimony to the fact that her hand was little. . . . Although she manifests no feeling towards Macbeth beyond the regard which ambition makes her yield, it is clear that he entertains for her the personal love which a beautiful woman would excite. . . . Moreover, the effect of remorse upon her own health proves the preponderance of nerve in her organization. Could the Lady Macbeth of Maclise, and of others who have painted this lady, have been capable of the fire and force of her character in the commission of her crimes, the remembrance of them would scarcely have disturbed the quiet of her after-years. We figure Lady Macbeth to have been a tawny or brown blonde Rachel, with more beauty, with gray and cruel eyes, but with the same slight, dry configuration and constitution, instinct with determined nerve-power.

NOTE BY THE EDITOR.—In a foot-note, Dr. Bucknill states that when he wrote the above he was not aware that Mrs. Siddons held a similar opinion as to Lady Macbeth's personal appearance. We append what Mrs. Siddons says on this subject in her "Remarks on the Character of Lady Macbeth:"

"In this astonishing creature one sees a woman in whose bosom the passion of ambition has almost obliterated all the characteristics of human nature; in whose composition are associated all the subjugating powers of intellect, and all the charms and graces of personal beauty. You will probably not agree with me as to the character of that beauty; yet, perhaps, this difference of opinion will be entirely attributable to the difficulty of your imagination disengaging itself from that idea of the person of her representative which you have been so long accustomed to contemplate. According to my notion, it is of that character which I believe is generally allowed to be most captivating to the other sex—fair, feminine, nay, perhaps, even fragile—

'Fair as the forms that, wove in Fancy's loom,
Float in light visions round the poet's head.'

"Such a combination only, respectable in energy and strength of mind, and captivating in feminine loveliness, could have composed a charm of such potency as to fascinate the mind of a hero so dauntless, a character so amiable, so honourable as Macbeth—to seduce him to brave all the dangers of the present and all the terrors of a future world; and we are constrained, even whilst we abhor his crimes, to pity the infatuated victim of such a thraldom."

Campbell, on the other hand, in his "Life of Mrs. Siddons," says of Lady Macbeth: "She is a splendid picture of evil, . . . a sort of sister of Milton's Lucifer; and, like him, we surely imagine her externally majestic and beautiful. Mrs. Siddons's idea of her having been a delicate and blonde beauty seems to me to be a pure caprice. The public would have ill exchanged such a representative of Lady Macbeth for the dark locks and the eagle eyes of Mrs. Siddons."

Maginn (*Shakespeare Papers*, 1860, p. 184) remarks: "Shakespeare gives us no hint as to her personal charms, except when he makes her describe her hand as 'little.' We may be sure that there were few 'more thoroughbred or fairer fingers' in the land of Scotland than those of its queen, whose bearing in public towards Duncan, Banquo, and the nobles is marked by elegance and majesty; and, in private, by affectionate anxiety for her sanguinary lord."

Fletcher (*Studies of Shakespeare*, cited on p. 24) says: "[Shakespeare] has combined in Macbeth an eminently masculine person with a spirit in other respects eminently feminine, but utterly wanting the feminine generosity of affection. To this character, thus contrasted within itself, he has opposed a female character presenting a contrast exactly the reverse of the former. No one doubts that he has shown us in the spirit of Lady Macbeth that masculine firmness of will which he has made wanting in her husband. The strictest analogy, then, would lead him to complete the harmonizing contrast of the two characters by enshrining this 'undaunted mettle' of hers in a frame as exquisitely feminine as her husband's is magnificently manly. This was requisite, also, in order to make her taunts of Macbeth's irresolution operate with the fullest intensity. Such sentiments from the lips of what is called a masculine looking or speaking woman have little moral energy compared with what they derive from the ardent utterance of a delicately feminine voice and nature. Mrs. Siddons, then, we believe, judged more correctly in this matter than the public."

The German critic Rötscher (translated by Mr. Furness in his edition of *Macbeth*, p. 467) says: "There are certain inferences to be drawn in regard to the personal appearance of Lady Macbeth. She enters reading her husband's letter containing the first announcement of the sayings of the weird sisters. The mighty passion of ambition bursts at once in Lady Macbeth's imagination into full flame by these few lines; she appears well-nigh intoxicated with that emotion; her whole appearance ought to be royal, as one for whose powerful features and majestic bearing the diadem is the befitting adornment. Her countenance ought to display noble and energetic outlines, from whose every feature mean desires are banished; it should presage demoniac forces, with never a trace of moral ugliness nor aught repellent. The glittering eye betrays the restless, busy ardor of the disposition, while the finely chiselled lips and the nostrils must eloquently express scorn of moral opposition, and a determined purpose in crime. Her queenly bearing, as well as the nobility of all her movements, proclaims her title to the highest earthly greatness and power. Lady Macbeth's looks ought to enchain, and yet, withal, chill us, for such features can awaken no human sympathy, and can only disclose the dominion of monstrous powers. Lady Macbeth, therefore, will have the more powerful effect the more majesty is thrown around her person, because she will be thereby at once removed to a region in which all ordinary standards are dwarfed, for we have here before us a nature in which dwells a spirit made up of savage elements, and which reveals its own peculiar laws in its projects as fearfully as in its ruin."

[*From Gervinus's "Shakespeare Commentaries."* *]

Lady Macbeth is more a dependent wife than an independent, masculine woman, in so far as she wishes the golden round rather for him than for herself; her whole ambition is for him and through him; of herself, and of elevation for herself, she never speaks. . . . We see in this marriage a union of esteem, aye, of deep reverence, rather than of affection. The poet has not left this unexplained. She has had children, but has reared none; this may have added another sting to Macbeth's jealousy of Banquo; but the most natural consequence is that the pair are drawn more closely together, and are more intent on the gratification each can afford the other. . . . When none of her golden expectations are fulfilled—when, instead of successful greatness, the ruin of the land and of her husband follows—then her powers suddenly collapse. Trusting in him, she could have endured forever the conflicts of conscience, of nature, and of a harrowing imagination, but, doubting him, she doubts herself also; like ivy, she had twined her fresh verd-

* Translated by Mr. Furness (see his ed. of *Macbeth*, p. 469) from the 3d German ed. (Leipzig, 1862).

ure around the branches of the kingly tree, but when the trunk totters, she falls to the ground; her iron heart dissolves in the fire of this affliction and of this false expectation. There have been regrets expressed that the transition in her from masculine strength to feminine weakness has not been more fully portrayed by the poet. It was, however, no gradual transition, but a sudden downfall. . . .

It is very noteworthy that for the murder of Banquo Macbeth employs the very incitements which had wrought most effectually upon himself: he appeals to the manhood of the murderers. . . .

As far as regards poetic justice in the fates of Duncan, Banquo, and Macduff, there lies in their several natures a contrast to Macbeth's. . . . King Duncan is characterized in history as a man of greater weakness than became a king; rebellions were frequent in his reign; he was no warrior to suppress them, no physiognomist to read treason in the face; after he had just passed through a painful experience through the treachery of the friendly thane of Cawdor, he at once, overlooking the modest Banquo, elevates Macbeth to this very thaneship, thereby pampering Macbeth's ambition, and suffers a cruel penalty for this blunder at the hands of the new thane, his own kinsman. The same lack of foresight ruins Banquo. He had been admitted to the secret of the weird sisters; pledged to openness towards Macbeth, he had an opportunity of convincing himself of his obduracy and secrecy; he surmises and suspects Macbeth's deed, yet he does nothing against him and nothing for himself; like, but with a difference, those cowardly impersonations of fear, the Doctor, Seyton, Ross, and the spying ironical Lennox, he suppresses his thoughts and wilfully shuts his eyes; he falls, having done nothing in a field full of dangers. Macduff is not quite so culpable in this respect; he is, therefore, punished, not in his own person, but in the fate of his family, which makes him the martyr-hero by whose hand Macbeth falls. . .

Macduff is, by nature, what Macbeth once was, a mixture of mildness and force; he is more than Macbeth, because he is without any admixture of ambition. When Malcolm accuses himself to Macduff of every imaginable vice, not a shadow of ambition to force himself into the usurper's place comes over Macduff. So noble, so blameless, so mild, Macduff lacks the goad of sharp ambition necessary to make him a victorious opponent of Macbeth: the poet, therefore, by the horrible extermination of his family, drains him of the milk of human kindness, and so fits him to be the conqueror of Macbeth.

[*From Dowden's "Shakspere."* *]

There is a line in the play of Macbeth, uttered as the evening shadows begin to gather on the day of Banquo's murder, which we may repeat to ourselves as a motto of the entire tragedy, "Good things of day begin to droop and drowse." It is the tragedy of the twilight and the setting-in of thick darkness upon a human soul. We assist at the spectacle of a terrible sunset in folded clouds of blood. To the last, however, one thin hand's-breadth of melancholy light remains—the sadness of the day without its strength. Macbeth is the prey of a profound world-weariness. And while a huge *ennui* pursues crime, the criminal is not yet in utter blackness of night. When the play opens, the sun is already dropping below the verge. And as at sunset strange winds arise, and gather the clouds to westward with mysterious pause and stir, so the play of Macbeth opens with movement of mysterious, spiritual powers, which are auxiliary of that awful shadow which first creeps and then strides across the moral horizon.

It need hardly be once more repeated that the Witches of Macbeth are not the broom-stick witches of vulgar, popular

* *Shakspere: a Critical Study of his Mind and Art*, by Edward Dowden (2d ed. London, 1876), p. 244 fol. (by permission).

tradition. If they are grotesque, they are also sublime. The weird sisters of our dramatist may take their place beside the terrible old women of Michael Angelo, who spin the destinies of man. . . . They tingle in every fibre with evil energy, as the tempest does with the electric current; their malignity is inexhaustible; they are wells of sin springing up into everlasting death; they have their raptures and ecstasies in crime; they snatch with delight at the relics of impiety and foul disease; they are the awful inspirers of murder, insanity, suicide. . . .

"The true reason for the first appearance of the witches," Coleridge has said, "is to strike the key-note of the character of the whole drama." They appear in a desert place, with thunder and lightning; it is the barren and blasted place where evil has obtained the mastery of things. Observe that the last words of the witches, in the opening scene of the play, are the first words which Macbeth himself utters.

> Fair is foul and foul is fair
> Hover through the fog and filthy air.*

Macbeth. "So foul and fair a day I have not seen." Shakspere intimates by this that although Macbeth has not yet set eyes upon these hags, the connection is already established between his soul and them. Their spells have already wrought upon his blood. When the three sisters meet Macbeth and Banquo upon the heath, it is Banquo to whom they are first visible in the gray, northern air. To Banquo they are objective—they are outside himself, and he can observe and describe their strange aspect, their wild attire, and their mysterious gesture. Macbeth is rapt in silence, and then with eager longing demands, "Speak if you can: what are you?" When they have given him the three Hails, as Glamis, as Cawdor, and as King, the hail of the past, of the

* Words uttered by all three witches, after each has singly spoken thrice.

present, of the future, Macbeth starts. "It is a full revelation of his criminal aptitudes," Mr. Hudson has well said, "that so startles and surprises him into a rapture of meditation." And besides this, Macbeth is startled to find that there is a terrible correspondence established between the baser instincts of his own heart and certain awful external agencies of evil. . . .

But beside the vague yet mastering inspiration of crime received from the witches, there is the more definite inspiration received from his wife. Macbeth is excitably imaginative, and his imagination alternately stimulates and enfeebles him. The facts in their clear-cut outline disappear in the dim atmosphere of surmise, desire, fear, hope, which the spirit of Macbeth effuses around the fact. But his wife sees things in the clearest and most definite outline. Her delicate frame is filled with high-strung nervous energy. With her to perceive is forthwith to decide, to decide is to act. Having resolved upon her end, a practical logic convinces her that the means are implied and determined. Macbeth resolves, and falters back from action; now he is restrained by his imagination, now by his fears, now by lingering velleities towards a loyal and honourable existence. He is unable to keep in check or put under restraint any one of the various incoherent powers of his nature, which impede and embarrass each the action of the other. Lady Macbeth gains, for the time, sufficient strength by throwing herself passionately into a single purpose, and by resolutely repressing all that is inconsistent with that purpose. Into the service of evil she carries some of the intensity and energy of asceticism—she cuts off from herself her better nature, she yields no weak paltering with conscience. "I have given suck," she exclaims, "and know how tender 'tis to love the babe that milks me;" she is unable to stab Duncan because he resembles her father in his sleep; she is appalled by the copious blood in which the old man lies, and the horror of the sight clings to her memory; the smell of the blood is hateful to her and almost insupportable; she had not been without apprehension that her feminine nature might fail to carry her through the terrible ordeal, through which she yet resolved that it should be compelled to pass. She must not waste an atom of her strength of will, which has to serve for two murderers—for her husband as well as for herself. She puts into requisition with the aid of wine and of stimulant words the reserve of nervous force which lay unused. No witches have given her "Hail;" no airy dagger marshals her the way she is going; nor is she afterwards haunted by the terrible vision of Banquo's gory head. As long as her will remains her own she can throw herself upon external facts, and maintain herself in relation with the definite, actual surroundings; it is in her sleep, when the will is incapable of action, that she is persecuted by the past which perpetually renews itself, not in ghostly shapes, but by the imagined recurrence of real and terrible incidents.

The fears of Lady Macbeth upon the night of Duncan's murder are the definite ones that the murderers may be detected, that some omission in the pre-arranged plan may occur, that she or her husband may be summoned to appear before the traces of their crime have been removed. More awful considerations would press in upon her and overwhelm her sanity, but that she forcibly repels them for the time:

> These deeds must not be thought
> After these ways; so, it will make us mad.

To her the sight of Duncan dead is as terrible as to Macbeth; but she takes the daggers from her husband; and with a forced jest, hideous in the self-violence which it implies, she steps forth into the dark corridor:

> If he do bleed
> I'll gild the faces of the grooms withal,
> For it must seem their guilt.

"A play of fancy here is like a gleam of ghastly sunshine striking across a stormy landscape."* The knocking at the gate clashes upon her overstrained nerves and thrills her; but she has determination and energy to direct the actions of Macbeth, and rouse him from the mood of abject depression which succeeded his crime. A white flame of resolution glows through her delicate organization, like light through an alabaster lamp:

> Infirm of purpose!
> Give me the daggers: the sleeping and the dead
> Are but as pictures: 'tis the eye of childhood
> That fears a painted devil.

If the hold which she possesses over her own faculties should relax for a moment, all would be lost. For dreadful deeds anticipated and resolved upon, she has strength, but the surprise of a novel horror, on which she has not counted, deprives her suddenly of consciousness; when Macbeth announces his butchery of Duncan's grooms, the lady swoons—not in feigning but in fact—and is borne away insensible.

Macbeth wastes himself in vague, imaginative remorse:

> Will not great Neptune's ocean wash this blood
> Clean from my hand? No, this my hand will rather
> The multitudinous seas incarnadine,
> Making the green one red.

Thus his imagination serves to dissipate the impression of his conscience. What is the worth of this vague, imaginative remorse? Macbeth retained enough of goodness to make him a haggard, miserable criminal; never enough to restrain him from a crime. His hand soon became subdued to what it worked in—the blood in which it paddled and plashed. And yet the loose, incoherent faculties, ever becoming more and more disorganized and disintegrated, somehow held together till the end. "My hands are of your colour," exclaims Lady Macbeth; "but I shame to wear a heart

* *Macbeth*, Clarendon Press Edition, p. 108

so white. A little water clears us of this deed." Yet it is she who has uttered no large words about "the multitudinous seas" who will rise in slumbery agitation, and with her accustomed action eagerly essay to remove from her little hand its ineffaceable stain, and with her delicate sense sicken at the smell of blood upon it, which "all the perfumes of Arabia will not sweeten;" and last, will loosen the terrible constriction of her heart with a sigh that longs to be perpetual. It is the queen, and not her husband, who is slain by conscience.

Yet the soul of Macbeth never quite disappears into the blackness of darkness. He is a cloud without water carried about of winds; a tree whose fruit withers, but not even to the last plucked up by the roots. For the dull ferocity of Macbeth is joyless. All his life has gone irretrievably astray, and he is aware of this. His suspicion becomes uncontrollable; his reign is a reign of terror; and as he drops deeper and deeper into the solitude and the gloom, his sense of error and misfortune, futile and unproductive as that sense is, increases. He lives under a dreary cloud, and all things look gray and cold. He has lived long enough, yet he clings to life; that which should accompany old age, "as honour, love, obedience, troops of friends," he may not look to have. Finally his sensibility has grown so dull that even the intelligence of his wife's death—the death of her who had been bound to him by such close communion in crime—hardly moves him, and seems little more than one additional incident in the weary, meaningless tale of human life:

> She should have died hereafter;
> There would have been a time for such a word.
> To-morrow, and to-morrow, and to-morrow,
> Creeps in this petty pace from day to day
> To the last syllable of recorded time;
> And all our yesterdays have lighted fools
> The way to dusty death. Out, out, brief candle!
> Life's but a walking shadow, a poor player

> That struts and frets his hour upon the stage,
> And then is heard no more ; it is a tale
> Told by an idiot, full of sound and fury,
> Signifying nothing.

This world-weariness, which has not the energy of Timon's despair, is yet less remote from the joy and glory of true living than is the worm-like vivacity of Iago. Macbeth remembers that he once knew there was such a thing as human goodness. He stands a haggard shadow against the hand's-breadth of pale sky which yields us sufficient light to see him. But Iago rises compact with fiend-like energy, seen brightly in the godless glare of hell. The end of Macbeth is savage, and almost brutal — a death without honour or loveliness. He fights now, not like "Bellona's bridegroom lapp'd in proof," but with a wild and animal clinging to life :

> They have tied me to a stake ; I cannot fly,
> But, bear-like, I must fight the course.

His followers desert him ; he feels himself taken in a trap. The powers of evil in which he had trusted turn against him and betray him. His courage becomes a desperate rage. We are in pain until the horrible necessity is accomplished.

GLAMIS CASTLE IN 1876.

MACBETH.

DRAMATIS PERSONÆ.

DUNCAN, King of Scotland.
MALCOLM, DONALBAIN, } his sons.
MACBETH, BANQUO, } generals of the king's army.
MACDUFF, LENNOX, ROSS, MENTEITH, ANGUS, CAITHNESS, } noblemen of Scotland.
FLEANCE, son to Banquo.
SIWARD Earl of Northumberland, general of the English forces.
Young SIWARD, his son.
SEYTON, an officer attending on Macbeth.

Boy, son to Macduff.
An English Doctor.
A Scotch Doctor.
A Sergeant.
A Porter.
An Old Man.
LADY MACBETH.
LADY MACDUFF.
Gentlewoman attending on Lady Macbeth.
HECATE.
Three Witches.
Apparitions.

Lords, Gentlemen, Officers, Soldiers, Murderers, Attendants, and Messengers.

SCENE: *Scotland; England.*

CAWDOR CASTLE.

ACT I.

SCENE I. *A Desert Place.*

Thunder and lightning. Enter three Witches.

First Witch. When shall we three meet again
In thunder, lightning, or in rain?

Second Witch. When the hurly-burly 's done,
When the battle 's lost and won.

Third Witch. That will be ere the set of sun.
First Witch. Where the place?
Second Witch. Upon the heath.
Third Witch. There to meet with Macbeth.
First Witch. I come, Graymalkin!
Second Witch. Paddock calls.
Third Witch. Anon. 10
All. Fair is foul, and foul is fair:
Hover through the fog and filthy air. [*Exeunt.*

SCENE II. *A Camp near Forres.*

Alarum within. Enter DUNCAN, MALCOLM, DONALBAIN, LENNOX, *with* Attendants, *meeting a bleeding* Sergeant.

Duncan. What bloody man is that? He can report,
As seemeth by his plight, of the revolt
The newest state.
Malcolm. This is the sergeant
Who like a good and hardy soldier fought
'Gainst my captivity.—Hail, brave friend!
Say to the king the knowledge of the broil
As thou didst leave it.
Sergeant. Doubtful it stood,
As two spent swimmers that do cling together
And choke their art. The merciless Macdonwald—
Worthy to be a rebel, for to that 10
The multiplying villanies of nature
Do swarm upon him—from the western isles
Of kerns and gallowglasses is supplied;
And Fortune, on his damned quarrel smiling,
Show'd like a rebel's whore: but all 's too weak;
For brave Macbeth—well he deserves that name—
Disdaining Fortune, with his brandish'd steel,
Which smok'd with bloody execution,
Like valour's minion carv'd out his passage

Till he fac'd the slave; 20
Which ne'er shook hands, nor bade farewell to him,
Till he unseam'd him from the nave to the chaps,
And fix'd his head upon our battlements.

Duncan. O valiant cousin! worthy gentleman!

Sergeant. As whence the sun gins his reflection
Shipwracking storms and direful thunders break,
So from that spring whence comfort seem'd to come
Discomfort swells. Mark, king of Scotland, mark:
No sooner justice had with valour arm'd
Compell'd these skipping kerns to trust their heels, 30
But the Norweyan lord, surveying vantage,
With furbish'd arms and new supplies of men
Began a fresh assault.

Duncan. Dismay'd not this
Our captains, Macbeth and Banquo?

Sergeant. Yes;
As sparrows eagles, or the hare the lion.
If I say sooth, I must report they were
As cannons overcharg'd with double cracks;
So they doubly redoubled strokes upon the foe:
Except they meant to bathe in reeking wounds,
Or memorize another Golgotha, 40
I cannot tell—
But I am faint, my gashes cry for help.

Duncan. So well thy words become thee as thy wounds;
They smack of honour both.—Go get him surgeons.
[*Exit Sergeant, attended.*
Who comes here?

Enter Ross.

Malcolm. The worthy thane of Ross.

Lennox. What a haste looks through his eyes! So should he look
That seems to speak things strange.

Ross. God save the king!

Duncan. Whence cam'st thou, worthy thane?

Ross. From Fife, great king;
Where the Norweyan banners flout the sky
And fan our people cold. Norway himself, 50
With terrible numbers,
Assisted by that most disloyal traitor,
The thane of Cawdor, began a dismal conflict;
Till that Bellona's bridegroom, lapp'd in proof,
Confronted him with self-comparisons,
Point against point rebellious, arm 'gainst arm,
Curbing his lavish spirit: and, to conclude,
The victory fell on us.

Duncan. Great happiness!

Ross. That now
Sweno, the Norways' king, craves composition;
Nor would we deign him burial of his men 60
Till he disbursed at Saint Colme's Inch
Ten thousand dollars to our general use.

Duncan. No more that thane of Cawdor shall deceive
Our bosom interest: go pronounce his present death,
And with his former title greet Macbeth.

Ross. I 'll see it done.

Duncan. What he hath lost noble Macbeth hath won.
[*Exeunt.*

SCENE III. *A Heath.*

Thunder. Enter the three Witches.

First Witch. Where hast thou been, sister?

Second Witch. Killing swine.

Third Witch. Sister, where thou?

First Witch. A sailor's wife had chestnuts in her lap,
And munch'd, and munch'd, and munch'd. 'Give me,' quoth I:

'Aroint thee, witch!' the rump-fed ronyon cries.
Her husband 's to Aleppo gone, master o' the Tiger:
But in a sieve I 'll thither sail,
And, like a rat without a tail,
I 'll do, I 'll do, and I 'll do. 10

Second Witch. I 'll give thee a wind.

First Witch. Thou 'rt kind.

Third Witch. And I another.

First Witch. I myself have all the other,
And the very ports they blow,
All the quarters that they know
I' the shipman's card.
I 'll drain him dry as hay:
Sleep shall neither night nor day
Hang upon his pent-house lid; 20
He shall live a man forbid:
Weary se'nnights nine times nine
Shall he dwindle, peak, and pine:
Though his bark cannot be lost,
Yet it shall be tempest-tost.
Look what I have.

Second Witch. Show me, show me.

First Witch. Here I have a pilot's thumb,
Wrack'd as homeward he did come. [*Drum within.*

Third Witch. A drum, a drum! 30
Macbeth doth come.

All. The weird sisters, hand in hand,
Posters of the sea and land,
Thus do go about, about:
Thrice to thine, and thrice to mine,
And thrice again, to make up nine.
Peace! the charm 's wound up.

Enter MACBETH *and* BANQUO.

Macbeth. So foul and fair a day I have not seen.

Banquo. How far is 't call'd to Forres? What are these
So wither'd and so wild in their attire, 40
That look not like the inhabitants o' the earth,
And yet are on 't?—Live you? or are you aught
That man may question? You seem to understand me,
By each at once her choppy finger laying
Upon her skinny lips: you should be women,
And yet your beards forbid me to interpret
That you are so.

Macbeth. Speak, if you can: what are you?

First Witch. All hail, Macbeth! hail to thee, thane of Glamis!

Second Witch. All hail, Macbeth! hail to thee, thane of Cawdor!

Third Witch. All hail, Macbeth, that shalt be king hereafter! 50

Banquo. Good sir, why do you start, and seem to fear
Things that do sound so fair?—I' the name of truth,
Are ye fantastical, or that indeed
Which outwardly ye show? My noble partner
You greet with present grace and great prediction
Of noble having and of royal hope,
That he seems rapt withal; to me you speak not.
If you can look into the seeds of time,
And say which grain will grow and which will not,
Speak then to me, who neither beg nor fear 60
Your favours nor your hate.

First Witch. Hail!

Second Witch. Hail!

Third Witch. Hail!

First Witch. Lesser than Macbeth, and greater.

Second Witch. Not so happy, yet much happier.

Third Witch. Thou shalt get kings, though thou be none:
So all hail, Macbeth and Banquo!

First Witch. Banquo and Macbeth, all hail!

Macbeth. Stay, you imperfect speakers, tell me more: 70
By Sinel's death I know I am thane of Glamis;
But how of Cawdor? the thane of Cawdor lives,
A prosperous gentleman; and to be king
Stands not within the prospect of belief,
No more than to be Cawdor. Say from whence
You owe this strange intelligence? or why
Upon this blasted heath you stop our way
With such prophetic greeting? speak, I charge you.
[*Witches vanish.*

Banquo. The earth hath bubbles as the water has,
And these are of them. Whither are they vanish'd? 80

Macbeth. Into the air; and what seem'd corporal melted
As breath into the wind. Would they had stay'd!

Banquo. Were such things here as we do speak about?
Or have we eaten on the insane root
That takes the reason prisoner?

Macbeth. Your children shall be kings.

Banquo. You shall be king.

Macbeth. And thane of Cawdor too: went it not so?

Banquo. To the selfsame tune and words. Who 's here?

Enter Ross *and* Angus.

Ross. The king hath happily receiv'd, Macbeth,
The news of thy success; and when he reads 90
Thy personal venture in the rebels' fight,
His wonders and his praises do contend
Which should be thine or his: silenc'd with that,
In viewing o'er the rest o' the selfsame day,
He finds thee in the stout Norweyan ranks,
Nothing afeard of what thyself didst make,
Strange images of death. As thick as tale

Came post with post, and every one did bear
Thy praises in his kingdom's great defence,
And pour'd them down before him.

Angus. We are sent 100
To give thee from our royal master thanks;
Only to herald thee into his sight,
Not pay thee.

Ross. And for an earnest of a greater honour,
He bade me, from him, call thee thane of Cawdor:
In which addition, hail, most worthy thane!
For it is thine.

Banquo. What, can the devil speak true?

Macbeth. The thane of Cawdor lives: why do you dress me
In borrow'd robes?

Angus. Who was the thane lives yet,
But under heavy judgment bears that life 110
Which he deserves to lose. Whether he was combin'd
With those of Norway, or did line the rebel
With hidden help and vantage, or that with both
He labour'd in his country's wrack, I know not;
But treasons capital, confess'd and prov'd,
Have overthrown him.

Macbeth. [*Aside*] Glamis, and thane of Cawdor!
The greatest is behind.—Thanks for your pains.—
Do you not hope your children shall be kings,
When those that gave the thane of Cawdor to me
Promis'd no less to them?

Banquo. That trusted home 120
Might yet enkindle you unto the crown,
Besides the thane of Cawdor. But 't is strange:
And oftentimes, to win us to our harm,
The instruments of darkness tell us truths,
Win us with honest trifles, to betray 's
In deepest consequence.—
Cousins, a word, I pray you.

Macbeth. [*Aside*] Two truths are told,
As happy prologues to the swelling act
Of the imperial theme.—I thank you, gentlemen.
[*Aside*] This supernatural soliciting 130
Cannot be ill, cannot be good: if ill,
Why hath it given me earnest of success,
Commencing in a truth? I am thane of Cawdor:
If good, why do I yield to that suggestion
Whose horrid image doth unfix my hair
And make my seated heart knock at my ribs,
Against the use of nature? Present fears
Are less than horrible imaginings:
My thought, whose murther yet is but fantastical,
Shakes so my single state of man that function 140
Is smother'd in surmise, and nothing is
But what is not.

Banquo. Look how our partner 's rapt.

Macbeth. [*Aside*] If chance will have me king, why, chance may crown me,
Without my stir.

Banquo. New honours come upon him,
Like our strange garments, cleave not to their mould
But with the aid of use.

Macbeth. [*Aside*] Come what come may,
Time and the hour runs through the roughest day.

Banquo. Worthy Macbeth, we stay upon your leisure.

Macbeth. Give me your favour: my dull brain was wrought
With things forgotten. Kind gentlemen, your pains 150
Are register'd where every day I turn
The leaf to read them. Let us toward the king.—
Think upon what hath chanc'd, and at more time,
The interim having weigh'd it, let us speak
Our free hearts each to other.

Banquo. Very gladly.

Macbeth. Till then, enough.—Come, friends. [*Exeunt.*

SCENE IV. *Forres. The Palace.*

Flourish. Enter DUNCAN, MALCOLM, DONALBAIN, LENNOX, *and* Attendants.

Duncan. Is execution done on Cawdor? Are not
Those in commission yet return'd?
Malcolm. My liege,
They are not yet come back. But I have spoke
With one that saw him die, who did report
That very frankly he confess'd his treasons,
Implor'd your highness' pardon, and set forth
A deep repentance: nothing in his life
Became him like the leaving it; he died
As one that had been studied in his death
To throw away the dearest thing he owed 10
As 't were a careless trifle.
Duncan. There 's no art
To find the mind's construction in the face:
He was a gentleman on whom I built
An absolute trust.—

Enter MACBETH, BANQUO, ROSS, *and* ANGUS.

O worthiest cousin!
The sin of my ingratitude even now
Was heavy on me: thou art so far before
That swiftest wing of recompense is slow
To overtake thee. Would thou hadst less deserv'd,
That the proportion both of thanks and payment
Might have been mine! only I have left to say, 20
More is thy due than more than all can pay.
Macbeth. The service and the loyalty I owe,
In doing it, pays itself. Your highness' part
Is to receive our duties: and our duties
Are to your throne and state children and servants;

Which do but what they should, by doing every thing
Safe toward your love and honour.
Duncan. Welcome hither:
I have begun to plant thee, and will labour
To make thee full of growing.—Noble Banquo,
That hast no less deserv'd, nor must be known 30
No less to have done so, let me infold thee
And hold thee to my heart.
Banquo. There if I grow,
The harvest is your own.
Duncan. My plenteous joys,
Wanton in fulness, seek to hide themselves
In drops of sorrow.—Sons, kinsmen, thanes,
And you whose places are the nearest, know
We will establish our estate upon
Our eldest, Malcolm, whom we name hereafter
The Prince of Cumberland; which honour must
Not unaccompanied invest him only, 40
But signs of nobleness, like stars, shall shine
On all deservers.—From hence to Inverness,
And bind us further to you.
Macbeth. The rest is labour, which is not us'd for you.
I 'll be myself the harbinger and make joyful
The hearing of my wife with your approach;
So humbly take my leave.
Duncan. My worthy Cawdor!
Macbeth. [*Aside*] The Prince of Cumberland! that is a step
On which I must fall down, or else o'erleap,
For in my way it lies. Stars, hide your fires! 50
Let not light see my black and deep desires:
The eye wink at the hand; yet let that be
Which the eye fears, when it is done, to see. [*Exit.*
Duncan. True, worthy Banquo: he is full so valiant,
And in his commendations I am fed;
It is a banquet to me. Let 's after him,

Whose care is gone before to bid us welcome:
It is a peerless kinsman. [*Flourish. Exeunt.*

SCENE V. *Inverness. A Room in Macbeth's Castle.*

Enter LADY MACBETH, *reading a letter.*

Lady Macbeth [Reads]. *They met me in the day of success: and I have learned by the perfectest report, they have more in them than mortal knowledge. When I burned in desire to question them further, they made themselves air, into which they vanished. Whiles I stood rapt in the wonder of it, came missives from the king, who all-hailed me 'Thane of Cawdor;' by which title, before, these weird sisters saluted me, and referred me to the coming on of time, with 'Hail, king that shalt be!' This have I thought good to deliver thee, my dearest partner of greatness, that thou mightst not lose the dues of rejoicing, by being ignorant of what greatness is promised thee. Lay it to thy heart, and farewell.*

Glamis thou art, and Cawdor, and shalt be 13
What thou art promis'd. Yet do I fear thy nature;
It is too full o' the milk of human kindness
To catch the nearest way. Thou wouldst be great;
Art not without ambition, but without
The illness should attend it: what thou wouldst highly,
That wouldst thou holily; wouldst not play false,
And yet wouldst wrongly win: thou 'dst have, great Glamis,
That which cries, 'Thus thou must do, if thou have it;' 21
And that which rather thou dost fear to do
Than wishest should be undone. Hie thee hither,
That I may pour my spirits in thine ear,
And chastise with the valour of my tongue
All that impedes thee from the golden round
Which fate and metaphysical aid doth seem
To have thee crown'd withal.

Enter a Messenger.

What is your tidings?

Messenger. The king comes here to-night.

Lady Macbeth. Thou 'rt mad to say it:
Is not thy master with him? who, were 't so, 30
Would have inform'd for preparation.

Messenger. So please you, it is true: our thane is coming.
One of my fellows had the speed of him,
Who, almost dead for breath, had scarcely more
Than would make up his message.

Lady Macbeth. Give him tending;
He brings great news. [*Exit Messenger.*
The raven himself is hoarse
That croaks the fatal entrance of Duncan
Under my battlements. Come, you spirits
That tend on mortal thoughts, unsex me here,
And fill me from the crown to the toe top-full 40
Of direst cruelty! make thick my blood;
Stop up the access and passage to remorse,
That no compunctious visitings of nature
Shake my fell purpose, nor keep peace between
The effect and it! Come to my woman's breasts,
And take my milk for gall, you murthering ministers,
Wherever in your sightless substances
You wait on nature's mischief! Come, thick night,
And pall thee in the dunnest smoke of hell,
That my keen knife see not the wound it makes, 50
Nor heaven peep through the blanket of the dark,
To cry 'Hold, hold!'

Enter Macbeth.

Great Glamis! worthy Cawdor!
Greater than both, by the all-hail hereafter!
Thy letters have transported me beyond

This ignorant present, and I feel now
The future in the instant.

Macbeth. My dearest love,
Duncan comes here to-night.

Lady Macbeth. And when goes hence?

Macbeth. To-morrow, as he purposes.

Lady Macbeth. O, never
Shall sun that morrow see!
Your face, my thane, is as a book where men 60
May read strange matters. To beguile the time,
Look like the time; bear welcome in your eye,
Your hand, your tongue: look like the innocent flower,
But be the serpent under 't. He that 's coming
Must be provided for: and you shall put
This night's great business into my dispatch;
Which shall to all our nights and days to come
Give solely sovereign sway and masterdom.

Macbeth. We will speak further.

Lady Macbeth. Only look up clear;
To alter favour ever is to fear: 70
Leave all the rest to me. [*Exeunt.*

SCENE VI. *Before Macbeth's Castle.*

Hautboys and torches. Enter DUNCAN, MALCOLM, DONALBAIN, BANQUO, LENNOX, MACDUFF, ROSS, ANGUS, *and* Attendants.

Duncan. This castle hath a pleasant seat; the air
Nimbly and sweetly recommends itself
Unto our gentle senses.

Banquo. This guest of summer.
The temple-haunting martlet, does approve
By his lov'd mansionry that the heaven's breath
Smells wooingly here: no jutty, frieze,
Buttress, nor coign of vantage, but this bird

Hath made his pendent bed and procreant cradle:
Where they most breed and haunt, I have observ'd
The air is delicate.

Enter LADY MACBETH.

Duncan. See, see, our honour'd hostess! 10
The love that follows us sometime is our trouble,
Which still we thank as love. Herein I teach you
How you shall bid God 'ield us for your pains
And thank us for your trouble.

Lady Macbeth. All our service
In every point twice done and then done double
Were poor and single business, to contend
Against those honours deep and broad wherewith
Your majesty loads our house: for those of old,
And the late dignities heap'd up to them,
We rest your hermits.

Duncan. Where 's the thane of Cawdor? 20
We cours'd him at the heels, and had a purpose
To be his purveyor; but he rides well,
And his great love, sharp as his spur, hath holp him
To his home before us. Fair and noble hostess,
We are your guest to-night.

Lady Macbeth. Your servants ever
Have theirs, themselves, and what is theirs, in compt,
To make their audit at your highness' pleasure,
Still to return your own.

Duncan. Give me your hand;
Conduct me to mine host: we love him highly,
And shall continue our graces towards him. 30
By your leave, hostess. [*Exeunt.*

SCENE VII. *Macbeth's Castle.*

Hautboys and torches. Enter a Sewer, *and divers* Servants *with dishes and service, and pass over the stage. Then enter* MACBETH.

Macbeth. If it were done when 't is done, then 't were well
It were done quickly: if the assassination
Could trammel up the consequence, and catch
With his surcease success; that but this blow
Might be the be-all and the end-all here,
But here, upon this bank and shoal of time,
We 'd jump the life to come. But in these cases
We still have judgment here; that we but teach
Bloody instructions, which being taught return
To plague the inventor: this even-handed justice 10
Commends the ingredients of our poison'd chalice
To our own lips. He 's here in double trust:
First, as I am his kinsman and his subject,
Strong both against the deed; then, as his host,
Who should against his murtherer shut the door,
Not bear the knife myself. Besides, this Duncan
Hath borne his faculties so meek, hath been
So clear in his great office, that his virtues
Will plead like angels trumpet-tongu'd against
The deep damnation of his taking-off; 20
And pity, like a naked new-born babe,
Striding the blast, or heaven's cherubin, hors'd
Upon the sightless couriers of the air,
Shall blow the horrid deed in every eye,
That tears shall drown the wind. I have no spur
To prick the sides of my intent, but only
Vaulting ambition, which o'erleaps itself
And falls on the other.

Enter LADY MACBETH.

How now! what news?

Lady Macbeth. He has almost supp'd: why have you left the chamber?

Macbeth. Hath he ask'd for me?

Lady Macbeth. Know you not he has? 30

Macbeth. We will proceed no further in this business:
He hath honour'd me of late; and I have bought
Golden opinions from all sorts of people,
Which would be worn now in their newest gloss,
Not cast aside so soon.

Lady Macbeth. Was the hope drunk
Wherein you dress'd yourself? hath it slept since?
And wakes it now, to look so green and pale
At what it did so freely? From this time
Such I account thy love. Art thou afeard
To be the same in thine own act and valour 40
As thou art in desire? Wouldst thou have that
Which thou esteem'st the ornament of life,
And live a coward in thine own esteem,
Letting 'I dare not' wait upon 'I would,'
Like the poor cat i' the adage?

Macbeth. Prithee, peace:
I dare do all that may become a man;
Who dares do more is none.

Lady Macbeth. What beast was 't then
That made you break this enterprise to me?
When you durst do it, then you were a man;
And, to be more than what you were, you would 50
Be so much more the man. Nor time nor place
Did then adhere, and yet you would make both:
They have made themselves, and that their fitness now
Does unmake you. I have given suck, and know
How tender 't is to love the babe that milks me:

I would, while it was smiling in my face,
Have pluck'd my nipple from his boneless gums
And dash'd the brains out, had I so sworn as you
Have done to this.

Macbeth. If we should fail?

Lady Macbeth. We fail.
But screw your courage to the sticking-place, 60
And we 'll not fail. When Duncan is asleep—
Whereto the rather shall his day's hard journey
Soundly invite him—his two chamberlains
Will I with wine and wassail so convince
That memory, the warder of the brain,
Shall be a fume, and the receipt of reason
A limbeck only: when in swinish sleep
Their drenched natures lie as in a death,
What cannot you and I perform upon
The unguarded Duncan? what not put upon 70
His spongy officers, who shall bear the guilt
Of our great quell?

Macbeth. Bring forth men-children only;
For thy undaunted mettle should compose
Nothing but males. Will it not be receiv'd,
When we have mark'd with blood those sleepy two
Of his own chamber and us'd their very daggers,
That they have done 't?

Lady Macbeth. Who dares receive it other,
As we shall make our griefs and clamour roar
Upon his death?

Macbeth. I am settled, and bend up
Each corporal agent to this terrible feat. 80
Away, and mock the time with fairest show:
False face must hide what the false heart doth know.

[*Exeunt.*

SCONE.

ACT II.

Scene I. *Court of Macbeth's Castle.*

Enter Banquo, *and* Fleance *bearing a torch before him.*

Banquo. How goes the night, boy?
Fleance. The moon is down, I have not heard the clock.
Banquo. And she goes down at twelve.
Fleance. I take 't, 't is later, sir.
Banquo. Hold, take my sword.—There 's husbandry in heaven;
Their candles are all out.—Take thee that too.—
A heavy summons lies like lead upon me,
And yet I would not sleep. Merciful powers,
Restrain in me the cursed thoughts that nature
Gives way to in repose!—

Enter MACBETH, *and a* Servant *with a torch.*

Give me my sword.—

Who 's there? 10

Macbeth. A friend.

Banquo. What, sir, not yet at rest? The king 's abed:
He hath been in unusual pleasure, and
Sent forth great largess to your offices.
This diamond he greets your wife withal,
By the name of most kind hostess; and shut up
In measureless content.

Macbeth. Being unprepar'd,
Our will became the servant to defect,
Which else should free have wrought.

Banquo. All 's well.
I dreamt last night of the three weird sisters: 20
To you they have show'd some truth.

Macbeth. I think not of them:
Yet, when we can entreat an hour to serve,
We would spend it in some words upon that business,
If you would grant the time.

Banquo. At your kind'st leisure.

Macbeth. If you shall cleave to my consent, when 't is,
It shall make honour for you.

Banquo. So I lose none
In seeking to augment it, but still keep
My bosom franchis'd and allegiance clear,
I shall be counsell'd.

Macbeth. Good repose the while!

Banquo. Thanks, sir: the like to you! 30

[*Exeunt Banquo and Fleance.*

Macbeth. Go bid thy mistress, when my drink is ready,
She strike upon the bell. Get thee to bed.— [*Exit Servant.*
Is this a dagger which I see before me,
The handle toward my hand?—Come, let me clutch thee.

I have thee not, and yet I see thee still.
Art thou not, fatal vision, sensible
To feeling as to sight? or art thou but
A dagger of the mind, a false creation,
Proceeding from the heat-oppressed brain?
I see thee yet, in form as palpable 40
As this which now I draw.
Thou marshall'st me the way that I was going;
And such an instrument I was to use.—
Mine eyes are made the fools o' the other senses,
Or else worth all the rest: I see thee still;
And on thy blade and dudgeon gouts of blood,
Which was not so before.—There 's no such thing:
It is the bloody business which informs
Thus to mine eyes.—Now o'er the one half world
Nature seems dead, and wicked dreams abuse 50
The curtain'd sleep; witchcraft celebrates
Pale Hecate's offerings, and wither'd murther,
Alarum'd by his sentinel the wolf,
Whose howl 's his watch, thus with his stealthy pace,
With Tarquin's ravishing strides, towards his design
Moves like a ghost.—Thou sure and firm-set earth,
Hear not my steps, which way they walk, for fear
Thy very stones prate of my whereabout,
And take the present horror from the time,
Which now suits with it.—Whiles I threat he lives: 60
Words to the heat of deeds too cool breath gives.

[*A bell rings.*

I go, and it is done; the bell invites me.—
Hear it not, Duncan, for it is a knell
That summons thee to heaven or to hell. [*Exit.*

SCENE II. *The Same.*

Enter LADY MACBETH.

Lady Macbeth. That which hath made them drunk hath made me bold;
What hath quench'd them hath given me fire.—Hark! Peace!
It was the owl that shriek'd, the fatal bellman,
Which gives the stern'st good-night. He is about it:
The doors are open, and the surfeited grooms
Do mock their charge with snores; I have drugg'd their possets,
That death and nature do contend about them,
Whether they live or die.

Macbeth. [*Within*] Who 's there? what, ho!

Lady Macbeth. Alack, I am afraid they have awak'd,
And 't is not done. The attempt and not the deed 10
Confounds us. Hark! I laid their daggers ready;
He could not miss 'em. Had he not resembled
My father as he slept, I had done 't.—My husband!

Enter MACBETH.

Macbeth. I have done the deed. Didst thou not hear a noise?

Lady Macbeth. I heard the owl scream and the crickets cry.
Did not you speak?

Macbeth. When?

Lady Macbeth. Now.

Macbeth. As I descended?

Lady Macbeth. Ay.

Macbeth. Hark!
Who lies i' the second chamber?

Lady Macbeth. Donalbain.

Macbeth. This is a sorry sight. [*Looking on his hands.* 20

Lady Macbeth. A foolish thought, to say a sorry sight.
Macbeth. There 's one did laugh in 's sleep, and one cried 'Murther!'
That they did wake each other: I stood and heard them:
But they did say their prayers, and address'd them
Again to sleep.
Lady Macbeth. There are two lodg'd together.
Macbeth. One cried 'God bless us!' and 'Amen' the other;
As they had seen me with these hangman's hands,
Listening their fear. I could not say 'Amen'
When they did say 'God bless us!'
Lady Macbeth. Consider it not so deeply. 30
Macbeth. But wherefore could not I pronounce 'Amen?'
I had most need of blessing, and 'Amen'
Stuck in my throat.
Lady Macbeth. These deeds must not be thought
After these ways; so, it will make us mad.
Macbeth. Methought I heard a voice cry 'Sleep no more!
Macbeth does murther sleep'—the innocent sleep,
Sleep that knits up the ravell'd sleave of care,
The death of each day's life, sore labour's bath,
Balm of hurt minds, great nature's second course,
Chief nourisher in life's feast,—
Lady Macbeth. What do you mean? 40
Macbeth. Still it cried 'Sleep no more!' to all the house:
'Glamis hath murther'd sleep, and therefore Cawdor
Shall sleep no more; Macbeth shall sleep no more.'
Lady Macbeth. Who was it that thus cried? Why, worthy thane,
You do unbend your noble strength, to think
So brainsickly of things. Go get some water,
And wash this filthy witness from your hand.
Why did you bring these daggers from the place?
They must lie there: go carry them, and smear
The sleepy grooms with blood.

Macbeth. I 'll go no more: 50
I am afraid to think what I have done;
Look on 't again I dare not.

Lady Macbeth. Infirm of purpose!
Give me the daggers: the sleeping and the dead
Are but as pictures; 't is the eye of childhood
That fears a painted devil. If he do bleed,
I 'll gild the faces of the grooms withal;
For it must seem their guilt. [*Exit. Knocking within.*

Macbeth. Whence is that knocking?
How is 't with me, when every noise appals me?
What hands are here? Ha! they pluck out mine eyes.
Will all great Neptune's ocean wash this blood 60
Clean from my hand? No; this my hand will rather
The multitudinous seas incarnadine,
Making the green one red.

Re-enter LADY MACBETH.

Lady Macbeth. My hands are of your colour; but I shame
To wear a heart so white. [*Knocking within.*] I hear a knocking
At the south entry: retire we to our chamber.
A little water clears us of this deed:
How easy is it, then! Your constancy
Hath left you unattended. [*Knocking within.*] Hark! more knocking.
Get on your nightgown, lest occasion call us 70
And show us to be watchers. Be not lost
So poorly in your thoughts.

Macbeth. To know my deed, 't were best not know myself.
[*Knocking within.*
Wake Duncan with thy knocking! I would thou couldst!
[*Exeunt.*

SCENE III. *The Same.*

Enter a Porter. *Knocking within.*

Porter. Here 's a knocking indeed! If a man were porter of hell-gate, he should have old turning the key. [*Knocking within.*] Knock, knock, knock! Who 's there, i' the name of Beelzebub? Here 's a farmer, that hanged himself on th' expectation of plenty: come in time; have napkins enow about you; here you 'll sweat for 't. [*Knocking within.*] Knock, knock! Who 's there, in th' other devil's name? Faith, here 's an equivocator, that could swear in both the scales against either scale; who committed treason enough for God's sake, yet could not equivocate to heaven: O, come in, equivocator. [*Knocking within.*] Knock, knock, knock! Who 's there? Faith, here 's an English tailor come hither, for stealing out of a French hose: come in, tailor; here you may roast your goose. [*Knocking within.*] Knock, knock; never at quiet! What are you? But this place is too cold for hell. I 'll devil-porter it no further: I had thought to have let in some of all professions, that go the primrose way to the everlasting bonfire.—[*Knocking within.*] Anon, anon! I pray you, remember the porter. [*Opens the gate.*

Enter MACDUFF *and* LENNOX.

Macduff. Was it so late, friend, ere you went to bed, 20
That you do lie so late?

Porter. Faith, sir, we were carousing till the second cock.

Macduff. Is thy master stirring?

Enter MACBETH.

Our knocking has awak'd him; here he comes.

Lennox. Good morrow, noble sir.

Macbeth. Good morrow, both.

Macduff. Is the king stirring, worthy thane?

Macbeth. Not yet.

Macduff. He did command me to call timely on him:
I have almost slipp'd the hour.

Macbeth. I 'll bring you to him.

Macduff. I know this is a joyful trouble to you;
But yet 't is one. 30

Macbeth. The labour we delight in physics pain.
This is the door.

Macduff. I 'll make so bold to call,
For 't is my limited service. [*Exit.*

Lennox. Goes the king hence to day?

Macbeth. He does: he did appoint so.

Lennox. The night has been unruly; where we lay,
Our chimneys were blown down, and, as they say,
Lamentings heard i' the air, strange screams of death,
And prophesying with accents terrible
Of dire combustion and confus'd events
New hatch'd to the woeful time; the obscure bird 40
Clamour'd the livelong night; some say the earth
Was feverous and did shake.

Macbeth. 'T was a rough night.

Lennox. My young remembrance cannot parallel
A fellow to it.

Re-enter MACDUFF.

Macduff. O horror, horror, horror! Tongue nor heart
Cannot conceive nor name thee!

Macbeth. } *Lennox.* } What 's the matter?

Macduff. Confusion now hath made his masterpiece.
Most sacrilegious murther hath broke ope
The Lord's anointed temple, and stole thence
The life o' the building.

Macbeth. What is 't you say? the life? 50

Lennox. Mean you his majesty?

Macduff. Approach the chamber, and destroy your sight
With a new Gorgon. Do not bid me speak;
See, and then speak yourselves. [*Exeunt Macbeth and Lennox.*
Awake, awake!
Ring the alarum-bell.—Murther and treason!—
Banquo and Donalbain!—Malcolm! awake!
Shake off this downy sleep, death's counterfeit,
And look on death itself! up, up, and see
The great doom's image!—Malcolm! Banquo!
As from your graves rise up, and walk like sprites, 60
To countenance this horror. Ring the bell. [*Bell rings.*

Enter LADY MACBETH.

Lady Macbeth. What 's the business,
That such a hideous trumpet calls to parley
The sleepers of the house? speak, speak!

Macduff. O gentle lady,
'T is not for you to hear what I can speak:
The repetition, in a woman's ear,
Would murther as it fell.—

Enter BANQUO.

O Banquo, Banquo!
Our royal master 's murther'd.

Lady Macbeth. Woe, alas!
What, in our house?

Banquo. Too cruel any where.
Dear Duff, I prithee, contradict thyself, 71
And say it is not so.

Re-enter MACBETH *and* LENNOX.

Macbeth. Had I but died an hour before this chance,
I had liv'd a blessed time; for from this instant
There 's nothing serious in mortality:

All is but toys: renown and grace is dead;
The wine of life is drawn, and the mere lees
Is left this vault to brag of.

Enter MALCOLM *and* DONALBAIN.

Donalbain. What is amiss?
Macbeth. You are, and do not know 't:
The spring, the head, the fountain of your blood
Is stopp'd,—the very source of it is stopp'd. 80
Macduff. Your royal father 's murther'd.
Malcolm. O, by whom?
Lennox. Those of his chamber, as it seem'd, had done 't.
Their hands and faces were all badg'd with blood;
So were their daggers, which unwip'd we found
Upon their pillows:
They star'd, and were distracted; no man's life
Was to be trusted with them.
Macbeth. O, yet I do repent me of my fury,
That I did kill them.
Macduff. Wherefore did you so?
Macbeth. Who can be wise, amaz'd, temperate and furious,
Loyal and neutral, in a moment? No man: 90
The expedition of my violent love
Outrun the pauser reason. Here lay Duncan,
His silver skin lac'd with his golden blood,
And his gash'd stabs look'd like a breach in nature
For ruin's wasteful entrance; there, the murtherers,
Steep'd in the colours of their trade, their daggers
Unmannerly breech'd with gore: who could refrain,
That had a heart to love, and in that heart
Courage to make 's love known?
Lady Macbeth. Help me hence, ho! 100
Macduff. Look to the lady.

Malcolm. [*Aside to Donalbain*] Why do we hold our tongues,
That most may claim this argument for ours?

Donalbain. [*Aside to Malcolm*] What should be spoken here, where our fate,
Hid in an auger-hole, may rush, and seize us?
Let 's away;
Our tears are not yet brew'd.

Malcolm. [*Aside to Donalbain*] Nor our strong sorrow
Upon the foot of motion.

Banquo. Look to the lady:—
[*Lady Macbeth is carried out.*
And when we have our naked frailties hid,
That suffer in exposure, let us meet,
And question this most bloody piece of work, 110
To know it further. Fears and scruples shake us:
In the great hand of God I stand, and thence
Against the undivulg'd pretence I fight
Of treasonous malice.

Macduff. And so do I.

All. So all.

Macbeth. Let 's briefly put on manly readiness,
And meet i' the hall together.

All. Well contented.
[*Exeunt all but Malcolm and Donalbain.*

Malcolm. What will you do? Let 's not consort with them:
To show an unfelt sorrow is an office
Which the false man does easy. I 'll to England.

Donalbain. To Ireland, I: our separated fortune 120
Shall keep us both the safer; where we are,
There 's daggers in men's smiles: the near in blood,
The nearer bloody.

Malcolm. This murtherous shaft that 's shot
Hath not yet lighted, and our safest way
Is to avoid the aim. Therefore, to horse;

And let us not be dainty of leave-taking,
But shift away: there 's warrant in that theft
Which steals itself when there 's no mercy left. [*Exeunt.*

SCENE IV. *Without the Castle.*

Enter ROSS *and an* old Man.

Old Man. Threescore and ten I can remember well:
Within the volume of which time I have seen
Hours dreadful and things strange; but this sore night
Hath trifled former knowings.

Ross. Ah, good father,
Thou seest, the heavens, as troubled with man's act,
Threaten his bloody stage: by the clock 't is day,
And yet dark night strangles the travelling lamp.
Is 't night's predominance, or the day's shame,
That darkness does the face of earth entomb,
When living light should kiss it?

Old Man. 'T is unnatural, 10
Even like the deed that 's done. On Tuesday last,
A falcon, towering in her pride of place,
Was by a mousing owl hawk'd at and kill'd.

Ross. And Duncan's horses — a thing most strange and certain—
Beauteous and swift, the minions of their race,
Turn'd wild in nature, broke their stalls, flung out,
Contending 'gainst obedience, as they would make
War with mankind.

Old Man. 'T is said they eat each other.

Ross. They did so, to the amazement of mine eyes
That look'd upon 't. Here comes the good Macduff.— 20

Enter MACDUFF.

How goes the world, sir, now?

Macduff. Why, see you not?

Ross. Is 't known who did this more than bloody deed?
Macduff. Those that Macbeth hath slain.
Ross. Alas, the day!
What good could they pretend?
Macduff. They were suborn'd:
Malcolm and Donalbain, the king's two sons,
Are stolen away and fled, which puts upon them
Suspicion of the deed.
Ross. 'Gainst nature still:
Thriftless ambition, that wilt ravin up
Thine own life's means! Then 't is most like
The sovereignty will fall upon Macbeth. 30
Macduff. He is already nam'd, and gone to Scone
To be invested.
Ross. Where is Duncan's body?
Macduff. Carried to Colme-kill,
The sacred storehouse of his predecessors
And guardian of their bones.
Ross. Will you to Scone?
Macduff. No, cousin, I 'll to Fife.
Ross. Well, I will thither.
Macduff. Well, may you see things well done there: adieu!
Lest our old robes sit easier than our new!
Ross. Farewell, father.
Old Man. God's benison go with you, and with those 40
That would make good of bad, and friends of foes!
[*Exeunt.*

FORRES.

ACT III.

SCENE I. *Forres. A Room in the Palace.*

Enter BANQUO.

Banquo. Thou hast it now,—king, Cawdor, Glamis, all,—
As the weird women promis'd, and I fear
Thou play'dst most foully for 't. Yet it was said
It should not stand in thy posterity,
But that myself should be the root and father
Of many kings. If there come truth from them—
As upon thee, Macbeth, their speeches shine—
Why, by the verities on thee made good,
May they not be my oracles as well
And set me up in hope? But hush! no more. 10

Sennet sounded. Enter MACBETH, *as king;* LADY MACBETH, *as queen;* LENNOX, ROSS, Lords, Ladies, *and* Attendants.

Macbeth. Here 's our chief guest.
Lady Macbeth. If he had been forgotten,
It had been as a gap in our great feast,
And all-thing unbecoming.
Macbeth. To-night we hold a solemn supper, sir,
And I 'll request your presence.
Banquo. Let your highness
Command upon me, to the which my duties
Are with a most indissoluble tie
For ever knit.
Macbeth. Ride you this afternoon?
Banquo. Ay, my good lord. 19
Macbeth. We should have else desir'd your good advice,
Which still hath been both grave and prosperous,
In this day's council; but we 'll take to-morrow.
Is 't far you ride?
Banquo. As far, my lord, as will fill up the time
'Twixt this and supper: go not my horse the better,
I must become a borrower of the night
For a dark hour or twain.
Macbeth. Fail not our feast.
Banquo. My lord, I will not.
Macbeth. We hear our bloody cousins are bestow'd
In England and in Ireland, not confessing 30
Their cruel parricide, filling their hearers
With strange invention: but of that to-morrow,
When therewithal we shall have cause of state
Craving us jointly. Hie you to horse: adieu,
Till you return at night. Goes Fleance with you?
Banquo. Ay, my good lord: our time does call upon 's.
Macbeth. I wish your horses swift and sure of foot;
And so I do commend you to their backs.

Farewell.— [*Exit Banquo.*
Let every man be master of his time 40
Till seven at night. To make society
The sweeter welcome, we will keep ourself
Till supper-time alone: while then, God be with you!
[*Exeunt all but Macbeth and an Attendant.*
Sirrah, a word with you: attend those men
Our pleasure?

Attendant. They are, my lord, without the palace gate.

Macbeth. Bring them before us.— [*Exit Attendant.*
To be thus is nothing;
But to be safely thus. Our fears in Banquo
Stick deep; and in his royalty of nature
Reigns that which would be fear'd: 't is much he dares, 50
And, to that dauntless temper of his mind,
He hath a wisdom that doth guide his valour
To act in safety. There is none but he
Whose being I do fear: and under him
My Genius is rebuk'd, as it is said
Mark Antony's was by Cæsar. He chid the sisters,
When first they put the name of king upon me,
And bade them speak to him; then prophet-like
They hail'd him father to a line of kings.
Upon my head they plac'd a fruitless crown, 60
And put a barren sceptre in my gripe,
Thence to be wrench'd with an unlineal hand,
No son of mine succeeding. If 't be so,
For Banquo's issue have I fil'd my mind;
For them the gracious Duncan have I murther'd;
Put rancours in the vessel of my peace
Only for them; and mine eternal jewel
Given to the common enemy of man,
To make them kings, the seed of Banquo kings!
Rather than so, come, fate, into the list, 70
And champion me to the utterance!—Who 's there?—

Re-enter Attendant, *with two* Murderers.

Now go to the door, and stay there till we call.—
[*Exit Attendant.*
Was it not yesterday we spoke together?
First Murderer. It was, so please your highness.
Macbeth. Well then, now
Have you consider'd of my speeches? Know
That it was he in the times past which held you
So under fortune, which you thought had been
Our innocent self. This I made good to you
In our last conference, pass'd in probation with you, 70
How you were borne in hand, how cross'd, the instruments,
Who wrought with them, and all things else that might
To half a soul and to a notion craz'd
Say 'Thus did Banquo.'
First Murderer. You made it known to us.
Macbeth. I did so, and went further, which is now
Our point of second meeting. Do you find
Your patience so predominant in your nature
That you can let this go? Are you so gospell'd
To pray for this good man and for his issue,
Whose heavy hand hath bow'd you to the grave
And beggar'd yours for ever?
First Murderer. We are men, my liege. 90
Macbeth. Ay, in the catalogue ye go for men,
As hounds and greyhounds, mongrels, spaniels, curs,
Shoughs, water-rugs, and demi-wolves, are clept
All by the name of dogs: the valued file
Distinguishes the swift, the slow, the subtle,
The housekeeper, the hunter, every one
According to the gift which bounteous nature
Hath in him clos'd; whereby he does receive
Particular addition, from the bill
That writes them all alike: and so of men. 100

Now if you have a station in the file,
Not i' the worst rank of manhood, say 't,
And I will put that business in your bosoms,
Whose execution takes your enemy off,
Grapples you to the heart and love of us,
Who wear our health but sickly in his life,
Which in his death were perfect.

Second Murderer. I am one, my liege,
Whom the vile blows and buffets of the world
Have so incens'd that I am reckless what
I do to spite the world.

First Murderer. And I another 110
So weary with disasters, tugg'd with fortune,
That I would set my life on any chance,
To mend it or be rid on 't.

Macbeth. Both of you
Know Banquo was your enemy.

Both Murderers. True, my lord.

Macbeth. So is he mine, and in such bloody distance
That every minute of his being thrusts
Against my near'st of life: and though I could
With barefac'd power sweep him from my sight
And bid my will avouch it, yet I must not,
For certain friends that are both his and mine, 120
Whose loves I may not drop, but wail his fall
Who I myself struck down: and thence it is,
That I to your assistance do make love,
Masking the business from the common eye
For sundry weighty reasons.

Second Murderer. We shall, my lord,
Perform what you command us.

First Murderer. Though our lives—

Macbeth. Your spirits shine through you. Within this hour at most
I will advise you where to plant yourselves,

Acquaint you with the perfect spy o' the time,
The moment on 't; for 't must be done to-night, 130
And something from the palace; always thought
That I require a clearness: and with him—
To leave no rubs nor botches in the work—
Fleance his son, that keeps him company,
Whose absence is no less material to me
Than is his father's, must embrace the fate
Of that dark hour. Resolve yourselves apart:
I 'll come to you anon.

Both Murderers. We are resolv'd, my lord.

Macbeth. I 'll call upon you straight: abide within.

[*Exeunt Murderers.*

It is concluded: Banquo, thy soul's flight, 140
If it find heaven, must find it out to-night. [*Exit.*

SCENE II. *The Same. Another Room.*

Enter LADY MACBETH *and a* Servant.

Lady Macbeth. Is Banquo gone from court?

Servant. Ay, madam, but returns again to-night.

Lady Macbeth. Say to the king, I would attend his leisure
For a few words.

Servant. Madam, I will. [*Exit.*

Lady Macbeth. Nought 's had, all 's spent,
Where our desire is got without content:
'T is safer to be that which we destroy
Than by destruction dwell in doubtful joy.

Enter MACBETH.

How now, my lord! why do you keep alone,
Of sorriest fancies your companions making,
Using those thoughts which should indeed have died 10
With them they think on? Things without all remedy
Should be without regard: what 's done is done.

Macbeth. We have scotch'd the snake, not kill'd it:
She 'll close and be herself, whilst our poor malice
Remains in danger of her former tooth.
But let the frame of things disjoint, both the worlds suffer,
Ere we will eat our meal in fear, and sleep
In the affliction of these terrible dreams
That shake us nightly; better be with the dead,
Whom we, to gain our peace, have sent to peace, 20
Than on the torture of the mind to lie
In restless ecstasy. Duncan is in his grave;
After life's fitful fever he sleeps well;
Treason has done his worst: nor steel, nor poison,
Malice domestic, foreign levy, nothing,
Can touch him further.

Lady Macbeth. Come on;
Gentle my lord, sleek o'er your rugged looks;
Be bright and jovial among your guests to-night.

Macbeth. So shall I, love; and so, I pray, be you:
Let your remembrance apply to Banquo; 30
Present him eminence, both with eye and tongue:
Unsafe the while that we
Must lave our honours in these flattering streams,
And make our faces visards to our hearts,
Disguising what they are.

Lady Macbeth. You must leave this.

Macbeth. O, full of scorpions is my mind, dear wife!
Thou know'st that Banquo, and his Fleance, lives.

Lady Macbeth. But in them nature's copy 's not eterne.

Macbeth. There 's comfort yet; they are assailable;
Then be thou jocund. Ere the bat hath flown 40
His cloister'd flight, ere to black Hecate's summons
The shard-borne beetle with his drowsy hums
Hath rung night's yawning peal, there shall be done
A deed of dreadful note.

Lady Macbeth. What 's to be done?

Macbeth. Be innocent of the knowledge, dearest chuck,

Till thou applaud the deed.—Come, seeling night,
Scarf up the tender eye of pitiful day,
And with thy bloody and invisible hand
Cancel and tear to pieces that great bond
Which keeps me pale!—Light thickens, and the crow 50
Makes wing to the rooky wood:
Good things of day begin to droop and drowse,
Whiles night's black agents to their preys do rouse.
Thou marvell'st at my words; but hold thee still:
Things bad begun make strong themselves by ill.
So, prithee, go with me. [*Exeunt.*

SCENE III. *A Park near the Palace.*

Enter three Murderers.

First Murderer. But who did bid thee join with us?
Third Murderer. Macbeth.
Second Murderer. He needs not our mistrust, since he delivers
Our offices and what we have to do
To the direction just.
First Murderer. Then stand with us.
The west yet glimmers with some streaks of day:
Now spurs the lated traveller apace
To gain the timely inn, and near approaches
The subject of our watch.
Third Murderer. Hark! I hear horses.
Banquo. [*Within*] Give us a light there, ho!
Second Murderer. Then 't is he: the rest
That are within the note of expectation 10
Already are i' the court.
First Murderer. His horses go about.
Third Murderer. Almost a mile: but he does usually,
So all men do, from hence to the palace gate
Make it their walk.
Second Murderer. A light, a light!

Enter BANQUO, *and* FLEANCE *with a Torch.*

Third Murderer. 'T is he.

First Murderer. Stand to 't.

Banquo. It will be rain to-night.

First Murderer. Let it come down.

[*They set upon Banquo.*

Banquo. O, treachery! Fly, good Fleance, fly, fly, fly!
Thou mayst revenge.—O slave! [*Dies. Fleance escapes.*

Third Murderer. Who did strike out the light?

First Murderer. Was 't not the way?

Third Murderer. There 's but one down; the son is fled.

Second Murderer. We have lost
Best half of our affair. 21

First Murderer. Well, let 's away and say how much is done. [*Exeunt.*

SCENE IV. *Hall in the Palace.*

A Banquet prepared. Enter MACBETH, LADY MACBETH, ROSS, LENNOX, Lords, *and* Attendants.

Macbeth. You know your own degrees; sit down: at first
And last the hearty welcome.

Lords. Thanks to your majesty.

Macbeth. Ourself will mingle with society
And play the humble host.
Our hostess keeps her state, but in best time
We will require her welcome.

Lady Macbeth. Pronounce it for me, sir, to all our friends;
For my heart speaks they are welcome.

First Murderer *appears at the door.*

Macbeth. See, they encounter thee with their hearts' thanks.—
Both sides are even: here I 'll sit i' the midst. 10

Be large in mirth ; anon we 'll drink a measure
The table round.—[*Approaching the door*] There 's blood upon thy face.

Murderer. 'T is Banquo's then.

Macbeth. 'T is better thee without than he within.
Is he dispatch'd?

Murderer. My lord, his throat is cut ; that I did for him.

Macbeth. Thou art the best o' the cut-throats : yet he 's good
That did the like for Fleance : if thou didst it,
Thou art the nonpareil.

Murderer. Most royal sir,
Fleance is scap'd. 20

Macbeth. [*Aside*] Then comes my fit again : I had else been perfect,
Whole as the marble, founded as the rock,
As broad and general as the casing air ;
But now I am cabin'd, cribb'd, confin'd, bound in
To saucy doubts and fears.—But Banquo 's safe?

Murderer. Ay, my good lord : safe in a ditch he bides,
With twenty trenched gashes on his head,
The least a death to nature.

Macbeth. Thanks for that.
[*Aside*] There the grown serpent lies ; the worm that 's fled
Hath nature that in time will venom breed, 30
No teeth for the present.—Get thee gone : to-morrow
We 'll hear ourselves again. [*Exit Murderer.*

Lady Macbeth. My royal lord,
You do not give the cheer ; the feast is sold
That is not often vouch'd, while 't is a-making,
'T is given with welcome : to feed were best at home ;
From thence the sauce to meat is ceremony ;
Meeting were bare without it.

Macbeth. Sweet remembrancer !

Now good digestion wait on appetite,
And health on both!
Lennox. May 't please your highness sit.
[*The Ghost of Banquo enters, and sits in Macbeth's place.*
Macbeth. Here had we now our country's honour roof'd,
Were the grac'd person of our Banquo present; 41
Who may I rather challenge for unkindness
Than pity for mischance!
Ross. His absence, sir,
Lays blame upon his promise. Please 't your highness
To grace us with your royal company.
Macbeth. The table 's full.
Lennox. Here is a place reserv'd, sir.
Macbeth. Where?
Lennox. Here, my good lord. What is 't that moves your highness?
Macbeth. Which of you have done this?
Lords. What, my good lord?
Macbeth. Thou canst not say I did it: never shake 50
Thy gory locks at me.
Ross. Gentlemen, rise: his highness is not well.
Lady Macbeth. Sit, worthy friends, my lord is often thus,
And hath been from his youth: pray you, keep seat;
The fit is momentary; upon a thought
He will again be well. If much you note him,
You shall offend him and extend his passion;
Feed, and regard him not.—Are you a man?
Macbeth. Ay, and a bold one, that dare look on that
Which might appal the devil.
Lady Macbeth. O proper stuff! 60
This is the very painting of your fear:
This is the air-drawn dagger which, you said,
Led you to Duncan. O, these flaws and starts,
Impostors to true fear, would well become
A woman's story at a winter's fire,

Authoriz'd by her grandam. Shame itself!
Why do you make such faces? When all 's done,
You look but on a stool.

Macbeth. Prithee, see there! behold! look! lo! how say you?—
Why, what care I? If thou canst nod, speak too.— 70
If charnel-houses and our graves must send
Those that we bury back, our monuments
Shall be the maws of kites. [*Ghost vanishes.*

Lady Macbeth. What, quite unmann'd in folly?

Macbeth. If I stand here, I saw him.

Lady Macbeth. Fie, for shame!

Macbeth. Blood hath been shed ere now, i' the olden time,
Ere human statute purg'd the gentle weal;
Ay, and since too, murthers have been perform'd
Too terrible for the ear: the time has been,
That when the brains were out the man would die,
And there an end; but now they rise again, 80
With twenty mortal murthers on their crowns,
And push us from our stools. This is more strange
Than such a murther is.

Lady Macbeth. My worthy lord,
Your noble friends do lack you.

Macbeth. I do forget.—
Do not muse at me, my most worthy friends;
I have a strange infirmity, which is nothing
To those that know me. Come, love and health to all;
Then I 'll sit down.—Give me some wine, fill full.—
I drink to the general joy o' the whole table,
And to our dear friend Banquo, whom we miss; 90
Would he were here! to all and him we thirst,
And all to all.

Lords. Our duties, and the pledge.

Re-enter Ghost.

Macbeth. Avaunt! and quit my sight! let the earth hide thee!
Thy bones are marrowless, thy blood is cold;
Thou hast no speculation in those eyes
Which thou dost glare with.

Lady Macbeth. Think of this, good peers,
But as a thing of custom: 't is no other;
Only it spoils the pleasure of the time.

Macbeth. What man dare, I dare:
Approach thou like the rugged Russian bear, 100
The arm'd rhinoceros, or the Hyrcan tiger;
Take any shape but that, and my firm nerves
Shall never tremble: or be alive again,
And dare me to the desert with thy sword;
If trembling I inhabit then, protest me
The baby of a girl. Hence, horrible shadow!
Unreal mockery, hence! [*Ghost vanishes.*
Why, so: being gone,
I am a man again.—Pray you, sit still.

Lady Macbeth. You have displac'd the mirth, broke the good meeting,
With most admir'd disorder.

Macbeth. Can such things be, 110
And overcome us like a summer's cloud,
Without our special wonder? You make me strange
Even to the disposition that I owe,
When now I think you can behold such sights,
And keep the natural ruby of your cheeks,
When mine is blanch'd with fear.

Ross. What sights, my lord?

Lady Macbeth. I pray you, speak not; he grows worse and worse;
Question enrages him. At once, good night:

Stand not upon the order of your going,
But go at once.
Lennox. Good night; and better health 120
Attend his majesty!
Lady Macbeth. A kind good night to all!
[*Exeunt all but Macbeth and Lady Macbeth.*
Macbeth. It will have blood, they say; blood will have blood:
Stones have been known to move and trees to speak;
Augurs and understood relations have
By magot-pies and choughs and rooks brought forth
The secret'st man of blood.—What is the night?
Lady Macbeth. Almost at odds with morning, which is which.
Macbeth. How say'st thou, that Macduff denies his person
At our great bidding?
Lady Macbeth. Did you send to him, sir?
Macbeth. I hear it by the way, but I will send: 130
There 's not a one of them but in his house
I keep a servant fee'd. I will to-morrow,
And betimes I will, to the weird sisters:
More shall they speak, for now I am bent to know,
By the worst means, the worst. For mine own good
All causes shall give way: I am in blood
Stepp'd in so far that, should I wade no more,
Returning were as tedious as go o'er.
Strange things I have in head that will to hand,
Which must be acted ere they may be scann'd. 140
Lady Macbeth. You lack the season of all natures, sleep.
Macbeth. Come, we 'll to sleep. My strange and self-abuse
Is the initiate fear that wants hard use:
We are yet but young in deed. [*Exeunt.*

SCENE V. *A Heath.*

Thunder. Enter the three Witches, *meeting* HECATE.

First Witch. Why, how now, Hecate! you look angerly.

Hecate. Have I not reason, beldams as you are,
Saucy and overbold? How did you dare
To trade and traffic with Macbeth
In riddles and affairs of death;
And I, the mistress of your charms,
The close contriver of all harms,
Was never call'd to bear my part,
Or show the glory of our art?
And, which is worse, all you have done 10
Hath been but for a wayward son,
Spiteful and wrathful; who, as others do,
Loves for his own ends, not for you.
But make amends now: get you gone,
And at the pit of Acheron
Meet me i' the morning: thither he
Will come to know his destiny.
Your vessels and your spells provide,
Your charms and every thing beside.
I am for the air; this night I 'll spend 20
Unto a dismal and a fatal end:
Great business must be wrought ere noon.
Upon the corner of the moon
There hangs a vaporous drop profound;
I 'll catch it ere it come to ground:
And that, distill'd by magic sleights,
Shall raise such artificial sprites
As by the strength of their illusion
Shall draw him on to his confusion.
He shall spurn fate, scorn death, and bear 30
His hopes 'bove wisdom, grace, and fear:

And you all know security
Is mortals' chiefest enemy.

[*Music and a song within:* 'Come away, come away,' etc.

Hark! I am call'd; my little spirit, see,
Sits in a foggy cloud, and stays for me. [*Exit.*

First Witch. Come, let 's make haste; she 'll soon be back again. [*Exeunt.*

SCENE VI. *Forres. The Palace.*

Enter LENNOX *and another* Lord.

Lennox. My former speeches have but hit your thoughts,
Which can interpret farther: only I say
Things have been strangely borne. The gracious Duncan
Was pitied of Macbeth:—marry, he was dead;
And the right-valiant Banquo walk'd too late;
Whom, you may say, if 't please you, Fleance kill'd,
For Fleance fled: men must not walk too late.
Who cannot want the thought, how monstrous
It was for Malcolm and for Donalbain
To kill their gracious father? damned fact! 10
How it did grieve Macbeth! did he not straight
In pious rage the two delinquents tear,
That were the slaves of drink and thralls of sleep?
Was not that nobly done? Ay, and wisely too;
For 't would have anger'd any heart alive
To hear the men deny 't. So that, I say,
He has borne all things well: and I do think
That had he Duncan's sons under his key—
As, an 't please heaven, he shall not—they should find
What 't were to kill a father; so should Fleance. 20
But, peace! for from broad words, and 'cause he fail'd
His presence at the tyrant's feast, I hear
Macduff lives in disgrace. Sir, can you tell
Where he bestows himself?

Lord. The son of Duncan,
From whom this tyrant holds the due of birth,
Lives in the English court, and is receiv'd
Of the most pious Edward with such grace
That the malevolence of fortune nothing
Takes from his high respect. Thither Macduff
Is gone to pray the holy king, upon his aid 30
To wake Northumberland and warlike Siward;
That by help of these, with Him above
To ratify the work, we may again
Give to our tables meat, sleep to our nights,
Free from our feasts and banquets bloody knives,
Do faithful homage and receive free honours;
All which we pine for now. And this report
Hath so exasperate the king that he
Prepares for some attempt of war.

Lennox. Sent he to Macduff

Lord. He did: and with an absolute 'Sir, not I,' 40
The cloudy messenger turns me his back,
And hums, as who should say 'You 'll rue the time
That clogs me with this answer.'

Lennox. And that well might
Advise him to a caution, to hold what distance
His wisdom can provide. Some holy angel
Fly to the court of England and unfold
His message ere he come, that a swift blessing
May soon return to this our suffering country
Under a hand accurs'd!

Lord. I 'll send my prayers with him!

[*Exeunt.*

THE DUNSINANE RANGE.

ACT IV.

SCENE I. *A Cavern. In the Middle, a Boiling Cauldron Thunder. Enter the three* Witches.

First Witch. Thrice the brinded cat hath mew'd.
Second Witch. Thrice and once the hedge-pig whin'd.
Third Witch. Harpier cries,—'t is time, 't is time.
First Witch. Round about the cauldron go;
In the poison'd entrails throw.
Toad, that under cold stone
Days and nights has thirty-one
Swelter'd venom sleeping got,
Boil thou first i' the charmed pot.
All. Double, double toil and trouble; 10
Fire burn and cauldron bubble.

G

Second Witch. Fillet of a fenny snake,
In the cauldron boil and bake;
Eye of newt and toe of frog,
Wool of bat and tongue of dog,
Adder's fork and blind-worm's sting,
Lizard's leg and howlet's wing,
For a charm of powerful trouble,
Like a hell-broth boil and bubble.
All. Double, double toil and trouble; 20
Fire burn and cauldron bubble.
Third Witch. Scale of dragon, tooth of wolf,
Witches' mummy, maw and gulf
Of the ravin'd salt-sea shark,
Root of hemlock digg'd i' the dark,
Liver of blaspheming Jew,
Gall of goat, and slips of yew
Sliver'd in the moon's eclipse,
Nose of Turk and Tartar's lips,
Finger of birth-strangled babe 30
Ditch-deliver'd by a drab,
Make the gruel thick and slab:
Add thereto a tiger's chaudron,
For the ingredients of our cauldron.
All. Double, double toil and trouble;
Fire burn and cauldron bubble.
Second Witch. Cool it with a baboon's blood,
Then the charm is firm and good.

Enter HECATE.

Hecate. O, well done! I commend your pains;
And every one shall share i' the gains: 40
And now about the cauldron sing,
Like elves and fairies in a ring,
Enchanting all that you put in.
[*Music and a song:* 'Black spirits,' etc. *Hecate retires.*

Second Witch. By the pricking of my thumbs,
Something wicked this way comes.
Open, locks,
Whoever knocks!

Enter MACBETH.

Macbeth. How now, you secret, black, and midnight hags!
What is 't you do?
All. A deed without a name.
Macbeth. I conjure you, by that which you profess, 50
Howe'er you come to know it, answer me:
Though you untie the winds and let them fight
Against the churches; though the yesty waves
Confound and swallow navigation up;
Though bladed corn be lodg'd and trees blown down;
Though castles topple on their warders' heads;
Though palaces and pyramids do slope
Their heads to their foundations; though the treasure
Of nature's germens tumble all together,
Even till destruction sicken; answer me 60
To what I ask you.
First Witch. Speak.
Second Witch. Demand.
Third Witch. We 'll answer.
First Witch. Say, if thou 'dst rather hear it from our mouths,
Or from our masters.
Macbeth. Call 'em; let me see 'em.
First Witch. Pour in sow's blood, that hath eaten
Her nine farrow; grease that 's sweaten
From the murtherer's gibbet throw
Into the flame.
All. Come, high or low;
Thyself and office deftly show!

Thunder. *First* Apparition: *an armed Head.*

Macbeth. Tell me, thou unknown power,—

First Witch. He knows thy thought:
Hear his speech, but say thou nought. 70

First Apparition. Macbeth! Macbeth! Macbeth! beware Macduff;
Beware the thane of Fife. Dismiss me: enough. [*Descends.*

Macbeth. Whate'er thou art, for thy good caution thanks;
Thou hast harp'd my fear aright: but one word more,—

First Witch. He will not be commanded: here 's another,
More potent than the first.

Thunder. *Second* Apparition: *a bloody Child.*

Second Apparition. Macbeth! Macbeth! Macbeth!

Macbeth. Had I three ears, I 'd hear thee.

Second Apparition. Be bloody, bold, and resolute; laugh to scorn
The power of man, for none of woman born 80
Shall harm Macbeth. [*Descends.*

Macbeth. Then live, Macduff: what need I fear of thee?
But yet I 'll make assurance double sure,
And take a bond of fate: thou shalt not live;
That I may tell pale-hearted fear it lies,
And sleep in spite of thunder.

Thunder. *Third* Apparition: *a Child crowned, with a tree in his hand.*

What is this,
That rises like the issue of a king,
And wears upon his baby brow the round
And top of sovereignty?

All. Listen, but speak not to 't.

Third Apparition. Be lion-mettled, proud, and take no care
Who chafes, who frets, or where conspirers are: 91

Macbeth shall never vanquish'd be until
Great Birnam wood to high Dunsinane hill
Shall come against him. [*Descends.*

Macbeth. That will never be:
Who can impress the forest, bid the tree
Unfix his earth-bound root? Sweet bodements! good!
Rebellion's head, rise never, till the wood
Of Birnam rise, and our high-plac'd Macbeth
Shall live the lease of nature, pay his breath
To time and mortal custom. Yet my heart 100
Throbs to know one thing: tell me,—if your art
Can tell so much,—shall Banquo's issue ever
Reign in this kingdom?

All. Seek to know no more.

Macbeth. I will be satisfied: deny me this,
And an eternal curse fall on you! Let me know—
Why sinks that cauldron? and what noise is this?
[*Hautboys.*

First Witch. Show!

Second Witch. Show!

Third Witch. Show!

All. Show his eyes, and grieve his heart; 110
Come like shadows, so depart!

A show of eight Kings, *the last with a glass in his hand; Banquo's Ghost following.*

Macbeth. Thou art too like the spirit of Banquo; down!
Thy crown does sear mine eyeballs.—And thy hair,
Thou other gold-bound brow, is like the first.—
A third is like the former.—Filthy hags!
Why do you show me this?—A fourth!—Start, eyes!—
What, will the line stretch out to the crack of doom?—
Another yet!—A seventh!—I'll see no more:—
And yet the eighth appears, who bears a glass
Which shows me many more; and some I see 120

That twofold balls and treble sceptres carry:
Horrible sight!—Now I see 't is true;
For the blood-bolter'd Banquo smiles upon me,
And points at them for his.— [*Apparitions vanish.*
What, is this so?

First Witch. Ay, sir, all this is so: but why
Stands Macbeth thus amazedly?
Come, sisters, cheer we up his sprights,
And show the best of our delights:
I 'll charm the air to give a sound,
While you perform your antic round, 130
That this great king may kindly say,
Our duties did his welcome pay.

[*Music. The Witches dance, and then vanish, with Hecate.*

Macbeth. Where are they? Gone? Let this pernicious hour
Stand aye accursed in the calendar!—
Come in, without there!

Enter LENNOX.

Lennox. What 's your grace's will?

Macbeth. Saw you the weird sisters?

Lennox. No, my lord.

Macbeth. Came they not by you?

Lennox. No indeed, my lord.

Macbeth. Infected be the air whereon they ride;
And damn'd all those that trust them!—I did hear
The galloping of horse: who was 't came by? 140

Lennox. 'T is two or three, my lord, that bring you word
Macduff is fled to England.

Macbeth. Fled to England!

Lennox. Ay, my good lord.

Macbeth. [*Aside*] Time, thou anticipat'st my dread exploits:
The flighty purpose never is o'ertook

Unless the deed go with it. From this moment
The very firstlings of my heart shall be
The firstlings of my hand. And even now,
To crown my thoughts with acts, be it thought and done:
The castle of Macduff I will surprise, 150
Seize upon Fife, give to the edge o' the sword
His wife, his babes, and all unfortunate souls
That trace him in his line. No boasting like a fool;
This deed I 'll do before this purpose cool.
But no more sights!—Where are these gentlemen?
Come, bring me where they are. [*Exeunt.*

SCENE II. *Fife. A Room in Macduff's Castle.*

Enter LADY MACDUFF, *her* SON, *and* ROSS.

Lady Macduff. What had he done, to make him fly the land?

Ross. You must have patience, madam.

Lady Macduff. He had none;
His flight was madness: when our actions do not,
Our fears do make us traitors.

Ross. You know not
Whether it was his wisdom or his fear.

Lady Macduff. Wisdom! to leave his wife, to leave his babes,
His mansion and his titles, in a place
From whence himself does fly? He loves us not;
He wants the natural touch: for the poor wren,
The most diminutive of birds, will fight, 10
Her young ones in her nest, against the owl.
All is the fear, and nothing is the love;
As little is the wisdom, where the flight
So runs against all reason.

Ross. My dearest coz,
I pray you, school yourself: but for your husband,

He is noble, wise, judicious, and best knows
The fits o' the season. I dare not speak much further;
But cruel are the times, when we are traitors
And do not know ourselves; when we hold rumour
From what we fear, yet know not what we fear, 20
But float upon a wild and violent sea
Each way and move. I take my leave of you;
Shall not be long but I 'll be here again.
Things at the worst will cease, or else climb upward
To what they were before. My pretty cousin,
Blessing upon you!

Lady Macduff. Father'd he is, and yet he 's fatherless.

Ross. I am so much a fool, should I stay longer,
It would be my disgrace and your discomfort:
I take my leave at once. [*Exit.*

Lady Macduff. Sirrah, your father 's dead: 30
And what will you do now? How will you live?

Son. As birds do, mother.

Lady Macduff. What, with worms and flies?

Son. With what I get, I mean; and so do they.

Lady Macduff. Poor bird! thou 'dst never fear the net nor lime,
The pitfall nor the gin.

Son. Why should I, mother? Poor birds they are not set for.
My father is not dead, for all your saying.

Lady Macduff. Yes, he is dead: how wilt thou do for a father?

Son. Nay, how will you do for a husband?

Lady Macduff. Why, I can buy me twenty at any market.

Son. Then you 'll buy 'em to sell again. 41

Lady Macduff. Thou speak'st with all thy wit, and yet, i' faith,
With wit enough for thee.

Son. Was my father a traitor, mother?

Lady Macduff. Ay, that he was.

Son. What is a traitor?

Lady Macduff. Why, one that swears and lies.

Son. And be all traitors that do so?

Lady Macduff. Every one that does so is a traitor, and must be hanged. 50

Son. And must they all be hanged that swear and lie?

Lady Macduff. Every one.

Son. Who must hang them?

Lady Macduff. Why, the honest men.

Son. Then the liars and swearers are fools, for there are liars and swearers enow to beat the honest men and hang up them.

Lady Macduff. Now, God help thee, poor monkey! But how wilt thou do for a father? 59

Son. If he were dead, you 'd weep for him: if you would not, it were a good sign that I should quickly have a new father.

Lady Macduff. Poor prattler, how thou talk'st!

Enter a Messenger.

Messenger. Bless you, fair dame! I am not to you known,
Though in your state of honour I am perfect.
I doubt some danger does approach you nearly:
If you will take a homely man's advice,
Be not found here; hence, with your little ones.
To fright you thus, methinks I am too savage;
To do worse to you were fell cruelty, 70
Which is too nigh your person. Heaven preserve you!
I dare abide no longer. [*Exit.*

Lady Macduff. Whither should I fly?
I have done no harm. But I remember now
I am in this earthly world, where to do harm
Is often laudable, to do good sometime
Accounted dangerous folly: why then, alas,

Do I put up that womanly defence,
To say I have done no harm?—

Enter Murderers.

What are these faces?

First Murderer. Where is your husband?

Lady Macduff. I hope, in no place so unsanctified 80
Where such as thou mayst find him.

First Murderer. He 's a traitor.

Son. Thou liest, thou shag-hair'd villain!

First Murderer. What, you egg!
[*Stabbing him.*
Young fry of treachery!

Son. He has kill'd me, mother:
Run away, I pray you! [*Dies.*

[*Exit Lady Macduff, crying* 'Murther!'
Exeunt Murderers, following her.

SCENE III. *England. Before the King's Palace.*

Enter MALCOLM *and* MACDUFF.

Malcolm. Let us seek out some desolate shade, and there
Weep our sad bosoms empty.

Macduff. Let us rather
Hold fast the mortal sword, and like good men
Bestride our down-fallen birthdom. Each new morn
New widows howl, new orphans cry, new sorrows
Strike heaven on the face, that it resounds
As if it felt with Scotland and yell'd out
Like syllable of dolour.

Malcolm. What I believe, I 'll wail;
What know, believe; and what I can redress,
As I shall find the time to friend, I will. 10
What you have spoke, it may be so perchance.
This tyrant, whose sole name blisters our tongues,

Was once thought honest: you have lov'd him well;
He hath not touch'd you yet. I am young; but something
You may deserve of him through me, and wisdom
To offer up a weak poor innocent lamb
To appease an angry god.

Macduff. I am not treacherous.

Malcolm. But Macbeth is.
A good and virtuous nature may recoil
In an imperial charge. But I shall crave your pardon; 20
That which you are my thoughts cannot transpose;
Angels are bright still, though the brightest fell;
Though all things foul would wear the brows of grace,
Yet grace must still look so.

Macduff. I have lost my hopes.

Malcolm. Perchance even there where I did find my doubts.
Why in that rawness left you wife and child,
Those precious motives, those strong knots of love,
Without leave-taking? I pray you,
Let not my jealousies be your dishonours,
But mine own safeties: you may be rightly just, 30
Whatever I shall think.

Macduff. Bleed, bleed, poor country!
Great tyranny, lay thou thy basis sure,
For goodness dare not check thee! wear thou thy wrongs;
The title is affeer'd!—Fare thee well, lord:
I would not be the villain that thou think'st
For the whole space that 's in the tyrant's grasp,
And the rich East to boot.

Malcolm. Be not offended:
I speak not as in absolute fear of you.
I think our country sinks beneath the yoke;
It weeps, it bleeds, and each new day a gash 40
Is added to her wounds: I think withal
There would be hands uplifted in my right;

And here from gracious England have I offer
Of goodly thousands; but for all this,
When I shall tread upon the tyrant's head,
Or wear it on my sword, yet my poor country
Shall have more vices than it had before,
More suffer, and more sundry ways than ever,
By him that shall succeed.

Macduff. What should he be?

Malcolm. It is myself I mean; in whom I know 50
All the particulars of vice so grafted
That, when they shall be open'd, black Macbeth
Will seem as pure as snow, and the poor state
Esteem him as a lamb, being compar'd
With my confineless harms.

Macduff. Not in the legions
Of horrid hell can come a devil more damn'd
In evils to top Macbeth.

Malcolm. I grant him bloody,
Luxurious, avaricious, false, deceitful,
Sudden, malicious, smacking of every sin
That has a name; but there 's no bottom, none, 60
In my voluptuousness: your wives, your daughters,
Your matrons and your maids, could not fill up
The cistern of my lust, and my desire
All continent impediments would o'erbear
That did oppose my will. Better Macbeth
Than such an one to reign.

Macduff. Boundless intemperance
In nature is a tyranny; it hath been
The untimely emptying of the happy throne,
And fall of many kings. But fear not yet
To take upon you what is yours; you may 70
Convey your pleasures in a spacious plenty,
And yet seem cold, the time you may so hoodwink.
We have willing dames enough; there cannot be

That vulture in you, to devour so many
As will to greatness dedicate themselves,
Finding it so inclin'd.
Malcolm. With this there grows
In my most ill-compos'd affection such
A stanchless avarice that, were I king,
I should cut off the nobles for their lands,
Desire his jewels and this other's house ; 80
And my more-having would be as a sauce
To make me hunger more, that I should forge
Quarrels unjust against the good and loyal,
Destroying them for wealth.
Macduff. This avarice
Sticks deeper, grows with more pernicious root
Than summer-seeming lust, and it hath been
The sword of our slain kings : yet do not fear ;
Scotland hath foisons to fill up your will,
Of your mere own. All these are portable,
With other graces weigh'd. 90
Malcolm. But I have none : the king-becoming graces,
As justice, verity, temperance, stableness,
Bounty, perseverance, mercy, lowliness,
Devotion, patience, courage, fortitude,
I have no relish of them, but abound
In the division of each several crime,
Acting it many ways. Nay, had I power, I should
Pour the sweet milk of concord into hell,
Uproar the universal peace, confound
All unity on earth.
Macduff. O Scotland, Scotland ! 100
Malcolm. If such a one be fit to govern, speak :
I am as I have spoken.
Macduff. Fit to govern !
No, not to live.—O nation miserable !
With an untitled tyrant bloody-scepter'd

When shalt thou see thy wholesome days again,
Since that the truest issue of thy throne
By his own interdiction stands accurs'd,
And does blaspheme his breed?—Thy royal father
Was a most sainted king: the queen that bore thee,
Oftener upon her knees than on her feet, 110
Died every day she liv'd.—Fare thee well!
These evils thou repeat'st upon thyself
Have banish'd me from Scotland.—O my breast,
Thy hope ends here!

Malcolm. Macduff, this noble passion,
Child of integrity, hath from my soul
Wip'd the black scruples, reconcil'd my thoughts
To thy good truth and honour. Devilish Macbeth
By many of these trains hath sought to win me
Into his power, and modest wisdom plucks me
From over-credulous haste: but God above 120
Deal between thee and me! for even now
I put myself to thy direction, and
Unspeak mine own detraction, here abjure
The taints and blames I laid upon myself,
For strangers to my nature. I am yet
Unknown to woman, never was forsworn,
Scarcely have coveted what was mine own,
At no time broke my faith, would not betray
The devil to his fellow, and delight
No less in truth than life: my first false speaking 130
Was this upon myself. What I am truly,
Is thine and my poor country's to command;
Whither indeed, before thy here-approach,
Old Siward, with ten thousand warlike men,
Already at a point, was setting forth.
Now we 'll together, and the chance of goodness
Be like our warranted quarrel! Why are you silent?

Macduff. Such welcome and unwelcome things at once
'T is hard to reconcile.

Enter a Doctor.

Malcolm. Well, more anon.—Comes the king forth, I pray
you? 140

Doctor. Ay, sir; there are a crew of wretched souls
That stay his cure: their malady convinces
The great assay of art; but at his touch,
Such sanctity hath heaven given his hand,
They presently amend.

Malcolm. I thank you, doctor. [*Exit Doctor.*

Macduff. What 's the disease he means?

Malcolm. 'T is call'd the evil:
A most miraculous work in this good king;
Which often, since my here-remain in England,
I have seen him do. How he solicits heaven,
Himself best knows: but strangely-visited people, 150
All swoln and ulcerous, pitiful to the eye,
The mere despair of surgery, he cures,
Hanging a golden stamp about their necks,
Put on with holy prayers; and 't is spoken,
To the succeeding royalty he leaves
The healing benediction. With this strange virtue,
He hath a heavenly gift of prophecy,
And sundry blessings hang about his throne
That speak him full of grace.

Enter Ross.

Macduff. See, who comes here?

Malcolm. My countryman; but yet I know him not. 160

Macduff. My ever-gentle cousin, welcome hither.

Malcolm. I know him now. Good God, betimes remove
The means that makes us strangers!

Ross. Sir, amen.

Macduff. Stands Scotland where it did?

Ross. Alas, poor country!
Almost afraid to know itself. It cannot

Be call'd our mother, but our grave ; where nothing,
But who knows nothing, is once seen to smile ;
Where sighs and groans and shrieks that rent the air
Are made, not mark'd ; where violent sorrow seems
A modern ecstasy : the dead man's knell 170
Is there scarce ask'd for who ; and good men's lives
Expire before the flowers in their caps,
Dying or ere they sicken.

Macduff. O, relation
Too nice, and yet too true!

Malcolm. What 's the newest grief?

Ross. That of an hour's age doth hiss the speaker ;
Each minute teems a new one.

Macduff. How does my wife?

Ross. Why, well.

Macduff. And all my children?

Ross. Well too.

Macduff. The tyrant has not batter'd at their peace?

Ross. No ; they were well at peace when I did leave 'em.

Macduff. Be not a niggard of your speech : how goes 't?

Ross. When I came hither to transport the tidings, 181
Which I have heavily borne, there ran a rumour
Of many worthy fellows that were out ;
Which was to my belief witness'd the rather,
For that I saw the tyrant's power a-foot.
Now is the time of help ; your eye in Scotland
Would create soldiers, make our women fight,
To doff their dire distresses.

Malcolm. Be 't their comfort
We are coming thither : gracious England hath
Lent us good Siward and ten thousand men ; 190
An older and a better soldier none
That Christendom gives out.

Ross. Would I could answer
This comfort with the like! But I have words

That would be howl'd out in the desert air,
Where hearing should not latch them.
Macduff. What concern they?
The general cause? or is it a fee-grief
Due to some single breast?
Ross. No mind that 's honest
But in it shares some woe, though the main part
Pertains to you alone.
Macduff. If it be mine,
Keep it not from me, quickly let me have it. 200
Ross. Let not your ears despise my tongue for ever,
Which shall possess them with the heaviest sound
That ever yet they heard.
Macduff. Hum! I guess at it.
Ross. Your castle is surpris'd; your wife and babes
Savagely slaughter'd: to relate the manner,
Were, on the quarry of these murther'd deer,
To add the death of you.
Malcolm. Merciful heaven!—
What, man! ne'er pull your hat upon your brows;
Give sorrow words: the grief that does not speak
Whispers the o'er-fraught heart, and bids it break. 210
Macduff. My children too?
Ross. Wife, children, servants, all.
That could be found.
Macduff. And I must be from thence!—
My wife kill'd too?
Ross. I have said.
Malcolm. Be comforted:
Let 's make us medicines of our great revenge,
To cure this deadly grief.
Macduff. He has no children.—All my pretty ones?
Did you say all?—O hell-kite!—All?
What, all my pretty chickens and their dam
At one fell swoop?

Malcolm. Dispute it like a man.

Macduff. I shall do so; 220

But I must also feel it as a man:
I cannot but remember such things were,
That were most precious to me.—Did heaven look on,
And would not take their part? Sinful Macduff,
They were all struck for thee! naught that I am,
Not for their own demerits, but for mine,
Fell slaughter on their souls. Heaven rest them now!

Malcolm. Be this the whetstone of your sword: let grief
Convert to anger; blunt not the heart, enrage it.

Macduff. O, I could play the woman with mine eyes, 230
And braggart with my tongue!—But, gentle heavens,
Cut short all intermission; front to front
Bring thou this fiend of Scotland and myself;
Within my sword's length set him; if he scape,
Heaven forgive him too!

Malcolm. This tune goes manly.
Come, go we to the king: our power is ready;
Our lack is nothing but our leave. Macbeth
Is ripe for shaking, and the powers above
Put on their instruments. Receive what cheer you may;
The night is long that never finds the day. 240

[*Exeunt.*

SEAL OF EDWARD THE CONFESSOR.

DUNKELD.

ACT V.

SCENE I. *Dunsinane. A Room in the Castle.*

Enter a Doctor of Physic *and a* Waiting Gentlewoman.

Doctor. I have two nights watched with you, but can perceive no truth in your report. When was it she last walked?

Gentlewoman. Since his majesty went into the field, I have seen her rise from her bed, throw her nightgown upon her, unlock her closet, take forth paper, fold it, write upon 't, read it, afterwards seal it, and again return to bed; yet all this while in a most fast sleep.

Doctor. A great perturbation in nature, to receive at once the benefit of sleep and do the effects of watching! In this slumbery agitation, besides her walking and other actual performances, what at any time have you heard her say? 11

Gentlewoman. That, sir, which I will not report after her.

Doctor. You may to me, and 't is most meet you should.

Gentlewoman. Neither to you nor any one, having no witness to confirm my speech.

Enter LADY MACBETH, *with a taper.*

Lo you, here she comes! This is her very guise; and, upon my life, fast asleep. Observe her; stand close.

Doctor. How came she by that light?

Gentlewoman. Why, it stood by her: she has light by her continually; 't is her command. 20

Doctor. You see, her eyes are open.

Gentlewoman. Ay, but their sense is shut.

Doctor. What is it she does now? Look, how she rubs her hands.

Gentlewoman. It is an accustomed action with her, to seem thus washing her hands: I have known her continue in this a quarter of an hour.

Lady Macbeth. Yet here 's a spot.

Doctor. Hark! she speaks: I will set down what comes from her, to satisfy my remembrance the more strongly. 30

Lady Macbeth. Out, damned spot! out, I say!—One: two: why, then 't is time to do 't.—Hell is murky!—Fie, my lord, fie! a soldier, and afeard? What need we fear who knows it, when none can call our power to account?—Yet who would have thought the old man to have had so much blood in him?

Doctor. Do you mark that?

Lady Macbeth. The thane of Fife had a wife: where is she now?—What, will these hands ne'er be clean?—No more o' that, my lord, no more o' that: you mar all with this starting. 41

Doctor. Go to, go to; you have known what you should not.

Gentlewoman. She has spoke what she should not, I am sure of that: heaven knows what she has known.

Lady Macbeth. Here 's the smell of the blood still: all the perfumes of Arabia will not sweeten this little hand. Oh, oh, oh!

Doctor. What a sigh is there! The heart is sorely charged. 50

Gentlewoman. I would not have such a heart in my bosom for the dignity of the whole body.

Doctor. Well, well, well,—

Gentlewoman. Pray God it be, sir.

Doctor. This disease is beyond my practice: yet I have known those which have walked in their sleep who have died holily in their beds.

Lady Macbeth. Wash your hands, put on your nightgown; look not so pale.—I tell you yet again, Banquo 's buried; he cannot come out on 's grave. 60

Doctor. Even so?

Lady Macbeth. To bed, to bed! there 's knocking at the gate: come, come, come, come, give me your hand. What 's done cannot be undone. To bed, to bed, to bed! [*Exit.*

Doctor. Will she go now to bed?

Gentlewoman. Directly.

Doctor. Foul whisperings are abroad. Unnatural deeds
Do breed unnatural troubles: infected minds
To their deaf pillows will discharge their secrets.
More needs she the divine than the physician.— 70
God, God forgive us all!—Look after her;
Remove from her the means of all annoyance,
And still keep eyes upon her. So, good night:
My mind she has mated, and amaz'd my sight.
I think, but dare not speak.

Gentlewoman. Good night, good doctor.

[*Exeunt.*

SCENE II. *The Country near Dunsinane.*

Drum and colours. Enter MENTEITH, CAITHNESS, ANGUS, LENNOX, *and* Soldiers.

Menteith. The English power is near, led on by Malcolm,
His uncle Siward, and the good Macduff.
Revenges burn in them; for their dear causes
Would to the bleeding and the grim alarm
Excite the mortified man.

Angus. Near Birnam wood
Shall we well meet them; that way are they coming.

Caithness. Who knows if Donalbain be with his brother?

Lennox. For certain, sir, he is not. I have a file
Of all the gentry: there is Siward's son,
And many unrough youths, that even now 10
Protest their first of manhood.

Menteith. What does the tyrant?

Caithness. Great Dunsinane he strongly fortifies.
Some say he 's mad; others, that lesser hate him,
Do call it valiant fury: but, for certain,
He cannot buckle his distemper'd cause
Within the belt of rule.

Angus. Now does he feel
His secret murthers sticking on his hands;
Now minutely revolts upbraid his faith-breach:
Those he commands move only in command,
Nothing in love; now does he feel his title 20
Hang loose about him, like a giant's robe
Upon a dwarfish thief.

Menteith. Who then shall blame
His pester'd senses to recoil and start,
When all that is within him does condemn
Itself for being there?

Caithness. Well, march we on,

To give obedience where 't is truly owed :
Meet we the medicine of the sickly weal,
And with him pour we in our country's purge
Each drop of us.

Lennox. Or so much as it needs,
To dew the sovereign flower and drown the weeds. 30
Make we our march towards Birnam. [*Exeunt, marching.*

SCENE III. *Dunsinane. A Room in the Castle.*

Enter MACBETH, Doctor, *and* Attendants.

Macbeth. Bring me no more reports ; let them fly all :
Till Birnam wood remove to Dunsinane,
I cannot taint with fear. What 's the boy Malcolm ?
Was he not born of woman ? The spirits that know
All mortal consequences have pronounc'd me thus :
'Fear not, Macbeth ; no man that 's born of woman
Shall e'er have power upon thee.' Then fly, false thanes,
And mingle with the English epicures :
The mind I sway by and the heart I bear
Shall never sag with doubt nor shake with fear. 10

Enter a Servant.

The devil damn thee black, thou cream-fac'd loon !
Where gott'st thou that goose look ?

Servant. There is ten thousand—

Macbeth. Geese, villain ?

Servant. Soldiers, sir.

Macbeth. Go prick thy face, and over-red thy fear,
Thou lily-liver'd boy. What soldiers, patch ?
Death of thy soul ! those linen cheeks of thine
Are counsellors to fear. What soldiers, whey-face ?

Servant. The English force, so please you.

Macbeth. Take thy face hence.— [*Exit Servant.*
Seyton !—I am sick at heart,

When I behold—Seyton, I say!—This push 20
Will cheer me ever, or dis-ease me now.
I have liv'd long enough: my way of life
Is fallen into the sear, the yellow leaf,
And that which should accompany old age,
As honour, love, obedience, troops of friends,
I must not look to have; but, in their stead,
Curses, not loud but deep, mouth-honour, breath,
Which the poor heart would fain deny, and dare not.—
Seyton!

Enter SEYTON.

Seyton. What 's your gracious pleasure?
Macbeth. What news more? 30
Seyton. All is confirm'd, my lord, which was reported.
Macbeth. I 'll fight till from my bones my flesh be hack'd.
Give me my armour.
Seyton. 'T is not needed yet.
Macbeth. I 'll put it on.
Send out moe horses, skirr the country round;
Hang those that talk of fear. Give me mine armour.—
How does your patient, doctor?
Doctor. Not so sick, my lord,
As she is troubled with thick-coming fancies,
That keep her from her rest.
Macbeth. Cure her of that.
Canst thou not minister to a mind diseas'd, 40
Pluck from the memory a rooted sorrow,
Raze out the written troubles of the brain,
And with some sweet oblivious antidote
Cleanse the stuff'd bosom of that perilous stuff
Which weighs upon the heart?
Doctor. Therein the patient
Must minister to himself.
Macbeth. Throw physic to the dogs, I 'll none of it.—

Come, put mine armour on; give me my staff.—
Seyton, send out.—Doctor, the thanes fly from me.—
Come, sir, dispatch.—If thou couldst, doctor, cast 50
The water of my land, find her disease,
And purge it to a sound and pristine health,
I would applaud thee to the very echo,
That should applaud again.—Pull 't off, I say.—
What rhubarb, senna, or what purgative drug,
Would scour these English hence? Hear'st thou of them?

Doctor. Ay, my good lord; your royal preparation
Makes us hear something.

Macbeth. Bring it after me.—
I will not be afraid of death and bane 59
Till Birnam forest come to Dunsinane. [*Exit.*

Doctor. Were I from Dunsinane away and clear,
Profit again should hardly draw me here. [*Exit.*

SCENE IV. *Country near Birnam Wood.*

Drum and colours. Enter MALCOLM, *old* SIWARD *and his* SON, MACDUFF, MENTEITH, CAITHNESS, ANGUS, LENNOX, ROSS, *and* Soldiers, *marching.*

Malcolm. Cousins, I hope the days are near at hand
That chambers will be safe.

Menteith. We doubt it nothing.

Siward. What wood is this before us?

Menteith. The wood of Birnam.

Malcolm. Let every soldier hew him down a bough,
And bear 't before him; thereby shall we shadow
The numbers of our host, and make discovery
Err in report of us.

Soldiers. It shall be done.

Siward. We learn no other but the confident tyrant
Keeps still in Dunsinane, and will endure
Our setting down before 't.

Malcolm. 'T is his main hope; 10
For where there is advantage to be given,
Both more and less have given him the revolt,
And none serve with him but constrained things
Whose hearts are absent too.

Macduff. Let our just censures
Attend the true event, and put we on
Industrious soldiership.

Siward. The time approaches
That will with due decision make us know
What we shall say we have and what we owe.
Thoughts speculative their unsure hopes relate,
But certain issue strokes must arbitrate; 20
Towards which advance the war. [*Exeunt, marching.*

SCENE V. *Dunsinane. Within the Castle.*

Enter MACBETH, SEYTON, *and* Soldiers, *with drum and colours.*

Macbeth. Hang out our banners on the outward walls;
The cry is still 'They come!' Our castle's strength
Will laugh a siege to scorn; here let them lie
Till famine and the ague eat them up.
Were they not forc'd with those that should be ours,
We might have met them dareful, beard to beard,
And beat them backward home. [*A cry of women within.*
What is that noise?

Seyton. It is the cry of women, my good lord. [*Exit.*

Macbeth. I have almost forgot the taste of fears:
The time has been, my senses would have cool'd 10
To hear a night-shriek, and my fell of hair
Would at a dismal treatise rouse and stir
As life were in 't. I have supp'd full with horrors;
Direness, familiar to my slaughterous thoughts,
Cannot once start me.—

Re-enter SEYTON.

Wherefore was that cry?

Seyton. The queen, my lord, is dead.

Macbeth. She should have died hereafter;
There would have been a time for such a word.
To-morrow, and to-morrow, and to-morrow,
Creeps in this petty pace from day to day 20
To the last syllable of recorded time,
And all our yesterdays have lighted fools
The way to dusty death. Out, out, brief candle!
Life 's but a walking shadow, a poor player
That struts and frets his hour upon the stage
And then is heard no more; it is a tale
Told by an idiot, full of sound and fury,
Signifying nothing.—

Enter a Messenger.

Thou com'st to use thy tongue; thy story quickly.

Messenger. Gracious my lord, 30
I should report that which I say I saw,
But know not how to do it.

Macbeth. Well, say, sir.

Messenger. As I did stand my watch upon the hill,
I look'd toward Birnam, and anon, methought,
The wood began to move.

Macbeth. Liar and slave!

Messenger. Let me endure your wrath, if 't be not so:
Within this three mile may you see it coming;
I say, a moving grove.

Macbeth. If thou speak'st false,
Upon the next tree shalt thou hang alive
Till famine cling thee; if thy speech be sooth, 40
I care not if thou dost for me as much.—
I pull in resolution, and begin

To doubt the equivocation of the fiend
That lies like truth: 'Fear not, till Birnam wood
Do come to Dunsinane;' and now a wood
Comes toward Dunsinane.—Arm, arm, and out!—
If this which he avouches does appear,
There is nor flying hence nor tarrying here.
I gin to be aweary of the sun,
And wish the estate o' the world were now undone.— 50
Ring the alarum-bell!—Blow, wind! come, wrack!
At least we 'll die with harness on our back. [*Exeunt.*

SCENE VI. *Dunsinane. Before the Castle.*

Drum and colours. Enter MALCOLM, *old* SIWARD, MACDUFF, *and their* Army, *with boughs.*

Malcolm. Now near enough: your leavy screens throw down,
And show like those you are.—You, worthy uncle,
Shall with my cousin, your right-noble son,
Lead our first battle; worthy Macduff and we
Shall take upon 's what else remains to do,
According to our order.

Siward. Fare you well.
Do we but find the tyrant's power to-night,
Let us be beaten, if we cannot fight.

Macduff. Make all our trumpets speak; give them all breath,
Those clamorous harbingers of blood and death. [*Exeunt.*

SCENE VII. *Another Part of the Field.*

Alarums. Enter MACBETH.

Macbeth. They have tied me to a stake; I cannot fly,
But, bear-like, I must fight the course. What 's he
That was not born of woman? Such a one
Am I to fear, or none.

Enter young SIWARD.

Young Siward. What is thy name?

Macbeth. Thou 'lt be afraid to hear it.

Young Siward. No; though thou call'st thyself a hotter name
Than any is in hell.

Macbeth. My name 's Macbeth.

Young Siward. The devil himself could not pronounce a title
More hateful to mine ear.

Macbeth. No, nor more fearful. 9

Young Siward. Thou liest, abhorred tyrant; with my sword
I 'll prove the lie thou speak'st.

[*They fight, and young Siward is slain.*

Macbeth. Thou wast born of woman.—
But swords I smile at, weapons laugh to scorn,
Brandish'd by man that 's of a woman born. [*Exit.*

Alarums. Enter MACDUFF.

Macduff. That way the noise is.—Tyrant, show thy face!
If thou be'st slain and with no stroke of mine,
My wife and children's ghosts will haunt me still.
I cannot strike at wretched kerns, whose arms
Are hir'd to bear their staves: either thou, Macbeth,
Or else my sword with an unbatter'd edge
I sheathe again undeeded. There thou shouldst be; 20
By this great clatter, one of greatest note
Seems bruited. Let me find him, fortune!
And more I beg not. [*Exit. Alarums.*

Enter MALCOLM *and old* SIWARD.

Siward. This way, my lord. The castle 's gently render'd:
The tyrant's people on both sides do fight;
The noble thanes do bravely in the war;

The day almost itself professes yours,
And little is to do.

Malcolm. We have met with foes
That strike beside us.

Siward. Enter, sir, the castle.

[*Exeunt. Alarum.*

SCENE VIII. *Another Part of the Field.*

Enter MACBETH.

Macbeth. Why should I play the Roman fool, and die
On mine own sword? whiles I see lives, the gashes
Do better upon them.

Enter MACDUFF.

Macduff. Turn, hell-hound, turn!

Macbeth. Of all men else I have avoided thee:
But get thee back; my soul is too much charg'd
With blood of thine already.

Macduff. I have no words;
My voice is in my sword, thou bloodier villain
Than terms can give thee out! [*They fight.*

Macbeth. Thou losest labour.
As easy mayst thou the intrenchant air
With thy keen sword impress as make me bleed: 10
Let fall thy blade on vulnerable crests;
I bear a charmed life, which must not yield
To one of woman born.

Macduff. Despair thy charm,
And let the angel whom thou still hast serv'd
Tell thee, Macduff was from his mother's womb
Untimely ripp'd.

Macbeth. Accursed be that tongue that tells me so,
For it hath cow'd my better part of man!
And be these juggling fiends no more believ'd,

That palter with us in a double sense; 20
That keep the word of promise to our ear,
And break it to our hope.—I 'll not fight with thee.

Macduff. Then yield thee, coward,
And live to be the show and gaze o' the time:
We 'll have thee, as our rarer monsters are,
Painted upon a pole, and underwrit,
'Here may you see the tyrant.'

Macbeth. I will not yield,
To kiss the ground before young Malcolm's feet,
And to be baited with the rabble's curse.
Though Birnam wood be come to Dunsinane, 30
And thou oppos'd, being of no woman born,
Yet I will try the last. Before my body
I throw my warlike shield: lay on, Macduff,
And damn'd be him that first cries 'Hold, enough!'

[*Exeunt, fighting. Alarums.*

Retreat. Flourish. Enter, with drum and colours, MALCOLM, *old* SIWARD, ROSS, *the other* Thanes, *and* Soldiers.

Malcolm. I would the friends we miss were safe arriv'd.

Siward. Some must go off; and yet, by these I see,
So great a day as this is cheaply bought.

Malcolm. Macduff is missing, and your noble son.

Ross. Your son, my lord, has paid a soldier's debt:
He only liv'd but till he was a man; 40
The which no sooner had his prowess confirm'd
In the unshrinking station where he fought,
But iike a man he died.

Siward. Then he is dead?

Ross. Ay, and brought off the field: your cause of sorrow
Must not be measur'd by his worth, for then
It hath no end.

Siward. Had he his hurts before?

Ross. Ay, on the front.

Siward. Why then, God's soldier be he!
Had I as many sons as I have hairs,
I would not wish them to a fairer death;
And so his knell is knoll'd.

Malcolm. He's worth more sorrow, 50
And that I 'll spend for him.

Siward. He 's worth no more:
They say he parted well and paid his score;
And so God be with him! Here comes newer comfort.

Re-enter MACDUFF, *with* MACBETH'S *head.*

Macduff. Hail, king! for so thou art. Behold, where stands
The usurper's cursed head; the time is free.
I see thee compass'd with thy kingdom's pearl,
That speak my salutation in their minds;
Whose voices I desire aloud with mine:
Hail, King of Scotland!

All. Hail, King of Scotland! [*Flourish.*

Malcolm. We shall not spend a large expense of time 60
Before we reckon with your several loves,
And make us even with you. My thanes and kinsmen,
Henceforth be earls, the first that ever Scotland
In such an honour nam'd. What's more to do,
Which would be planted newly with the time,—
As calling home our exil'd friends abroad
That fled the snares of watchful tyranny,
Producing forth the cruel ministers
Of this dead butcher and his fiend-like queen,
Who, as 't is thought, by self and violent hands 70
Took off her life,—this, and what needful else
That calls upon us, by the grace of Grace
We will perform in measure, time, and place:
So, thanks to all at once and to each one,
Whom we invite to see us crown'd at Scone.

[*Flourish. Exeunt.*

NOTES.

ABBREVIATIONS USED IN THE NOTES.

Abbott (or Gr.), Abbott's *Shakespearian Grammar* (third edition).
A. S., Anglo-Saxon.
A. V., Authorized Version of the Bible (1611).
B. and F., Beaumont and Fletcher.
B. J., Ben Jonson.
C., Craik's *English of Shakespeare* (Rolfe's edition).
Camb. ed., "Cambridge edition" of *Shakespeare*, edited by Clark and Wright.
Cf. (*confer*), compare.
Coll., Collier.
Coll. MS., Manuscript Corrections of Second Folio, edited by Collier.
C. P. ed., "Clarendon Press" edition of *Macbeth* (Oxford, 1869).
D., Dyce.
F. Q., Spenser's *Faërie Queene*.
Furness, "New Variorum" edition of *Macbeth* (Philadelphia, 1873).
H., Hudson.
Hen. VIII. (followed by reference to *page*), Rolfe's edition of *Henry VIII.*
Hunter, Joseph Hunter's *New Illustrations*, etc. (see p. 32, foot-note).
Id. (*idem*), the same.
J. C. (followed by reference to *page*), Rolfe's edition of *Julius Cæsar.*
J. Hunter, John Hunter's edition of *Macbeth* (London, 1869).
K., Knight.
Mätzner, *English Grammar*, trans. by Grece (London, 1874).
Mer., Rolfe's edition of *The Merchant of Venice.*
Moberly, C. E. Moberly's edition of *Macbeth* (London, 1872).
Nares, *Glossary*, edited by Halliwell and Wright (London, 1859).
Prol., Prologue.
Rich. II. (followed by reference to *page*), Rolfe's edition of *Richard II.*
S., Shakespeare.
Schmidt, A. Schmidt's *Shakespeare-Lexicon* (Berlin, 1874).
Shep. Kal., Spenser's *Shepherd's Kalendar.*
Sr., Singer.
St., Staunton.
Temp. (followed by reference to *page*), Rolfe's edition of *The Tempest.*
Theo., Theobald.
V., Verplanck.
W., White.
Walker, Wm. Sidney Walker's *Critical Examination of the Text of Shakespeare* (London, 1860).
Warb., Warburton.
Weiss, *Wit, Humor, and Shakespeare*, by John Weiss (Boston, 1876).
Wb., Webster's Dictionary (revised quarto edition of 1864).
Worc., Worcester's Dictionary (quarto edition).

The abbreviations of the names of Shakespeare's Plays will be readily understood; as *T. N.* for *Twelfth Night*, *Cor.* for *Coriolanus*, 3 *Hen. VI.* for *The Third Part of King Henry the Sixth*, etc. *P. P.* refers to *The Passionate Pilgrim; V. and A.* to *Venus and Adonis; L. C.* to *Lover's Complaint;* and *Sonn.* to the *Sonnets.*

NOTES.

IONA.

INTRODUCTION.

THE following extracts from Holinshed contain all the passages referred to throughout the play by the various commentators. The text here given is that of the edition of 1587, which, as already stated (p. 13), was undoubtedly the one that Shakespeare used.*

"It appears that King Duffe, who commenced his reign 'in the yeare after the incarnation 968, as saith Hector Boetius,' treated 'diuers robbers and pillers of the common people' in a style which created no small offence; some were executed, and the rest were obliged 'either to get them ouer into Ireland, either else to learne some manuall occupation wherewith to get their liuing, yea though they were neuer so great gen-

* For these extracts and the thread of narrative connecting them, we are indebted to Mr. Furness's edition of *Macbeth*, p. 355 fol. We have added a few explanatory footnotes.

tlemen borne.' There was therefore great murmuring at such rigorous reforms. But,

" 'In the meane time the king [Duffe] fell into a languishing disease, not so greeuous as strange, for that none of his physicians could perceiue what to make of it. For there was seene in him no token, that either choler, melancholie, flegme, or any other vicious humor did any thing abound, whereby his bodie should be brought into such decaie and consumption (so as there remained vnneth* anie thing vpon him saue skin and bone).

" 'And sithens it appeared manifestlie by all outward signes and tokens, that naturall moisture did nothing faile in the vitall spirits, his colour also was fresh and faire to behold, with such liuelines of looks, that more was not to be wished for; he had also a temperat desire and appetite to his meate & drinke, but yet could he not sleepe in the night time by any prouocations that could be deuised, but still fell into exceeding sweats, which by no means might be restreined. The physicians perceiuing all their medicines to want due effect, yet to put him in some comfort of helpe, declared to him that they would send for some cunning physicians into forreigne parts, who happilie being inured with such kind of diseases, should easilie cure him, namelie so soone as the spring of the yeare was once come, which of it selfe should helpe much thervnto.'

" The Chronicle goes on to state that the 'king being sicke yet he regarded iustice to be executed,' and that a rebellion which arose was kept from his knowledge, 'for doubt of increasing his sicknes.' It then proceeds:

" 'But about that present time there was a murmuring amongst the people, how the king was vexed with no naturall sicknesse, but by sorcerie and magicall art, practised by a sort of witches dwelling in a towne of Murreyland, called Fores.

" 'Wherevpon, albeit the author of this secret talke was not knowne: yet being brought to the kings eare, it caused him to send foorthwith certeine wittie persons thither, to inquire of the truth. They that were thus sent, dissembling the cause of their iornie, were receiued in the darke of the night into the castell of Fores by the lieutenant of the same, called Donwald, who continuing faithfull to the king, had kept that castell against the rebels to the kings vse. Vnto him therefore these messengers declared the cause of their comming, requiring his aid for the accomplishment of the kings pleasure.

" 'The souldiers, which laie there in garrison had an inkling that there was some such matter in hand as was talked of amongst the people; by reason that one of them kept as concubine a yoong woman, which was daughter to one of the witches as his paramour, who told him the whole maner vsed by hir mother & other hir companions, with their intent also, which was to make awaie the king. The souldier hauing learned this of his lemman,† told the same to his fellowes, who made re-

* Scarcely, hardly. Cf. 2 *Hen. VI.* ii 4. 8:

> " Uneath may she endure the flinty streets
> To tread them with her tender-feeling feet."—(*Ed.*)

† Leman; i. e. mistress, paramour. Cf. *T. N.* ii. 3. 26; 2 *Hen. IV.* v. 3. 49.—(*Ed.*)

port to Donwald, and hee shewed it to the kings messengers, and therwith sent for the yoong damosell which the souldier kept, as then being within the castell, and caused hir vpon streict examination to confesse the whole matter as she had seene and knew. Wherevpon learning by hir confession in what house in the towne it was where they wrought there mischiefous mysterie, he sent foorth souldiers, about the middest of the night, who breaking into the house, found one of the witches rosting vpon a woodden broch an image of wax at the fier, resembling in each feature the kings person, made and deuised (as is to be thought) by craft and art of the diuell: an other of them sat reciting certeine words of inchantment, and still basted the image with a certeine liquor verie busilie.

i. 3. 23.

"'The souldiers finding them occupied in this wise, tooke them togither with the image, and led them into the castell, where being streictlie examined for what purpose they went about such manner of inchantment, they answered, to the end to make away the king: for as the image did waste afore the fire, so did the bodie of the king breake foorth in sweat.* And as for the words of inchantment, they serued to keepe him still waking from sleepe, so that as the wax euer melted, so did the kings flesh: by the which meanes it should haue come to passe, that when the wax was once cleane consumed, the death of the king should immediatlie follow. So were they taught by euill spirits, and hired to worke the feat by the nobles of Murrey land. The standers by, that heard such an abhominable tale told by these witches, streightwaies brake the image, and caused the witches (according as they had well deserued) to bee burnt to death.

"'It was said that the king, at the verie same time that these things were a dooing within the castell of Fores, was deliuered of his languor, and slept that night without anie sweat breaking foorth vpon him at all, & the next daie being restored to his strength, was able to doo anie maner of thing that lay in man to doo, as though he had not beene sicke before anie thing at all. But howsoeuer it came to passe, truth it is, that when he was restored to his perfect health, he gathered a power of men, & with the same went into Murrey land against the rebels there, and chasing them from thence, he pursued them into Rosse, and from Rosse into Cathnesse, where apprehending them, he brought them backe vnto Fores, and there caused them to be hanged vp, on gallows and gibets.

"'Amongest them there were also certeine yoong gentlemen, right beautifull and goodlie personages, being neere of kin vnto Donwald capteine of the castell, and had beene persuaded to be partakers with the other rebels, more through the fraudulent counsell of diuerse wicked persons, than of their owne accord; wherevpon the foresaid Donwald

---

* So the witch in Theocritus melts a waxen image, and says:

> *ὡς τοῦτον τὸν καρὸν ἐγὼ συν δαίμονι τάκω,*
> *ὡς τάκοιθ' ὑπ' ἔρωτος ὁ Μύνδιος αὐτίκα Δελφις.*

Virgil has imitated this in *Ecl.* viii. 80:

> Limus ut hic durescit, et haec ut cera liquescit
> Uno eodemque igni, sic nostro Daphnis amore.

Cf. also Horace, *Epod.* xvii. 76 and *Sat.* i. 8. 30.—(*Ed.*)

lamenting their case, made earnest labor and sute to the king to haue begged their pardon; but hauing a plaine deniall, he conceiued such an inward malice towards the king, (though he shewed it not outwardlie at the first) that the same continued still boiling in his stomach, and ceased not, till through setting on of his wife, and in reuenge of such vnthankefulnesse, hee found meanes to murther the king within the foresaid castell of Fores where he vsed to soiourne. For the king being in that countrie, was accustomed to lie most commonlie within the same castell, hauing a speciall trust in Donwald, as a man whom he neuer suspected.

"'But Donwald, not forgetting the reproch which his linage had susteined by the execution of those his kinsmen, whome the king for a spectacle to the people had caused to be hanged, could not but shew manifest tokens of great griefe at home amongst his familie: which his wife perceiuing, ceassed not to trauell with him, till she vnderstood what the cause was of his displeasure. Which at length when she had learned by his owne relation, she as one that bare no lesse malice in hir heart towards the king, for the like cause on hir behalfe, than hir husband did for his friends, counselled him (sith the king oftentimes vsed to lodge in his house without anie gard about him, other than the garrison of the castell, which was wholie at his commandement) to make him awaie, and shewed him the meanes wherby he might soonest accomplish it.

"'Donwald thus being the more kindled in wrath by the words of his wife, determined to follow hir aduise in the execution of so heinous an act. Whervpon deuising with himselfe for a while, which way hee might best accomplish his cursssed intent, at length he gat opportunitie, and sped his purpose as followeth. It chanced that the king vpon the daie before he purposed to depart foorth of the castell, was long in his oratorie at his praiers, and there continued till it was late in the night. At the last, comming foorth, he called such afore him as had faithfullie serued him in pursute and apprehension of the rebels, and giuing them heartie thanks, he bestowed sundrie honorable gifts amongst them, of the which number Donwald was one, as he that had beene euer accounted a most faithfull seruant to the king.

"'At length, hauing talked with them a long time, he got him into his priuie chamber, onelie with two of his chamberlains, who hauing brought him to bed, came foorth againe, and then fell to banketting with Donwald and his wife, who had prepared diuerse delicate dishes, and sundrie sorts of drinks for their reare supper or collation, wherat they sate vp so long, till they had charged their stomachs with such full gorges, that their heads were no sooner got to the pillow, but asleepe they were so fast, that a man might haue remooued the chamber ouer them, sooner than to haue awaked them out of their droonken sleepe.

i. 7. 63.

"'Then Donwald, though he abhorred the act greatlie in his heart, yet through instigation of his wife, hee called foure of his seruants vnto him (whome he had made priuie to his wicked intent before, and framed to his purpose with large gifts) and now declaring vnto them, after what sort they should worke the feat, they gladlie obeied his instructions, &

speedilie going about the murther, they enter the chamber (in which the king laie) a little before cocks crow, where they secretlie cut his throte as he lay sleeping, without anie buskling* at all: and immediatlie by a posterne gate they caried foorth the dead bodie into the fields, and throwing it vpon an horsse there prouided readie for that purpose, they conuey it vnto a place, about two miles distant from the castell, where they staied, and gat certeine labourers to helpe them to turne the course of a little riuer running through the fields there, and digging a deepe hole in the chanell, they burie the bodie in the same, ramming it vp with stones and grauell so closelie, that setting the water in the right course againe, no man could perceiue that anie thing had beene newlie digged there. This they did by order appointed them by Donwald as is reported, for that the bodie should not be found, & by bleeding (when Donwald should be present) declare him to be guiltie of the murther. For such an opinion men haue, that the dead corps of anie man being slaine, will bleed abundantlie if the murtherer be present. But for what consideration soeuer they buried him there, they had no sooner finished the work, but that they slue them whose helpe they vsed herein, and streightwaies therevpon fled into Orknie.

" 'Donwald, about the time that the murther was in dooing, got him amongst them that kept the watch, and so continued in companie with them all the residue of the night. But in the morning when the noise was raised in the kings chamber how the king was slaine, his bodie conueied away, and the bed all beraied with bloud; he with the watch ran thither, as though he had knowne nothing of the matter, and breaking into the chamber, and finding cakes of bloud in the bed, and on the floore about the sides of it, he foorthwith slue the chamberleins, as guiltie of that heinous murther, and then like a mad man running to and fro, he ransacked euerie corner within the castell, as though it had beene to haue seene if he might haue found either the bodie, or anie of the murtherers hid in anie priuie place: but at length comming to the posterne gate, and finding it open, he burdened the chamberleins, whome he had slaine, with all the fault, they hauing the keies of the gates committed to their keeping all the night, and therefore it could not be otherwise (said he) but that they were of counsell in the committing of that most detestable murther.

" 'Finallie, such was his ouer earnest diligence in the seuere inquisition and triall of the offendors heerein, that some of the lords began to mislike the matter, and to smell foorth shrewd tokens, that he should not be altogither cleare himselfe. But for so much as they were in that countrie, where hee had the whole rule, what by reason of his friends and authoritie togither, they doubted to vtter what they thought, till time and place should better serue therevnto, and heerevpon got them awaie euerie man to his home. For the space of six moneths togither, after this heinous murther thus committed, there appeered no sunne by day, nor moone by night in anie part of the realme, but still was the skie couered with continuall clouds, and sometimes suche outragious

ii. 4. 10.

* Bustling, commotion.—(*Ed.*)

windes arose, with lightenings and tempests, that the people were in great feare of present destruction.' (pp. 149–151.) *

" 'Monstrous sights also that were seene within the Scotish kingdome that yeere' [that is, of King Duffe's murder, A.D. 972] 'were these, horsses in Louthian, being of singular beautie and swiftnesse, did eate their owne flesh, and would in no wise taste anie other meate. In Angus there was a gentlewoman brought foorth a child without eies, nose, hand, or foot. There was a sparhawke also strangled by an owle.' (p. 152.)

ii. 4. 15.

ii. 4. 13.

"Thus far the Chronicle of King Duffe supplied Shakespeare with some of the details and accessories of his tragedy; and we now turn to the history of the hero himself, Macbeth. But there is one other incident recorded by Holinshed, on one of the few intermediate pages of his Chronicle, between the stories of King Duffe and Macbeth, which I cannot but think attracted Shakespeare's notice as he passed from one story to the other, and which was afterward worked up by him in connection with Duncan's murder.† As far as I am aware, it has never been noted by any editor or commentator. It seems that Kenneth, the brother, and one of the successors of Duffe, was a virtuous and able prince, and would have left an unstained name had not the ambition to have his son succeed him tempted him to poison secretly his nephew Malcome, the son of Duff and the heir apparent to the throne. Kenneth then obtained from a council at Scone the ratification of his son as his successor. 'Thus might he seeme happie to all men,' continues Holinshed (p. 158), 'but yet to himselfe he seemed most vnhappie as he that could not but still live in continuall feare, least his wicked practise concerning the death of Malcome Duffe should come to light and knowledge of the world. For so commeth it to passe, that such as are pricked in conscience for anie secret offense committed, haue euer an vnquiet mind.' [What follows suggested, I think, to Shakespeare 'the voice,' at ii. 2. 35, that cried 'sleep no more.'] 'And (as the fame goeth) it chanced that a voice was heard as he was in bed in the night time to take his rest, vttering vnto him these or the like woords in effect: "Thinke not Kenneth that the wicked slaughter of Malcome Duffe by thee contriued, is kept secret from the knowledge of the eternall God," &c. . . . The king with this voice being striken into great dread and terror, passed that night without anie sleepe comming in his eies.'

" 'After Malcolme' [that is, 'after the incarnation of our Saviour 1034 yeeres,'] 'succeeded his nephue Duncane, the sonne of his daughter Beatrice: for Malcolme had two daughters, the one which was this Beatrice, being giuen in marriage vnto one Abbanath Crinen, a man of great nobilitie, and thane of the Isles and west part of Scotland, bare of that mariage the foresaid Duncane; The other called Doada, was maried vnto Sinell the thane of Glammis, by whome she had issue one Makbeth a valiant gentleman, and one that if he had not beene

i. 3. 71.

---

* These references are to the pages of Holinshed.—(*Ed.*)

† The reader will bear in mind (see p. 131, foot-note) that we are quoting Mr. Furness here, and that it is to him that this interesting discovery is due.—(*Ed.*)

somewhat cruell of nature, might haue beene thought most woorthie the gouernement of a realme. On the other part, Duncane was so soft and gentle of nature, that the people wished the inclinations and maners of these two cousins to haue beene so tempered and enterchangeablie bestowed betwixt them, that where the one had too much clemencie, and the other of crueltie, the meane vertue betwixt these two extremities might haue reigned by indifferent partition in them both, so should Duncane haue proued a woorthie king, and Makbeth an excellent capteine. The beginning of Duncans reigne was verie quiet and peaceable, without anie notable trouble ; but after it was perceiued how negligent he was in punishing offendors, manie misruled persons tooke occasion thereof to trouble the peace and quiet state of the common-wealth, by seditious commotions which first had their beginnings in this wise.

" 'Banquho the thane of Lochquhaber, of whom the house of the Stewards is descended, the which by order of linage hath now for a long time inioied the crowne of Scotland, euen till these our daies, as he gathered the finances due to the king, and further punished somewhat sharpelie such as were notorious offendors, being assailed by a number of rebels inhabiting in that countrie, and spoiled of the monie and all other things, had much a doo to get awaie with life, after he had receiued sundrie grieuous wounds amongst them. Yet escaping their hands, after hee was somewhat recouered of his hurts and was able to ride, he repaired to the court, where making his complaint to the king in most earnest wise, he purchased at length that the offendors were sent for by a sergeant at armes, to appeare to make answer vnto such matters as should be laid to their charge : but they augmenting their mischiefous act with a more wicked deed, after they had misused the messenger with sundrie kinds of reproches, they finallie slue him also.

" 'Then doubting not but for such contemptuous demeanor against the kings regall authoritie, they should be inuaded with all the power the king could make, Makdowald one of great estimation among them, making first a confederacie with his neerest friends and kinsmen, tooke vpon him to be chiefe capteine of all such rebels, as would stand against the king, in maintenance of their grieuous offenses latelie committed against him. Manie slanderous words also, and railing tants this Makdowald vttered against his prince, calling him a faint-hearted milkesop, more meet to gouerne a sort of idle moonks in some cloister, than to haue the rule of such valiant and hardie men of warre as the Scots were. He vsed also such subtill persuasions and forged allurements, that in a small time he had gotten togither a mightie power of men : for out of the westerne Isles there came vnto him a great multitude of people, offering themselues to assist him in that rebellious quarell, and out of Ireland in hope of the spoile came no small number of Kernes and Galloglasses, offering gladlie to serue vnder him, whither it should please him to lead them.

i. 2. 14.

" 'Makdowald thus hauing a mightie puissance about him, incountered with such of the kings people as were sent against him into Lochquhaber, and discomfiting them, by mere force tooke their capteine Malcolme, and after the end of the battell smote off his head. This ouerthrow being notified to the king, did put him in woonderfull feare, by reason of his small skill in warlike affaires. Calling therefore his nobles to a councell, he asked of them their best aduise for the subduing of Makdowald & other the rebels. Here, in sundrie heads (as euer it happeneth) were sundrie opinions, which they vttered according to euerie man his skill. At length Makbeth speaking much against the kings softnes, and ouermuch slacknesse in punishing offendors, whereby they had such time to assemble togither, he promised notwithstanding, if the charge were committed vnto him and vnto Banquho, so to order the matter, that the rebels should be shortly vanquished & quite put downe, and that not so much as one of them should be found to make resistance within the countrie.

" 'And euen so it came to passe: for being sent foorth with a new power, at his entring into Lochquhaber, the fame of his comming put the enimies in such feare, that a great number of them stale secretlie awaie from their capteine Makdowald, who neuerthelesse inforced thereto, gaue battell vnto Makbeth, with the residue which remained with him: but being ouercome, and fleeing for refuge into a castell (within the which his wife & children were inclosed) at length when he saw how he could neither defend the hold anie longer against his enimies, nor yet vpon surrender be suffered to depart with life saued, hee first slue his wife and children, and lastlie himselfe, least if he had yeelded simplie, he should haue beene executed in most cruell wise for an example to other. Makbeth entring into the castell by the gates, as then set open, found the carcasse of Macdowald lieng dead there amongst the residue of the slaine bodies, which when he beheld, remitting no peece of his cruell nature with that pitifull sight, he caused the head to be cut off, and set vpon a poles end, and so sent it as a present to the king who as then laie at Bertha. The headlesse trunke he commanded to bee hoong vp vpon an high paire of gallowes.

" 'Them of the westerne Isles suing for pardon, in that they had aided Makdowald in his tratorous enterprise, he fined at great sums of moneie: and those whome he tooke in Lochquhaber, being come thither to beare armor against the king, he put to execution. Hervpon the Ilandmen conceiued a deadlie grudge towards him, calling him a couenant-breaker, a bloudie tyrant, & a cruell murtherer of them whome the kings mercie had pardoned. With which reprochfull words Makbeth being kindled in wrathfull ire against them, had passed ouer with an armie into the Isles, to haue taken reuenge vpon them for their liberall * talke, had he not beene otherwise persuaded by some of his friends, and partlie pacified by gifts presented vnto him on the behalfe of the Ilandmen, seeking to auoid his displeasure. Thus was iustice and law restored againe to the old accustomed course, by the diligent means of Makbeth. Immediatlie wherevpon woord came that Sueno king of Norway was arriued in Fife with a puissant armie, to subdue the whole realme of Scotland.' (pp. 168, 169.)

---

* Too free. S. uses it in a similar sense = licentious, wanton. Cf. *Much Ado*, iv. 1. 93; *Ham.* iv. 7. 171; *Oth.* ii. 1. 165, etc.—(*Ed.*)

" 'The crueltie of this Sueno was such, that he neither spared man, woman, nor child, of what age, condition or degree soeuer they were. Whereof when K. Duncane was certified, he set all slouthfull and lingering delaies apart, and began to assemble an armie in most speedie wise, like a verie valiant capteine: for oftentimes it happeneth, that a dull coward and slouthfull person, constreined by necessitie, becommeth verie hardie and actiue. Therefore when his whole power was come togither, he diuided the same into three battels. The first was led by Makbeth, the second by Banquho, & the king himselfe gouerned in the maine battell or middle ward, wherein were appointed to attend and wait upon his person the most part of all the residue of the Scotish nobilitie.

v. 6. 4.

" 'The armie of Scotishmen being thus ordered, came vnto Culros, where incountering with the enimies, after a sore and cruell foughten battell, Sueno remained victorious, and Malcolme with his Scots discomfited. Howbeit the Danes were so broken by this battell, that they were not able to make long chase on their enimies, but kept themselues all night in order of battell, for doubt least the Scots assembling togither againe, might haue set vpon them at some aduantage. On the morrow, when the fields were discouered, and that it was perceiued how no enimies were to be found abrode, they gathered the spoile, which they diuided amongst them, according to the law of armes. Then was it ordeined by commandement of Sueno, that no souldier should hurt either man, woman, or child, except such as were found with weapon in hand readie to make resistance, for he hoped now to conquer the realme without further bloudshed.

" 'But when knowledge was giuen how Duncane was fled to the castell of Bertha, and that Makbeth was gathering a new power to withstand the incursions of the Danes, Sueno raised his tents & comming to the said castell, laid a strong siege round about it. Duncane seeing himselfe thus enuironed by his enimies, sent a secret message by counsell of Banquho to Makbeth, commanding him to abide at Inchcuthill, till he heard from him some other newes. In the meane time Duncane fell in fained communication with Sueno, as though he would haue yeelded vp the castell into his hands, vnder certeine conditions, and this did he to driue time, and to put his enimies out of all suspicion of anie enterprise ment against them, till all things were brought to passe that might serue for the purpose. At length, when they were fallen at a point for rendring vp the hold, Duncane offered to send foorth of the castell into the campe greate prouision of vittels to refresh the armie, which offer was gladlie accepted of the Danes, for that they had beene in great penurie of sustenance manie daies before.

iv. 3. 135.

" 'The Scots heerevpon tooke the iuice of mekilwoort berries, and mixed the same in their ale and bread, sending it thus spiced & confectioned, in great abundance vnto their enimies. They reioising that they had got meate and drinke sufficient to satisfie their bellies, fell to eating and drinking after such greedie wise, that it seemed they stroue who might deuoure and swallow vp most, till the operation of the berries spread in such sort through all the parts of their bodies,

i. 3. 84.

that they were in the end brought into a fast dead sleepe, that in manner it was vnpossible to awake them. Then foorthwith Duncane sent vnto Makbeth, commanding him with all diligence to come and set vpon the enimies, being in easie point to be ouercome. Makbeth making no delaie, came with his people to the place where his enimies were lodged, and first killing the watch, afterwards entered the campe, and made such slaughter on all sides without anie resistance that it was a woonderfull matter to behold, for the Danes were so heauie of sleepe that the most part of them were slaine and neuer stirred: other that were awakened either by the noise or other waies foorth, were so amazed and dizzie headed vpon their wakening, that they were not able to make anie defense: so that of the whole number there escaped no more but onelie Sueno himselfe and ten other persons, by whose helpe he got to his ships lieng at rode in the mouth of Taie.

"'The most part of the mariners, when they heard what plentie of meate and drinke the Scots had sent vnto the campe, came from the sea thither to be partakers thereof, and so were slaine amongst their fellowes: by meanes whereof when Sueno perceiued how through lacke of mariners he should not be able to conueie awaie his nauie, he furnished one ship throughlie with such as were left, and in the same sailed backe into Norwaie, cursing the time that he set forward on this infortunate iournie. The other ships which he left behind him, within three daies after his departure from thence, were tossed so togither by violence of an east wind, that beating and rushing one against another, they sunke there, and lie in the same place euen vnto these daies, to the great danger of other such ships as come on that coast: for being couered with the floud when the tide commeth, at the ebbing againe of the same, some part of them appeere aboue water.

"'The place where the Danish vessels were thus lost, is yet called Drownelow sands. This ouerthrow receiued in manner afore said by Sueno, was verie displeasant to him and his people, as should appeere, in that it was a custome manie yeeres after, that no knights were made in Norwaie, except they were first sworne to reuenge the slaughter of their countriemen and friends thus slaine in Scotland. The Scots hauing woone so notable a victorie, after they had gathered & divided the spoile of the field, caused solemne processions to be made in all places of the realme, and thanks to be giuen to almightie God, that had sent them so faire a day ouer their enimies. But whilest the people were thus at their processions, woord was brought that a new fleet of Danes was arriued at Kingcorne, sent thither by Canute king of England, in reuenge of his brother Suenos ouerthrow. To resist these enimies, which were alreadie landed, and busie in spoiling the countrie; Makbeth and Banquho were sent with the kings authoritie, who hauing with them a conuenient power, incountred the enimies, slue part of them, and chased the other to their ships. They that escaped and got once to their ships, obteined of Makbeth for a great summe of gold, that such of their friends as were slaine at this last bickering, might be buried in saint Colmes Inch. In memorie whereof, manie old sepultures are yet in the said Inch, there to be seene grauen with the armes of the Danes,

i. 2. 62.

as the maner of burieng noble men still is, and heeretofore hath beene vsed.

" 'A peace was also concluded at the same time betwixt the Danes and Scotishmen, ratified (as some haue written) in this wise: That from thencefoorth the Danes should neuer come into Scotland to make anie warres against the Scots by anie maner of meanes. And these were the warres that Duncane had with forren enimies, in the seventh yeere of his reigne. Shortlie after happened a strange and vncouth woonder, which afterward was the cause of much trouble in the realme of Scotland, as ye shall after heare. It fortuned as Makbeth and Banquho iournied towards Fores, where the king then laie, they went sporting by the waie togither without other companie, saue onelie themselues, passing thorough the woods and fields, when suddenlie in the middest of a laund, there met them three women in strange and wild apparell, resembling creatures of elder world, whome when they attentiuelie beheld, woondering much at the sight, the first of them spake and said; All haile Makbeth, thane of Glammis (for he had latelie entered into that dignitie and office by the death of his father Sinell). The second of them said; Haile Makbeth thane of Cawder. But the third said; All haile Makbeth that heereafter shalt be king of Scotland.

i. 2. 1.

i. 3. 71.

" 'Then Banquho; What manner of women (saith he) are you, that seeme so little fauourable vnto me, whereas to my fellow heere, besides high offices, ye assigne also the kingdome, appointing foorth nothing for me at all? Yes (saith the first of them) we promise greater benefits vnto thee, than vnto him, for he shall reigne in deed, but with an vnluckie end: neither shall he leaue anie issue behind him to succeed in his place, where contrarilie thou in deed shalt not reigne at all, but of thee those shall be borne which shall gouern the Scotish kingdome by long order of continuall descent. Herewith the foresaid women vanished immediatlie out of their sight. This was reputed at the first but some vaine fantasticall illusion by Mackbeth and Banquho, insomuch that Banquho would call Mackbeth in iest king of Scotland; and Mackbeth againe would call him in sport likewise, the father of manie kings. But afterwards the common opinion was, that these women were either the weird sisters, that is (as ye would say) the goddesses of destinie, or else some nymphs or feiries, indued with knowledge of prophesie by their necromanticall science, bicause euerie thing came to passe as they had spoken. For shortlie after, the thane of Cawder being condemned at Fores of treason against the king committed; his lands, liuings, and offices were giuen of the kings liberalitie to Mackbeth.

i. 3. 53.

" 'The same night after, at supper, Banquho iested with him and said; Now Mackbeth thou hast obteined those things which the two former sisters prophesied, there remaineth onelie for thee to purchase that which the third said should come to passe. Wherevpon Mackbeth reuoluing the thing in his mind, began euen then to deuise how he might atteine to the kingdome: but yet he thought with himselfe that he must tarie a time, which should aduance him thereto (by the diuine prouidence) as it had come to passe in his former preferment. But shortlie after it chanced

v. 2. 2. that king Duncane, hauing two sonnes by his wife which was the daughter of Siward earle of Northumberland, he made the elder of them called Malcolme prince of Cumberland, as it were thereby i. 4. 39. to appoint him his successor in the kingdome, immediatlie after his deceasse. Mackbeth sore troubled herewith, for that he saw by this means his hope sore hindered (where, by the old lawes of the realme, the ordinance was, that if he that should succeed were not of able age to take the charge vpon himselfe, he that was next of bloud vnto him should be admitted) he began to take counsell how he might vsurpe the kingdome by force, hauing a iust quarell so to doo (as he tooke the matter) for that Duncane did what in him lay to defraud him of all maner of title and claime, which he might in time to come, pretend vnto the crowne.

"'The woords of the three weird sisters also (of whom before ye haue heard) greatlie incouraged him herevnto, but speciallie his wife lay sore vpon him to attempt the thing, as she that was verie ambitious, burning in vnquenchable desire to beare the name of a queene. At length therefore, communicating his purposed intent with his trustie friends, amongst whome Banquho was the chiefest, vpon confidence of their promised aid, he slue the king at Enuerns, or (as some say) at Botgosuane, in the sixt yeare of his reigne. Then hauing a companie about him of such as he had made priuie to his enterprise, he caused himselfe to be proclamed ii. 4. 31. king, and foorthwith went vnto Scone, where (by common consent) he receiued the inuesture of the kingdome according to the accustomed maner. The bodie of Duncane was first conueied vnto Elgine, & there buried in kinglie wise; but afterwards it was remoued and ii. 4. 34. conueied vnto Colmekill, and there laid in a sepulture amongst his predecessors, in the yeare after the birth of our Sauiour, 1046.

"'Malcolme Cammore and Donald Bane the sons of king Duncane, for feare of their liues (which they might well know that Mackbeth would seeke to bring to end for his more sure confirmation in the estate) fled into Cumberland, where Malcolme remained, till time that saint Edward the sonne of Etheldred recouered the dominion of England from the Danish power, the which Edward receiued Malcolme by way of most friendlie enterteinment: but Donald passed ouer into Ireland, where he was tenderlie cherished by the king of that land. Mackbeth, after the departure thus of Duncanes sonnes, vsed great liberalitie towards the nobles of the realme, thereby to win their fauour, and when he saw that no man went about to trouble him, he set his whole intention to mainteine iustice, and to punish all enormities and abuses, which had chanced through the feeble and slouthfull administration of Duncane.' (pp. 169–171.)

"[And so vigorously did Macbeth carry out his reforms, that 'these theeues, barrettors, and other oppressors of the innocent people' . . . 'were streight waies apprehended by armed men, and trussed vp in halters on gibbets, according as they had iustlie deserued. The residue of misdooers that were left, were punished and tamed in such sort, that manie yeares after all theft and reiffings were little heard of, the people inioieng the blissefull benefit of good peace and tranquilitie. Mackbeth shewing himselfe thus a most diligent punisher of all iniuries and wrongs attempted by anie disordered persons within his realme, was accounted the sure defense and buckler of innocent people; and hereto he also applied his whole indeuor, to cause yoong men to exercise themselues in vertuous maners, and men of the church to attend their diuine seruice according to their vocations.

"'He caused to be slaine sundrie thanes, as of Cathnes, Sutherland, Stranauerne, and Ros, because through them and their seditious attempts, much trouble dailie rose in the realme.' . . . 'To be briefe, such were the woorthie dooings and princelie acts of this Mackbeth in the administration of the realme, that if he had atteined therevnto by rightfull means, and continued in vprightnesse of iustice as he began, till the end of his reigne, he might well haue beene numbred amongest the most noble princes that anie where had reigned. He made manie holesome laws and statutes for the publike weale of his subiects.' [Holinshed here 'sets foorth according to Hector Boetius' some of the laws made by Macbeth, and for one of them the king certainly deserves a handsome notice from some of our most advanced reformers of the present day: 'The eldest daughter shall inherit hir fathers lands, as well as the eldest sonne should, if the father leave no sonne behind him.']

"'These and the like commendable lawes Makbeth caused to be put as then in vse, gouerning the realme for the space of ten yeares in equall iustice. But this was but a counterfet zeale of equitie shewed by him, partlie against his naturall inclination to purchase thereby the fauour of the people. Shortlie after, he began to shew what he was, in stead of equitie practising crueltie. For the pricke of conscience (as it chanceth euer in tyrants, and such as atteine to anie estate by vnrighteous means) caused him euer to feare, least he should be serued of the same cup as he had ministred to his predecessor. The woords also of the three weird sisters would not out of his mind, which as they promised him the kingdome, so likewise did they promise it at the same time vnto the posteritie of Banquho. He willed therefore the same Banquho with his sonne named Fleance, to come to a supper that he had prepared for them, which was in deed, as he had deuised, present death at the hands of certeine murderers, whom he hired to execute that deed, appointing them to meete with the same Banquho and his sonne without the palace, as they returned to their lodgings, and there to slea them, so that he would not haue his house slandered, but that in time to come he might cleare himselfe, if anie thing were laid to his charge vpon anie suspicion that might arise.

i. 7. 11.

iii. 1. 48.

iii. 1. 131.

"'It chanced yet by the benefit of the darke night, that though the father were slaine, the sonne yet by the helpe of almightie God reseruing him to better fortune, escaped that danger: and afterwards hauing some inkeling (by the admonition of some friends which he had in the court) how his life was sought no lesse than his fathers, who was slaine not by chancemedlie * (as by the handling of the matter Makbeth woould haue

* The old law term for manslaughter. Dalton, in his *Country Justice* (1620), says: "Manslaughter, otherwise called *chancemedley*, is the killing a man feloniously, . . . and yet without any malice forethought," etc.—(*Ed.*)

had it to appeare), but euen vpon a prepensed deuise: wherevpon to auoid further perill he fled into Wales.' (p. 172.)

"[The old historian here makes a digression in order to 'rehearse the originall line of those kings, which haue descended from the foresaid Banquho.' It will suffice here to note that (according to Holinshed) Fleance's great-grandson Alexander had two sons, from one of whom descended 'the earles of Leuenox and Dernlie,' and from the other came Walter Steward, who 'maried Margerie Bruce daughter to king Robert Bruce, by whome he had issue king Robert the second of that name' (p. 173), 'the first' (says French, *Shakespeareana Genealogica*, p. 291) 'of the dynasty of Stuart, which continued to occupy the throne until the son of Mary Queen of Scots, James, the sixth of the name, was called to the throne of England, as James the First.']

"'But to returne vnto Makbeth, in continuing the historie, and to begin where I left, ye shall vnderstand that after the contriued slaughter of Banquho, nothing prospered with the foresaid Makbeth: for in maner euerie man began to doubt his owne life, and durst vnneth appeare in the kings presence; and euen as there were manie that stood in feare of him, so likewise stood he in feare of manie, in such sort that he began to make those awaie by one surmised cauillation or other, whome he thought most able to worke him anie displeasure.

"'At length he found such sweetnesse by putting his nobles thus to death, that his earnest thirst after bloud in this behalfe might in no wise be satisfied: for ye must consider he wan double profite (as hee thought) hereby: for first they were rid out of the way whome he feared, and then againe his coffers were inriched by their goods which were forfeited to his vse, whereby he might the better mainteine a gard of armed men about him to defend his person from iniurie of them whom he had in anie suspicion. Further, to the end he might the more cruellie oppresse his subjects with all tyrantlike wrongs, he builded a strong castell on the top of an hie hill called Dunsinane, situate in Gowrie, ten miles from Perth, on such a proud height, that standing there aloft, a man might behold well neere all the countries of Angus, Fife, Stermond, and Ernedale, as it were lieng vnderneath him. This castell then being founded on the top of that high hill, put the realme to great charges before it was finished, for all the stuffe necessarie to the building could not be brought vp without much toile and businesse. But Makbeth being once determined to haue the worke go forward, caused the thanes of each shire within the realme to come and helpe towards that building, each man his course about.

"'At the last, when the turne fell vnto Makduffe thane of Fife to builde his part, he sent workemen with all needfull prouision, and commanded them to shew such diligence in euerie behalfe, that no occasion might bee giuen for the king to find fault with him, in that he came not himselfe as other had doone, which he refused to doo, for doubt least the king bearing him (as he partlie vnderstood) no great good will, would laie violent handes vpon him, as he had doone vpon diuerse other. Shortly after, Makbeth comming to behold how the worke went forward, and bicause he found not Makduffe there, he was sore offended, and said;

I perceiue this man will neuer obeie my commandements, till he be ridden with a snaffle: but I shall prouide well inough for him. Neither could he afterwards abide to looke vpon the said Makduffe, either for that he thought his puissance ouer great; either else for that he had learned of certeine wizzards, in whose words he put great confidence (for that the prophesie had happened so right, which the three faries or weird sisters had declared vnto him) how that he ought to take heed of Makduffe, who in time to come should seeke to destroie him.

" 'And suerlie herevpon had he put Makduffe to death, but that a certeine witch, whome hee had in great trust, had told that he should neuer be slaine with man borne of anie woman, nor vanquished till the wood of Bernane came to the castell of Dunsinane. By this prophesie Makbeth put all feare out of his heart, supposing he might doo what he would, without anie feare to be punished for the same, for by the one prophesie he beleeued it was vnpossible for anie man to vanquish him, and by the other vnpossible to slea him. This vaine hope caused him to doo manie outragious things, to the greeuous oppression of his subiects. At length Makduffe, to auoid perill of life, purposed with himselfe to passe into England, to procure Malcolme Cammore to claime the crowne of Scotland. But this was not so secretlie deuised by Makduffe, but that Makbeth had knowledge giuen him thereof: for kings (as is said) haue sharpe sight like vnto Lynx, and long ears like vnto Midas. For Makbeth had in euerie noble mans house one slie fellow or other in fee with him, to reueale all that was said or doone within the same, by which slight he oppressed the most part of the nobles of his realme.

iv. 1. 80.

iii. 4. 131.

" 'Immediatlie then, being aduertised whereabout Makduffe went, he came hastily with a great power into Fife, and foorthwith besieged the castell where Makduffe dwelled, trusting to haue found him therein. They that kept the house, without anie resistance opened the gates, and suffered him to enter, mistrusting none euill. But neuerthelesse Makbeth most cruellie caused the wife and children of Makduffe, with all other whom he found in that castell, to be slaine. Also he confiscated the goods of Makduffe, proclaimed him traitor, and confined him out of all the parts of his realme; but Makduffe was alreadie escaped out of danger, and gotten into England vnto Malcolme Cammore, to trie what purchase hee might make by means of his support to reuenge the slaughter so cruellie executed on his wife, his children, and other friends. At his comming vnto Malcolme, he declared into what great miserie the estate of Scotland was brought, by the detestable cruelties exercised by the tyrant Makbeth, hauing committed manie horrible slaughters and murders, both as well of the nobles as commons, for the which he was hated right mortallie of all his liege people, desiring nothing more than to be deliuered of that intollerable and most heauie yoke of thraldome, which they susteined at such a caitifes hands.

iv. 3.

" 'Malcolme hearing Makduffes woords, which he vttered in verie lamentable sort, for meere compassion and verie ruth that pearsed his sorowfull hart, bewailing the miserable state of his countrie, he fetched a deepe sigh; which Makduffe perceiuing, began to fall most earnestlie in hand with him, to enterprise the deliuering of the Scotish people out of the hands of so cruell and bloudie a tyrant, as Makbeth by too manie plaine experiments did shew himselfe to be: which was an easie matter for him to bring to passe, considering not onelie the good title he had, but also the earnest desire of the people to haue some occasioned ministred, whereby they might be reuenged of those notable iniuries, which they dailie susteined by the outragious crueltie of Makbeths misgouernance. Though Malcolme was verie sorowfull for the oppression of his countriemen the Scots, in maner as Makduffe had declared; yet doubting whether he were come as one that ment vnfeinedlie as he spake, or else as sent from Makbeth to betraie him, he thought to haue some further triall, and therevpon dissembling his mind at the first, he answered as followeth.

"'I am trulie verie sorie for the miserie chanced to my countrie of Scotland, but though I haue neuer so great affection to relieue the same, yet by reason of certeine incurable vices, which reigne in me, I am nothing meet thereto. First, such immoderate lust and voluptuous sensualitie (the abhominable founteine of all vices) followeth me, that if I were made king of Scots, I should seeke to defloure your maids and matrones, in such wise that mine intemperancie should be more importable vnto you than the bloudie tyrannie of Makbeth now is. Heereunto Makduffe answered: this suerly is a verie euill fault, for many noble princes and kings haue lost both liues and kingdomes for the same; neuerthelesse there are women enow in Scotland, and therefore follow my counsell, Make thy selfe king, and I shall conueie the matter so wiselie, that thou shalt be so satisfied at thy pleasure in such wise, that no man shall be aware thereof.

iv. 3. 71.

iv. 3. 72.

"'Then said Malcolme, I am also the most auaritious creature on the earth, so that if I were king, I should seeke so manie waies to get lands and goods, that I would slea the most part of all the nobles of Scotland by surmised accusations, to the end I might inioy their lands, goods, and possessions; and therefore to shew you what mischiefe may insue on you through mine vnsatiable couetousnes, I will rehearse vnto you a fable. There was a fox hauing a sore place on him ouerset with a swarme of flies, that continuallie sucked out hir bloud: and when one that came by and saw this manner, demanded whether she would haue the flies driuen beside hir, she answered no: for if these flies that are alreadie full, and by reason thereof sucke not verie egerlie, should be chased awaie, other that are emptie and fellie* an hungred, should light in their places, and sucke out the residue of my bloud farre more to my greeuance than these, which now being satisfied doo not much annoie me. Therefore saith Malcolme, suffer me to remaine where I am, least if I

* The obsolete adverb corresponding to the adjective *fell*, and = fiercely, cruelly. Cf. Spenser, *F. Q.* vi. 11, 48:

> "How many flyes, in whottest sommers day,
> Do seize upon some beast whose flesh is bare,
> That all the place with swarmes do overlay,
> And with their litle stings right felly fare," etc.—(*Ed.*)

atteine to the regiment of your realme, mine inquenchable auarice may prooue such; that ye would thinke the displeasures which now grieue you, should seeme easie in respect of the vnmeasurable outrage, which might insue through my comming amongst you.

" 'Makduffe to this made answer, how it was a far woorse fault than the other: for auarice is the root of all mischiefe, and for that crime the most part of our kings haue beene slaine and brought to their finall end. Yet notwithstanding follow my counsell, and take vpon thee the crowne, There is gold and riches inough in Scotland to satisfie thy greedie desire. Then said Malcolme againe, I am furthermore inclined to dissimulation, telling of leasings,* and all other kinds of deceit, so that I naturallie reioise in nothing so much, as to betraie & deceiue such as put anie trust or confidence in my woords. Then sith there is nothing that more becommeth a prince than constancie, veritie, truth, and iustice, with the other laudable fellowship of those faire and noble vertues which are comprehended onelie in soothfastnesse,† and that lieng vtterlie ouerthroweth the same; you see how vnable I am to gouerne anie prouince or region: and therefore sith you haue remedies to cloke and hide all the rest of my other vices, I praie you find shift to cloke this vice amongst the residue.

" 'Then said Makduffe: This yet is the woorst of all, and there I leaue thee, and therefore saie; Oh ye vnhappie and miserable Scotishmen, which are thus scourged with so manie and sundrie calamities, ech one aboue other! Ye haue one cursssed and wicked tyrant that now reigneth ouer you, without anie right or title, oppressing you with his most bloudie crueltie. This other that hath the right to the crowne, is so replet with the inconstant behauiour and manifest vices of Englishmen, that he is nothing woorthie to inioy it: for by his owne confession he is not onelie auaritious, and giuen to vnsatiable lust, but so false a traitor withall, that no trust is to be had vnto anie woord he speaketh. Adieu Scotland, for now I account my selfe a banished man for euer, without comfort or consolation: and with those woords the brackish teares trickled downe his cheekes verie abundantlie.

" 'At the last, when he was readie to depart, Malcolme tooke him by the sleeue, and said: Be of good comfort Makduffe, for I haue none of these vices before remembred, but haue iested with thee in this manner, onelie to prooue thy mind: for diuerse times heeretofore hath Makbeth sought by this manner of meanes to bring me into his hands, but the more slow I haue shewed my selfe to condescend to thy motion and request, the more diligence shall I vse in accomplishing the same. Incontinentlie heereupon they imbraced ech other, and promising to be faithfull the one to the other, they fell in consultation how they might best prouide for all their businesse, to bring the same to good effect. Soone after, Makduffe repairing to the borders of Scotland, addressed his letters with secret dispatch vnto the nobles of the realme, declaring how Mal-

* Falsehoods. Cf. Spenser, *F. Q.* ii. 9, 51: "And all that fained is, as leasings, tales, and lies." See also *Psalms*, iv. 2, v. 6; *T. N.* i. 5. 105; *Cor.* v. 2. 22.—(*Ed.*)

† Truthfulness. On *sooth* = truth, see note on i. 2. 36 below. Cf. *shamefastness* (= modesty), of which our modern *shamefacedness* is a corruption.—(*Ed.*)

colme was confederat with him, to come hastilie into Scotland to claime the crowne, and therefore he required them, sith he was right inheritor thereto, to assist him with their powers to recouer the same out of the hands of the wrongfull vsurper.

" 'In the meane time, Malcolme purchased such fauor at king Edwards hands, that old Siward earle of Northumberland, was appointed with ten thousand men to go with him into Scotland, to support him in this enterprise, for recouerie of his right. After these newes were spread abroad in Scotland, the nobles drew into two seuerall factions, the one taking part with Makbeth, and the other with Malcolme. Heereupon insued oftentimes sundrie bickerings, & diuerse light skirmishes: for those that were of Malcolmes side, would not ieopard to ioine with their enimies in a pight* field, till his comming out of England to their support. But after that Makbeth perceiued his enimies power to increase, by such aid as came to them foorth of England with his aduersarie Malcolme, he recoiled backe into Fife, there purposing to abide in campe fortified, at the castell of Dunsinane, and to fight with his enimies, if they ment to pursue him; howbeit some of his friends aduised him, that it should be best for him, either to make some agreement with Malcolme, or else to flee with all speed into the Iles, and to take his treasure with him, to the end he might wage † sundrie great princes of the realme to take his part, & reteine strangers, in whome he might better trust than in his owne subiects, which stale dailie from him: but he had such confidence in his prophesies, that he beleeued he should neuer be vanquished, till Birnane wood were brought to Dunsinane; nor yet to be slaine with anie man, that should be or was borne of anie woman.

v. 4. 11.

" 'Malcolme following hastilie after Makbeth, came the night before the battell vnto Birnane wood, and when his armie had rested a while there to refresh them, he commanded euerie man to get a bough of some tree or other of that wood in his hand, as big as he might beare, and to march foorth therewith in such wise, that on the next morrow they might come closelie and without sight in this manner within viewe of his enimies. On the morrow when Makbeth beheld them comming in this sort, he first maruelled what the matter ment, but in the end remembered himselfe that the prophesie which he had heard long before that time, of the comming of Birnane wood to Dunsinane castell, was likelie to be now fulfilled. Neuerthelesse, he brought his men in order of battell, and exhorted them to doo valiantlie, howbeit his enimies had scarsely cast from them their boughs, when Makbeth perceiuing their numbers, betooke him streict to flight, whom Makduffe pursued with great hatred euen till he came vnto Lunfannaine, where Makbeth perceiuing that Makduffe was hard at his backe, leapt beside his horsse, saieng;

v. 4.

---

* Pitched. Cf. *T. and C.* v. 10. 24:

> " You vile abominable tents,
> Thus proudly pight upon our Phrygian plains."—(*Ed.*)

† Hire, bribe. Cf. *Cor.* v. 6. 40:

> " I seem'd his follower, not partner, and
> He wag'd me with his countenance, as if
> I had been mercenary."—(*Ed.*)

Thou traitor, what meaneth it that thou shouldest thus in vaine follow me that am not appointed to be slaine by anie creature that is borne of a woman, come on therefore, and receiue thy reward which thou hast deserued for thy paines, and therwithall he lifted vp his swoord thinking to haue slaine him.

"'But Makduffe quicklie auoiding* from his horsse, yer he came at him, answered (with his naked swoord in his hand) saieng: It is true Makbeth, and now shall thy insatiable crueltie haue an end, for I am euen he that thy wizzards haue told thee of, who was neuer borne of my mother, but ripped out of her wombe: therewithall he stept vnto him, and slue him in the place. Then cutting his head from his shoulders, he set it vpon a pole, and brought it vnto Malcolme. This was the end of Makbeth, after he had reigned 17 yeeres ouer the Scotishmen. In the beginning of his reigne he accomplished manie woorthie acts, verie profitable to the common-wealth, (as ye haue heard) but afterward by illusion of the diuell, he defamed the same with most terrible crueltie. He was slaine in the yeere of the incarnation 1057, and in the 16 yeere of king Edwards reigne ouer the Englishmen.

v. 8. 53.

"'Malcolme Cammore thus recouering the relme (as ye haue heard) by support of king Edward, in the 16 yeere of the same Edwards reigne, he was crowned at Scone the 25 day of Aprill, in the yeere of our Lord 1057. Immediatlie after his coronation he called a parlement at Forfair, in the which he rewarded them with lands and liuings that had assisted him against Makbeth, aduancing them to fees and offices as he saw cause, & commanded that speciallie those that bare the surname of anie offices or lands, should haue and inioy the same. He created manie earles, lords, barons, and knights. Manie of them that before were thanes, were at this time made earles, as Fife, Menteth, Atholl, Leuenox, Murrey, Cathnes, Rosse, and Angus. These were the first earles that haue beene heard of amongst the Scotishmen, (as their histories doo make mention.)' (pp. 174–176.)

v. 8. 63.

"In the 'fift Chapter' of 'the eight Booke of the historie of England,' Shakespeare found the account of young Siward's death (v. 7.):

"'About the thirteenth yeare of king Edward his reigne (as some write) or rather about the nineteenth or twentith yeare, as should appeare by the Scotish writers, Siward the noble earle of Northumberland with a great power of horssemen went into Scotland, and in battell put to flight Mackbeth that had vsurped the crowne of Scotland, and that doone, placed Malcolme surnamed Camoir, the sonne of Duncane, sometime king of Scotland, in the gouernement of that realme, who afterward slue the said Mackbeth, and then reigned in quiet. Some of our English writers say that this Malcolme was king of Cumberland, but other report him to be sonne to the king of Cumberland. But heere is to be noted, that if Mackbeth reigned till the yeare 1061, and was then slaine by Malcolme, earle Siward was not at that battell; for as our writers doo testi-

---

* Withdrawing, dismounting. Cf. *W. T.* i. 2. 462: "Let us avoid;" *Cor.* iv. 5. 34: "here's no place for you; pray you, avoid." See also 1 *Sam.* xviii. 11.—(*Ed.*)

fie, he died in the yeare 1055, which was in the yeare next after (as the same writers affirme) that he vanquished Mackbeth in fight, and slue manie thousands of Scots, and all those Normans which (as ye haue heard) were withdrawen into Scotland, when they were driuen out of England.

" 'It is recorded also, that in the foresaid battell, in which earle Siward vanquished the Scots, one of Siwards sonnes chanced to be slaine, whereof although the father had good cause to be sorowfull, yet when he heard that he died of a wound which he had receiued in fighting stoutlie in the forepart of his bodie, and that with his face towards the enimie, he greatlie reioised thereat, to heare that he died so manfullie. But here is to be noted, that not now, but a little before (as Henrie Hunt. saith) that earle Siward went into Scotland himselfe in person, he sent his sonne with an armie to conquere the land, whose hap was there to be slaine; and when his father heard the newes, he demanded whether he receiued the wound whereof he died, in the forepart of the bodie, or in the hinder part: and when it was told him that he receiued it in the forepart; I reioise (saith he) euen with all my heart, for I would not wish either to my sonne nor to my selfe any other kind of death.' "

v. 8. 49.

KING MALCOLM'S GRAVESTONE, AT GLAMIS.

ACT I.

SCENE I.—1. Delius remarks (cf. Gr. 504) that this trochaic metre is elsewhere used by S. when supernatural beings are speaking; as in *Temp.* and *M. N. D.*

The folios put an interrogation mark at the end of the first line.

3. *Hurlyburly.* Doubtless an onomatopoetic word, as Peacham explained it in the *Garden of Eloquence* in 1577: "Onomatopeia, when we invent, devise, fayne, and make a name intimating the sound of that it signifyeth, as *hurlyburly*, for an *uprore* and *tumultuous stirre.*" *Hullabaloo* (which is not in Wb., though given by Worc. and Wedgwood) is probably a related word. S. uses *hurlyburly* only here and in 1 *Hen. IV.* v. 1. 78, where it is an adjective. He has *hurly* in the same sense in *T. of S.* iv. 1. 216: "amid this hurly;" *K. John*, iii. 4. 169: "Methinks I see this hurly all on foot;" and 2 *Hen. IV.* iii. 1. 25: "That with the hurly death itself awakes."

Cf. Latimer (sermon preached in 1550): "the chiefest cause of all this hurlyburly and commotion;" North's *Plutarch* (*Fabius*): "A marvellous tumult and hurlyburly;" Spenser, *F. Q.* v. 3, 30:

> "Thereof great hurly-burly moved was
> Throughout the hall for that same warlike horse."

5. *Set of sun.* The C. P. ed. cites *Rich. III.* v. 3. 19: "The weary sun hath made a golden set."

8. *Graymalkin.* Also spelled *Grimalkin;* it means a gray cat. *Mal-*

kin is a diminutive of *Mary*, and, like *maukin* (or *mawkin*) which is the same word, is often used as a common noun and contemptuously (=kitchen-wench); as in *Cor.* ii. 1. 224; *Per.* iv. 3. 34. Cf. Tennyson, *Princess*, v.: "a draggled mawkin." *Malkin* is the name of one of the witches in Middleton's *Witch*.

9. *Paddock.* A toad. R. Scot (*Discovery of Witchcraft*, 1584) says: "Some say they [witches] can keepe divels and spirits in the likenesse of todes and cats." Cf. *Ham.* iii. 4. 190.

The word sometimes means a frog; as in the North of England, according to Goldsmith. Cf. Chapman, *Cæsar and Pompey* (1607): "Paddockes, todes, and watersnakes." In New England "bull-paddock" is a popular synonym for bull-frog.

10. *Anon.* Presently, immediately; "especially by waiters, instead of the modern 'coming'" (Schmidt). Cf. 1 *Hen. IV.* ii. 1. 5; ii. 4. 29, 36, 41, 49, 58, etc.

11. *Fair is foul*, etc. "The meaning is, that *to us*, perverse and malignant as we are, *fair is foul, and foul is fair*" (Johnson). Cf. Spenser, *F. Q.* iv. 8, 32: "Then faire grew foule, and foule grew faire in sight."

SCENE II.—The C. P. editors believe that this scene was not written by S. They remark: "Making all allowance for corruption of text, the slovenly metre is not like Shakespeare's work, even when he is most careless. The bombastic phraseology of the sergeant is not like Shakespeare's language even when he is most bombastic. What is said of the thane of Cawdor, lines 52, 53, is inconsistent with what follows in scene iii. lines 72, 73, and 112 sqq. We may add that Shakespeare's good sense would hardly have tolerated the absurdity of sending a severely wounded soldier to carry the news of a victory."

On this last point Mr. Furnivall (*Trans. New Shaks. Soc.* 1874, p. 499) says: "Mr. Daniel has already answered this by showing (1.) that the sergeant is *not* sent; (2.) that no victory had been won when he left the field; (3.) that the man sent with news of the victory was Ross; (4.) that the wounded sergeant was only met by Duncan, etc." Cf. Weiss, p. 364.

1. *Bloody.* Bodenstedt (cited by Furness) remarks that "this word *bloody* reappears on almost every page, and runs like a red thread through the whole piece; in no other of Shakespeare's dramas is it so frequent."

3. *Sergeant.* Here a trisyllable. Gr. 479. In the stage direction of the folio we find "*a bleeding Captaine*," but "Serieant" in this line of the text.

5. *Hail.* Metrically equivalent to a dissyllable (Gr. 484).

6. *Say . . . the knowledge.* Tell what you know. *Say* often=tell. Cf. *Cymb.* iv. 2. 376: "say his name;" *C. of E.* i. 1. 29: "say, in brief, the cause," etc.

Broil. Battle; as often in S. Cf. 1 *Hen. IV.* i. 1. 3, 47; *Cor.* iii. 2. 81; *Oth.* i. 3. 87, etc.

7. On the measure, see Gr. 506.

9. *Choke their art.* "That is, drown each other by rendering their skill in swimming useless" (C. P. ed.). Cf. *Mark*, v. 13.

Macdonwald. The reading of 1st folio; the others have "Macdonnel." Holinshed calls him "Macdowald."

10. *To that.* To that end. Gr. 186. "His multiplied villainies fit him for that rebel's trade" (Moberly).

11. Mr. Fleay thinks that this line is Shakespeare's, retained by Middleton when he substituted this scene for the original one.

13. *Of kerns and gallowglasses.* *Of* = with; as often. See Gr. 171. *Kerns* were light-armed soldiers. See *Rich. II.* p. 175, note on *Rug-headed kerns.* *Gallowglasses* were heavy-armed troops. Cf. 2 *Hen. VI.* iv. 9. 26: "Of gallowglasses and stout kerns." S. takes both words from Holinshed (see p. 137). Cf. v. 7. 17 below. See also Drayton, *Heroical Epist.*:

> "Bruce now shall bring his Redshanks from the seas,
> From the isled Orcads and the Hebrides;
> And to his western havens give free pass
> To land the Kerne and Irish Galliglasse."

14. *Quarrel.* Johnson's emendation for the "quarry" of the early eds. As the word occurs in Holinshed's relation of this very fact, it is probably the right one, but many editors retain *quarry.* K. says: "We have it in the same sense in *Cor.* i. 1. 202; the 'damned quarry' being the doomed army of kerns and gallowglasses, who, although Fortune deceitfully smiled on them, fled before the sword of Macbeth and became his *quarry*—his prey."

For *quarrel* in this sense (=*cause* or *occasion* of a quarrel) cf. Bacon, *Essay* 8: "So as a Man may have a Quarrell to marry, when he will;" Latimer, *Sermon on Christmas Day:* "to live and die in God's quarrel," etc. Cf. iv. 3. 137: "our warranted quarrel."

15. *Show'd.* Appeared. Cf. *M. of V.* iv. 1. 196:

> "And earthly power doth then show likest God's
> When mercy seasons justice."

"The meaning is that Fortune, while she smiled on him, deceived him" (Malone).

19. *Minion.* Favourite, darling. It is the French *mignon.* Cf. *Temp.* iv. 1. 98: "Mars's hot minion;" and see note, *Temp.* p. 136.

21. *Which.* As D. remarks, if this is the right word, it is equivalent to *who.* Gr. 265. Probably there is some corruption of the text. Capell's emendation of "And ne'er" is adopted by Sr. and D. (2d ed.). "As the text stands, the meaning is, Macdonwald did not take leave of, nor bid farewell to, his antagonist till Macbeth had slain him" (C. P. ed.).

22. *Nave.* Navel. Warb. suggested "nape." Steevens cites Nash, *Dido* (1594): "Then from the navel to the throat at once He ript old Priam."

24. *Cousin.* Macbeth and Duncan were both grandsons of King Malcolm.

25. *Gins.* The 1st folio has "'gins" here (and "'gin" in v. 5. 49), the other folios "gins." In every other instance in which *gins* or *gan* occurs in the 1st folio (*Temp.* iii. 3. 106; *Cor.* ii. 2. 119; 2 *Hen. IV.* i. 1. 129; *Ham.* i. 5. 90; *Cymb.* ii. 3. 22, v. 3. 37, v. 5. 197) the apostrophe is omitted. Nares says, under *gin:* "Usually supposed to be a contraction of *begin,*

but shown by Mr. Todd to be the original word." Schmidt also gives it as a complete word, and recognizes *can* in *L. L. L.* iv. 3. 106 as its past tense—an old form which Spenser sometimes uses. Abbott (Gr. 460) does not give *'gin* in his list of words in which prefixes are dropped (though he gives some words that ought not to be there, as *get*=beget, *haviour*, *plain*=complain, *tend*=attend, etc.), nor does he refer any instance of *gin* or *gan* to § 460 in his "Index of Quotations." Richardson, in his *Dict.*, says: "*Gin*, and the pret. *gan*, are in common use with our old writers without the prefix *be*;" and one of his examples (Hakluyt's *Voyages*, vol. i. p. 187: "Therefore I ginne to wryte now of the see") proves that the word had not ceased to be used, even *in prose*, in the time of S. The editors often confound these obsolete simple words with contractions of their compounds now in use. See *Temp.* p. 118 (note on *Hests*), *Mer.* p. 153 (note on *Bated*), *J. C.* p. 182 (note on *Now some light*), and *Rich. II.* p. 162 (note on *Haviour*).

On the general meaning of this passage, Sr. says: "The allusion is to the storms that prevail in spring, at the vernal equinox—the equinoctial gales. The beginning of the reflection of the sun (cf. 'So from that spring') is the epoch of his passing from the severe to the mildest season, opening, however, with storms." The C. P. ed. explains it thus: "As thunder and storms sometimes come from the East, the quarter from which we expect the sunrise, so out of victory a new danger arises."

31. *Norweyan.* The spelling of the folio, as in line 52 and i. 3. 95 below.

Surveying vantage. Perceiving his opportunity. The phrase is used in a different sense in *Rich. III.* v. 3. 15: "Let us survey the vantage of the field."

32. *Furbish'd.* Burnished; that is, not before used in the fight, not yet stained with blood.

34. *Captains.* A trisyllable here. Gr. 477, 506.

36. *Sooth.* Truth. See foot-note, p. 147, and cf. v. 5. 40 below.

37. *Cracks.* Charges; an example of metonymy, the effect being put for the cause. For *crack*=report, cf. *Temp.* i. 2. 203 and *T. of A.* ii. 1. 3. Malone quotes the old play of *King John* (1591): "the echo of a cannon's crack."

38. *So they.* The C. P. editors prefer to put these words at the end of the preceding line. Sr. and D., following Steevens and Malone, make them a separate line.

On *doubly redoubled*, cf. *Rich. II.* i. 3. 80.

40. *Memorize.* Make memorable, render famous. The meaning is, "*make* another Golgotha, which should be celebrated and delivered down to posterity with as frequent mention as the first" (Heath). Halliwell cites Vicars, *Trans. of Virgil* (1632):

> "Though Grecian seas or shores me captiv'd quel'd,
> With annuall votes and due solemnities,
> And altar-decking gifts, I'd memorize."

Cf. also *Hen. VIII.* iii. 2. 52. For *Golgotha*, see *Mark*, xv. 22.

41. *I cannot tell.* J. Hunter explains this as="I know not what to say or think of it," and cites *T. of S.* iv. 3. 22: "I cannot tell: I fear 'tis choleric." On the measure, see Gr. 511.

43. *So well.* We should say, *as* well. See Gr. 275.

45. *Thane.* "An Anglo-Saxon nobleman, inferior in rank to an eorl and ealdorman" (Bosworth). See Wb.

46. *A haste.* The reading of the 1st folio; the other folios omit "a."

So should he look, etc. On *should*, see Gr. 323. The meaning is, "So should he look that appears to be on the point of speaking things strange" (Heath), or "whose appearance corresponds with the strangeness of his message" (C. P. ed.). *Teems*, *comes*, *seeks*, and *deems* have been needlessly suggested in place of *seems.* Cf. *Rich. II.* iii. 2. 194–197.

49. *Flout.* Mock. Malone quotes *K. John*, v. 1. 72: "Mocking the air with colours idly spread;" and adds: "The meaning seems to be, not that the Norweyan banners proudly insulted the sky; but that, the standards being taken by Duncan's forces, and fixed in the ground, the colours idly flapped about, serving only to cool the conquerors, instead of being proudly displayed by their former possessors." But, as the C. P. ed. suggests, "'flout the sky' seems better suited to the banners of a triumphant or defiant host." *Flout* must then be a historic present. Keightley reads:

> "Where the Norweyan banners
> Did flout the sky and fan our people cold."

51. Pope reads "With numbers terrible."

53. *Cawdor.* Cawdor Castle is about five miles south of Nairn and about fifteen from Inverness. The royal license to build it was granted by James II. in 1454. There is a tradition that a "wise man" counselled the Thane of Cawdor to load an ass with a chest full of gold, and to use the money in building a castle at the third hawthorn tree at which the beast should stop. The advice was followed, and the castle built round the tree, the trunk of which is still shown in the basement of the tower. The castle is still in excellent preservation, being used as a summer residence by the Earl of Cawdor.

54. *Till that.* On *that* as "a conjunctional affix," see Gr. 287.

Bellona's bridegroom. We have no doubt that S. means to compare Macbeth to Mars (cf. *Rich. II.* ii. 3. 100: "the Black Prince, that young Mars of men"), though Mars was not the husband of Bellona. Perhaps, as the C. P. ed. remarks, the expression may have been suggested by an imperfect recollection of Virgil, *Æn.* vii. 319: "Et Bellona manet te pronuba." Holinshed, though not in this connection, refers to "the goddesse of battell, called Bellona."

Lapp'd in proof. Clad in armour of proof. Cf. *Cymb.* v. 5. 360: "lapp'd In a most curious mantle;" and *Rich. II.* i. 3. 73: "Add proof unto mine armour with thy prayers" (see note in our ed.).

55. *Confronted him*, etc. "That is, gave him as good as he brought, showed he was his equal" (Warb.). *Him* refers to Norway.

56. The folio has "Point against Point, rebellious Arme 'gainst Arme," and many editors retain that pointing. *Rebellious* must in that case be =opposing, resisting. Theo. was the first to transpose the comma, giving *rebellious* the meaning it almost invariably has in S.

57. *Lavish.* Unrestrained, insolent. Cf. 2 *Hen. IV.* iv. 4. 62: "lavish manners;" and 1 *Hen. VI.* ii. 5. 47: "his lavish tongue."

58. *That now.* On the omission of *so*, see Gr. 283. Cf. i. 7. 8; ii. 2. 7; ii. 2. 23; iv. 3. 6; iv. 3. 82.

59. *Norways'.* Norwegians'. See Gr. 433.

Composition. Terms of peace. Cf. *M. for M.* i. 2. 2: "If the duke with the other dukes come not to composition with the king of Hungary, why then all the dukes fall upon the king."

61. *Saint Colme's Inch.* The Island of St. Columba, now Inchcolm, an islet in the Firth of Forth, about two miles south of Aberdour. Here are the remains of a monastery founded in 1123 by Alexander II., who had been driven on the island by stress of weather. There is also an oratory of rude construction, probably as old as the 9th century. St. Columba is said to have resided here for a time; but the island must not be confounded with Colmes-kill, Icolmkill, or Iona, *the* Island of St. Columba, on the west coast of Scotland, where "the gracious Duncan" (see ii. 4. 33 below) was laid beside his royal predecessors.

Inch (the Gaelic *inis*, island) is found in the names of many Scotch islands, as Inchkeith, Inchkenneth, Inchmurrin, Inchcruin, Clairinch, Torrinch, Bucinch, etc.

62. *Dollars.* Of course, an anachronism (as the C. P. ed. points out), the *thaler*, or dollar, having been first coined about 1518, in the Valley of St. Joachim, Bohemia. *Thaler* is probably derived from *thal*, valley.

64. *Bosom interest.* "Close and intimate affection" (C. P. ed.). Cf. *M. of V.* iii. 4. 17: "bosom lover." Schmidt explains *interest* here as = concern, advantage. On the measure, see Gr. 501.

Present. Immediate. Cf. *J. C.* ii. 2. 5: "Go bid the priests do present sacrifice;" 2 *Hen. IV.* iv. 3. 80: "To York, to present execution." So *presently* = instantly; as in *M. of V.* i. 1. 183: "Go presently inquire." See another example in the next note below.

Scene III.—2. "Witches seem to have been most suspected of malice against swine. Dr. Harsnet observes that, about that time, a sow could not be sick of the measles, nor a girl of the sullens, but some old woman was charged with witchcraft" (Johnson). Steevens cites *A Detection of Damnable Driftes practized by Three Witches*, etc. (1579): "she came on a tyme to the house of one Robert Lathburie, . . . who, dislyking her dealyng, sent her home emptie; but presently after her departure, his hogges fell sicke and died, to the number of twentie."

5. *Give me.* For the omission of the direct object, cf. *R. and J.* iv. 1. 121: "Give me, give me!"

6. *Aroint thee.* Cf. *Lear*, iii. 4. 129: "Aroint thee, witch, aroint thee!" The meaning is evidently "Away with thee!" but the derivation of *aroint* has been much disputed. Several authorities state that "Rynt thee!" or "'Roint thee!" is still used in Cheshire, chiefly by milkmaids in bidding a cow get out of the way. See Nares and Wb. In an old drawing representing the "Harrowing of Hell," Christ is in the act of releasing various souls from the mouth of the pit, while the appointed custodian appears to be blowing a horn as a signal of alarm; above his head is the legend, "Out out aroynt." The 3d and 4th folios have "Anoynt," which Johnson approved as consistent with the "common

account of witches, who are related to perform many supernatural acts by means of unguents, and particularly to fly to their hellish festivals."

Rump-fed. According to Colepepper this means fed on offal (kidneys, rumps, and other scraps being among the low perquisites of the kitchen given away to the poor); but more likely it means well-fed: "she fed on best joints, I hungry and begging for a chestnut" (Moberly). Nares (endorsed by Schmidt) thinks it means "fat-rumped."

Ronyon. "A scabby or mangy woman." See Wb. The word is used again in *M. W.* iv. 2. 195.

7. *Aleppo.* From this place there was a large caravan trade to Ispahan, Bussora, and Damascus. In Hakluyt's *Voyages* (1589) there are accounts of a voyage made to Aleppo by the ship Tiger of London, in 1583. Cf. *T. N.* v. 1. 65: "And this is he that did the Tiger board."

8. *A sieve.* A favourite craft with witches. Sir W. Davenant says, in his *Albovine* (1629): "He sits like a witch sailing in a sieve." Steevens quotes *Newes from Scotland, or the damnable Life of Dr. Fian, a notable Sorcerer*, etc., wherein it is told how sundry witches "went to sea, each one in a riddle or cive."

9. *Without a tail.* It was believed that a witch could take the form of any animal, but that the tail would be wanting. According to Sir F. Madden, one distinctive mark of a werwolf, or human being changed to a wolf, was the absence of a tail.

10. *I'll do.* "She threatens, in the shape of a rat, to gnaw through the hull of the Tiger and make her spring a leak" (C. P. ed.).

11. Steevens remarks that this free gift of a wind is to be considered as an act of sisterly friendship, for witches were supposed to sell them. Cf. Sumner's *Last Will and Testament* (1600):

> "in Ireland and Denmark both,
> Witches for gold will sell a man a wind,
> Which, in the corner of a napkin wrap'd,
> Shall blow him safe unto what coast he will."

The C. P. ed. quotes Drayton, *Moon-Calf*, line 865:

> "She could sell winds to any one that would
> Buy them for money, forcing them to hold
> What time she listed, tie them in a thread,
> Which ever as the seafarer undid,
> They rose or scantled, as his sails would drive,
> To the same port whereas he would arrive."

14. *Other.* See Gr. 12.

15. *And the very ports they blow.* That is, *to* which they blow. Johnson wished to read "various" for *very*, and Pope "points" for *ports*. The C. P. editors think that "orts" for *ports* "seems still more probable."

17. *The shipman's card.* The card of the compass. Some explain it as=chart. Halliwell quotes *The Loyal Subject:*

> "The card of goodness in your minds, that shews ye
> When ye sail false; the needle touch'd with honour,
> That through the blackest storms still points at happiness," etc.

Cf. also Pope, *Essay on Man*, ii. 108:

> "On life's vast ocean diversely we sail,
> Reason the card, but passion is the gale."

For *shipman*, cf. *T. and C.* v. 2. 172; also 1 *Kings*, ix. 27 and *Acts*, xxvii. 27, 30.

20. *Pent-house lid.* Malone cites Decker, *Gull's Horne-Booke:* "The two eyes are the glasse windowes, at which light disperses itself into every roome, having goodlie pent-houses of haire to overshaddow them." Cf. also Drayton, *David and Goliath:*

> "His brows, like two steep pent-houses, hung down
> Over his eyelids."

21. *Forbid.* Under a ban, or accursed.

22, 23. Probably suggested by Holinshed's account of the bewitching of King Duffe (see p. 133).

32. *Weird.* The folios have "weyward." Theo. substituted *weird*, which is Holinshed's word. "The weird sisters" is Gawin Douglas's translation of Virgil's "Parcae." For the derivation of *weird*, see Wb. For the dissyllabic pronunciation of the word, see Gr. 485; and cf. ii. 1. 20, iii. 4. 133, and iv. 1. 136.

33. *Posters.* "Speedy travellers" (Schmidt).

34. As the C. P. editors remark, the witches here take hold of hands and dance round in a ring nine times, three rounds for each witch, as a charm for the furtherance of their purposes. Multiples of three and nine were specially affected by witches, ancient and modern. See Ovid, *Met.* xiv. 58:

> "Ter novies carmen magico demurmurat ore;"

and vii. 189–191:

> "Ter se convertit; ter sumptis flumine crinem
> Irroravit aquis; ternis ululatibus ora
> Solvit."

38. *Foul and fair.* Perhaps referring to the sudden change in the weather, brought about by witchcraft; perhaps, as Elwin explains it, "*foul* with regard to the weather, and *fair* with reference to his victory."

According to Delius (quoted by Furness), "Macbeth enters engaged in talking with Banquo about the varying fortune of the day of battle which they had just experienced."

39. *Forres.* Forres is on the southern shore of the Moray Frith, about twenty-five miles from Inverness. At its western extremity there is a height commanding the river, the level country to the south, and the town. Here are the ruins of an ancient castle, a stronghold of the Earls of Moray. Some believe that it was the residence of Duncan, and afterwards of Macbeth, when the court was at Forres. Not far distant is the famous "blasted heath," of which Knight says: "There is not a more dreary piece of moorland to be found in all Scotland. It is without tree or shrub. A few patches of oats are visible here and there, and the eye reposes on a fir plantation at one extremity; but all around is bleak and brown, made up of peat and bog water, white stones and bushes of furze. The desolation of the scene in stormy weather, or when the twilight fogs are trailing over the pathless heath or settling down upon the pools, must be indescribable."

FORRES AND THE "BLASTED HEATH."

43. *That man may question.* "Are ye any beings with which man is permitted to hold converse, or of whom it is lawful to ask questions?" (Johnson).

45. *Should.* See Gr. 323, and cf. i. 2. 46 above.

46. *Beards.* St. quotes B. and F., *Honest Man's Fortune*, ii. 1:

> "And the women that
> Come to us, for disguises must wear beards;
> And that's, they say, a token of a witch."

Cf. also *M. W.* iv. 2. 202: "I think the 'oman is a witch indeed; I like not when a 'oman has a great peard."

48. *Glamis.* "In Scotland, always pronounced as a monosyllable, with the open sound of the first vowel, as in *alms*" (Seymour).

Glamis, or Glammis, is a village about twenty-five miles north-east of Perth, in a very beautiful situation.* Near by is Glamis Castle, "perhaps the finest and most picturesque of the Scottish castles now inhabited." In its present form, it dates back only to the 17th century, though portions of it are much older. The original castle was frequently used as a residence by the Scottish kings, especially by Alexander II. in 1263–64. Robert II. gave it to John Lyon, who had married his daughter, but in 1537 it reverted to the Crown, and James V. occupied it for some time.

Sir Walter Scott says: "I was only nineteen or twenty years old when I happened to pass a night in this magnificent old baronial castle. The hoary old pile contains much in its appearance, and in the traditions connected with it, impressive to the imagination. It was the scene of the murder of a Scottish king of great antiquity; not indeed the gracious Duncan, with whom the name naturally associates it, but Malcolm II. It contains also a curious monument of the peril of feudal times, being a secret chamber, the entrance to which, by the law or custom of the family, must only be known to three persons at once—the Earl of Strathmore, his heir-apparent, and any third person whom they may take into their confidence. The extreme antiquity of the building is vouched by the immense thickness of the walls, and the wild and straggling arrangement of the accommodation within doors. I was conducted to my apartment in a distant corner of the building; and I must own that, as I heard door after door shut, after my conductor had retired, I began to consider myself too far from the living and somewhat too near the dead."

In front of the manse at Glamis is an ancient sculptured obelisk (see cut, p. 150) called "King Malcolm's Gravestone," and here tradition says he was buried.

51. Coleridge comments on this speech and the context as follows:

"But O! how truly Shakespearian is the opening of Macbeth's character given in the *unpossessedness* of Banquo's mind, wholly present to the present object—an unsullied, unscarified mirror! And how strictly true to nature it is that Banquo, and not Macbeth himself, directs our notice to the effect produced on Macbeth's mind, rendered temptable by previous dalliance of the fancy with ambitious thoughts:

---

* See cut on p. 8; and for Glamis Castle, views on p. 9 (from a sketch by Creswick, made about 1840) and p. 46.

'Good sir, why do you start, and seem to fear
Things that do sound so fair?'

And then, again, still unintroitive, addresses the witches:

'I' the name of truth,
Are ye fantastical, or that indeed
Which outwardly ye show?'

Banquo's questions are those of natural curiosity—such as a girl would put after hearing a gipsy tell her school-fellow's fortune;—all perfectly general, or rather planless. But Macbeth, lost in thought, raises himself to speech only by the witches being about to depart:

'Stay, you imperfect speakers, tell me more;'

and all that follows is reasoning on a problem already discussed in his mind—on a hope which he welcomes, and the doubts concerning the attainment of which he wishes to have cleared up. Compare his eagerness—the keen eye with which he has pursued the witches' evanishing—

'Speak, I charge you,'

with the easily satisfied mind of the self-uninterested Banquo:

'The earth hath bubbles, as the water has,
And these are of them. Whither are they vanish'd?'

and then Macbeth's earnest reply—

'Into the air; and what seem'd corporal melted
As breath into the wind. *Would they had stay'd!*'

Is it too minute to notice the appropriateness of the simile 'as breath,' etc., in a cold climate?

Still again Banquo goes on wondering, like any common spectator:

'Were such things here as we do speak about?'

while Macbeth persists in recurring to the self-concerning:

'Your children shall be kings.
Banquo. You shall be king.
Macbeth. And thane of Cawdor too: went it not so?'

So surely is the guilt in its germ anterior to the supposed cause and immediate temptation! Before he can cool, the confirmation of the tempting half of the prophecy arrives, and the concatenating tendency of the imagination is fostered by the sudden coincidence:

'Glamis, and thane of Cawdor!
The greatest is behind.'

Oppose this to Banquo's simple surprise:

'What, can the devil speak true?'"

53. *Fantastical.* "That is, creatures of *fantasy*, or imagination" (Johnson). The word occurs in Holinshed's account of this interview with the weird sisters (see p. 141). Cf. line 139 below, and *Rich. II.* i. 3. 299.

54. *Show.* Appear. See on i. 2. 15. On *ye* followed by *you*, see Gr. 236.

55. "There is here a skilful reference to the thrice repeated 'Hail' of

the witches. 'Thane of Glamis' he was; that is the 'present grace;' but 'Thane of Cawdor' was only predicted; this is the 'noble having;' the prospect of royalty is only hope, 'of royal hope'" (Hunter).

56. *Having.* Possession, estate. Cf. *M. W.* iii. 2. 73: "The gentleman is of no having;" *T. of A.* ii. 2. 153:

> "The greatest of your having lacks a half
> To pay your present debts."

See also *Hen. VIII.* ii. 3. 23 and iii. 2. 159.

57. *That.* On the omission of *so*, see Gr. 283, and cf. i. 2. 58 above.

60. *Who neither beg*, etc. Who neither beg your favours nor fear your hate. Cf. ii. 3. 45 below. The C. P. ed. quotes *W. T.* iii. 2. 164:

> "Though I with death and with
> Reward did threaten and encourage him."

65. *Lesser.* Still sometimes used as an adjective, but never adverbially, as in *T. and C.* ii. 2. 8: "Though no man lesser fears the Greeks than I." See also v. 2. 13 below.

66. *Happy.* Fortunate; like the Latin *felix.* Cf. *Lear*, iv. 6. 230.

67. *Get.* Beget; but not a contraction of that word. See Wb. and note on i. 2. 25 above.

71. *Sinel.* The father of Macbeth, according to Holinshed. Ritson says his true name was Finleg (Finley); Dr. Beattie conjectured that it was Sinane, and that *Dunsinane* (the hill of Sinane) was derived from it.

72. Johnson asks: "How can Macbeth be ignorant of the state of the thane whom he has just defeated and taken prisoner (see i. 2. 50 fol.), or call him a *prosperous gentleman* who has forfeited his title and life by open rebellion? He cannot be supposed to dissemble, because nobody is present but Banquo, who was equally acquainted with Cawdor's treason?"

76. *Owe.* Own, have. Cf. *Rich. II.* iv. 1. 184: "That owes two buckets;" and see note in our ed.

80. *Of them.* Cf. *A. W.* ii. 5. 50: "I have kept of them tame;" *W. T.* iv. 4. 217: "You have of these pedlars," etc.

81. *Corporal.* Corporeal. S. never uses *corporeal* or *incorporeal.* He has *incorporal* in *Ham.* iii. 4. 118: "the incorporal air."

Elwin (quoted by Furness) says: "The emphasis should be laid on 'seem'd,' and the division of ideas is at 'corporal,' and there the rest should be made by the speaker; for the mind dwells first on the *seeming immateriality*, and then turns to the antithesis of *invisibility.* 'Melted' consequently belongs to the second line, which is uttered in accents of wonder, and with a rapidity illustrative of the act it describes."

84. *On.* Cf. *J. C.* i. 2. 71: "jealous on me;" *M. of V.* ii. 6. 67: "glad on't;" and see note, *Mer.* p. 143, or Gr. 138, 181.

The insane root is an example of "prolepsis;" *insane*=*making* insane. Steevens thinks that hemlock is meant, and quotes Greene, *Never too Late* (1616): "you have eaten of the roots of hemlock, that makes men's eyes conceit unseen objects." "Root of hemlock" is one of the ingredients of the witches' cauldron, iv. 1. 25. Douce cites Batman, *Uppon Bartholome de Prop. Rerum:* "*Henbane* . . . is called *insana*, mad, for the use thereof is perillous, for if it be eate or dronke, it breedeth madnesse, or slow lyknesse of sleepe." The C. P. editors suggest that it may be the deadly nightshade (*Atropa belladonna*), of which Gerard, in his *Herball*, says: "This kinde of Nightshade causeth sleepe, troubleth the minde, bringeth madnes, if a few of the berries be inwardly taken." Beisley (*Shakespeare's Garden*) says: "It is difficult to decide what plant S. meant. John Bauhin, in his *Historia Plantarum*, says: 'Hyoscyamus was called *herba insana*.'"

89. *Ross*. Some editors print the name *Rosse;* but as French (*Shakespeareana Genealogica*) points out, that is "an Irish dignity," and should not be confounded with this Scottish title, which "really belonged to Macbeth, who, long before the action of the play begins, was Thane, or more properly, Maormor of Ross by the death of his father, Finley."

91. *Rebels'*. The folios have "rebels." Delius and some other editors print "rebel's," taking "personal venture" to refer to Macbeth's single combat with Macdonald.

92, 93. "*Thine* refers to *praises*, *his* to *wonders*, and the meaning is: There is a conflict in the king's mind between his astonishment at the achievement and his admiration of the achiever; he knows not how sufficiently to express his own wonder and to praise Macbeth, so that he is reduced to silence. *That* refers to the mental conflict just described" (C. P. ed.).

"His wonder, which is his own, contends with his praise, which is yours" (Moberly).

Silenc'd with that is explained by Malone, "wrapped in silent wonder at the deeds performed by Macbeth;" by Moberly, "when he had done speaking of that;" by J. Hunter, "leaving that unsettled."

96. *Nothing afeard*. On *nothing* used adverbially, see Gr. 55. S. uses *afeard* 32 times and *afraid* 44 times (including the *poems* as well as the plays).

97. *As thick as tale*. The folio reading is "as thick as Tale Can post with post," etc. Rowe changed this to "as thick as hail Came post," etc. Johnson restored "tale," retaining "Came," and explained the passage, "posts arrived as fast as they could be counted." Sr., Coll., W., St., and H. follow Johnson; most of the other editors adopt Rowe's emendation in full. W. remarks: "To say that men arrived as thick as tale, *i. e.* as fast as they could be told, is an admissible hyperbole; to say that *men* arrived as thick as *hail*, *i. e.* as close together as hailstones in a storm, is equally absurd and extravagant. The expression, 'as thick as hail,' is never applied, either in common talk or in literature, I believe, except to inanimate objects which fall or fly, or have fallen or flown, with unsuccessive multitudinous rapidity." This latter point seems to have been overlooked by those who dwell on the fact that "thick as hail" is often used by the old writers. It must be admitted, on the other hand, that no parallel instance of "thick as tale" is to be found. The question is a very close one. If both readings were conjectural we should be inclined to adopt "hail;" but as "tale" is in the folio, and may possibly be right, we allow it to stand in the text.

100. *Sent*. Hunter conjectured "not sent;" but the sense is quite

clear as the text stands, for thanks are not payment, and Angus's speech thus suits much better with the one which follows (C. P. ed.).

106. *Addition.* Title. The C. P. ed. quotes Cowel, who says (*Law Dict.* s. v.) that it signifies "a title given to a man besides his Christian and surname, shewing his estate, degree, mystery, trade, place of dwelling," etc. Cf. *Cor.* i. 9. 66; *Hen. V.* v. 2. 467; *Ham.* i. 4. 20; *M. W.* ii. 2. 312, etc.

107. *Devil.* Metrically a monosyllable, like the Scotch *de'il.* Gr. 466. So *whether* in 111 just below.

108. See on line 72 above. Hunter (*New Illus.*, ii. 153, quoted by Furness) finds here an additional reason for fixing the date of the play in 1606. He says: "This passage has hitherto been taken as merely metaphorical; but it seems to me that Shakespeare really intended that the robes pertaining to the dignity of Thane of Cawdor, to which Macbeth was just elevated, should be produced on the stage by Ross and Angus; that in fact the ceremony of investiture should take place on the stage. It is at least more in accordance with the turn of the expression than to suppose that Macbeth spoke thus in mere metaphor.

"Now, it happened that this ancient ceremony of investiture had been lately gone through by Sir David Murray on his being created Lord Scone. We are told that he 'was with the greatest solemnity invested in that honour on the 7th of April, 1605, by a special commission, directed to the Earl Dumfermling, the Lord Chancellor, to that effect. The ceremony was in presence of the earls Angus, Sutherland, Marischal, Linlithgow; the lords Fleming, Drummond, and Thirlestane.' This particular investiture in a Scottish dignity probably suggested to Shakespeare the idea of introducing the investiture of Macbeth as Thane of Cawdor. The Earl of Angus, we see, appears both in the play and in the actual performance of the ceremony; and Sir David Murray, it may also be observed, received the dignity under circumstances not very unlike those under which Macbeth acquired the thanedom of Cawdor. He had a large share in saving the life of the king at the time of the Gowrie conspiracy, and the king gave him for his reward, first, the barony of Ruthven, which had belonged to the Earl of Gowrie, and next the lands of Scone, of which the Earl of Gowrie had been commendator, and had lost them by treason. 'What he hath lost noble Macbeth hath won.'"

109. *Who.* *He* who. See Gr. 251.

112. *Line.* Strengthen, fortify (Schmidt). Cf. 1 *Hen. IV.* ii. 3. 86: "To line his enterprise;" *Hen. V.* ii. 4. 7: "To line and new repair our towns of war."

113. *Vantage.* See on i. 2. 31.

114. *Wrack.* The spelling *wreck* is never found in the early eds. See *Rich. II.* p. 177.

120. *Trusted home.* Trusted completely. See Gr. 45. Cf. the expression still in use, "to strike home."

121. *Enkindle you unto.* "Incite you to hope for" (C. P. ed.). Cf. *A. Y. L.* i. 1. 179: "nothing remains but that I kindle the boy thither" (that is, incite him to it).

123. *And oftentimes*, etc. Flathe (*Shaks. in seiner Wirklichkeit*, quoted by Furness), who considers that Banquo is a silent accomplice in Macbeth's murderous designs, believing that these must be carried out in order to ensure the fulfilment of the prophecy with regard to his own posterity, remarks here: "This warning comes oddly enough from the lips of a man who has just questioned the witches himself with such haste and eagerness. Here we have the first glimpse of the deceit and falsehood practised by Banquo upon himself. . . .

"Banquo would so gladly esteem himself an honourable man; therefore he warns Macbeth, although as briefly as possible, against the devil. He knows that a mere warning will avail nothing, but he ignores this, wishing to be able to say to himself, when Macbeth has attained his end, 'I am guiltless, I warned him against the devil.' Had Banquo been really true, how differently he would have borne himself." . . .

126, 127. On the measure, see Gr. 454, 468, 513. On *cousins*, see *Rich. II.* p. 158, or Schmidt, s. v.

128. *Swelling act.* Cf. *Hen. V.* prol. 4:

> "princes to act,
> And monarchs to behold the swelling scene."

129. On the measure, see Gr. 461, 468.

130. *Soliciting.* "That is, incitement" (Johnson).

135. Cf. v. 5. 11–13.

136. *Seated.* "Fixed, firmly placed" (Steevens). Cf. Milton, *P. L.* vi. 644: "the seated hills."

137. *Present fears.* Warb. substituted "feats," whereon Coleridge comments as follows: "Mercy on this most wilful ingenuity of blundering, which, nevertheless, was the very Warburton of Warburton—his inmost being! *Fears* here are present fear-striking objects, *terribilia adstantia.*" For *fear* = object of fear, cf. *M. N. D.* v. 1. 21:

> "Or in the night, imagining some fear,
> How easy is a bush supposed a bear!"

139. *Fantastical.* See on i. 3. 53; and for the measure, Gr. 467. On *murther*, see *Rich. II.* p. 158.

140. *My single state of man.* St. remarks: "*Single* here bears the sense of *weak; my feeble government* (or *body politic*) of man. S.'s affluence of thought and language is so unbounded that he rarely repeats himself, but there is a remarkable affinity, both in idea and in expression, between the present passage and one in *J. C.* ii. 1. 63–69:

> 'Between the acting of a dreadful thing
> And the first motion, all the interim is
> Like a phantasma, or a hideous dream:
> The Genius and the moral instruments
> Are then in council; and the state of man,
> Like to a little kingdom, suffers then
> The nature of an insurrection.'"

Cf. also *T. and C.* ii. 3. 184:

> "'twixt his mental and his active parts
> Kingdom'd Achilles in commotion rages,
> And batters down himself."

Schmidt explains *single* here as=individual. For *single*=weak, unsupported, cf. *Temp.* i. 2. 432: "A single thing, as I am now."

That function, etc. "All powers of action are oppressed and crushed by one overwhelming image in the mind, and nothing is present to me but that which is really future. Of things now about me I have no perception, being intent wholly on that which has yet no existence" (Johnson).

For *surmise* the C. P. ed. cites *T. A.* ii. 3. 219:

"Aaron is gone; and my compassionate heart
Will not permit mine eyes once to behold
The thing whereat it trembles by surmise."

144. *Stir.* Motion, action. Cf. *Rich. II.* ii. 3. 51, and see note in our ed.

Come. Cf. *R. of L.* 1784: "Weak words, so thick come in his poor heart's aid." Gr. 295.

145. *Our strange garments.* That is, new ones.

147. *Time and the hour*, etc. "That is, *tempus et hora*, time and occasion, will carry the thing through, and bring it to some determined point and end, let its nature be what it will" (Mrs. Montagu). "*The hour* signifies *the appropriate hour*" (Elwin). On *runs*, see Gr. 336.

149. *Favour.* "Indulgence, pardon" (Steevens). Cf. *Hen. VIII.* i. 1. 168. Coleridge remarks here: "Lost in the prospective of his guilt, he turns round alarmed lest others may suspect what is passing in his own mind, and instantly invents the lie of ambition:

'my dull brain was wrought
With things *forgotten*;'

and immediately after pours forth the promising courtesies of a usurper in intention:

'Kind gentlemen, your pains
Are register'd where every day I turn
The leaf to read them.'"

Wrought=agitated. Cf. *W. T.* v. 3. 58:

"If I had thought the sight of my poor image
Would thus have wrought you."

The C. P. ed. cites *Oth.* v. 2. 345.

151. *Register'd.* "That is, in the tablets of his memory, like the μνήμονες δέλτοι φρενῶν (Æschylus, *Prom.* 789). Cf. *Ham.* i. 5. 98" (C. P. ed.).

154. *The interim.* The C. P. editors, following Steevens, think that "the *interim*, or intervening time, is here personified." Abbott considers it a case of the omission of a preposition (Gr. 202)=*in* the interim. Cf. iv. 3. 48: [in] "more sundry ways."

Scene IV.—1. *Are.* The reading of 2d folio; the 1st has "Or."

3. On *are come*, see Gr. 295; on *spoke*, Gr. 343.

8. *The leaving.* See Gr. 93.

9. *Had been studied.* "Had made it his study" (Schmidt). Cf. *M. of V.* ii. 2. 205:

"Like one well studied in a sad ostent
To please his grandam."

"The meaning is that he died as if he had studied to throw away his life as a careless trifle. The comma after *death* should be omitted" (Noble Butler). See Gr. 295.

10. *Owed.* See on i. 3. 76.

11. *As 't were.* See Gr. 107; and for *careless*=uncared-for, Gr. 3. Cf. *sightless*=invisible, in i. 7. 23.

The C. P. ed. cites here Euripides, *Medea*, 516–520:

> ὦ Ζεῦ, τί δὴ χρυσοῦ μὲν ὃς κίβδηλος ᾖ,
> τεκμήρι' ἀνθρώποισιν ὤπασας σαφῆ,
> ἀνδρῶν δ' ὅτῳ χρὴ τὸν κακὸν διειδέναι,
> οὐδεὶς χαρακτὴρ ἐμπέφυκε σώματι;

There 's no art, etc. "Duncan's childlike spirit makes a moment's pause of wonder at the act of treachery, and then flings itself, like Gloster in *King Lear*, with still more absolute trust and still more want of reflection, into the toils of a far deeper and darker treason. The pause on the word *trust*, shortening the line by two syllables, is in this point of view very suggestive" (Moberly).

19. *Proportion.* "The due proportion" (C. P. ed.). Cf. *T. and C.* i. 3. 87: "proportion, season, form."

20. *Mine.* In my power, mine to *give;* as *all* in the next line means all *I have.*

23. *Pays itself.* Is its own reward. Gr. 336.

27. *Safe toward.* "With sure tendency, with certain direction" (Seymour).

"Here in contrast with Duncan's 'plenteous joys,' Macbeth has nothing but the commonplaces of loyalty, in which he hides himself with 'our duties.' Note the exceeding effort of Macbeth's addresses to the king, his reasoning on his allegiance, and then especially when a new difficulty, the designation of a successor, suggests a new crime. This, however, seems the first distinct notion as to the plan of realizing his wishes; and here, therefore, with great propriety, Macbeth's cowardice of his own conscience discloses itself" (Coleridge).

30. *Nor.* We should now use *And.* Cf. *M. of V.* iii. 4. 11: "Nor shall not now." For double negatives in S., see Gr. 406.

32. *Grow.* Here used, as the C. P. ed. remarks, in the double sense of "to cling close" and "to increase." For the former, cf. *Hen. VIII.* v. 5. 50:

> "Peace, plenty, love, truth, terror,
> That were the servants to this chosen infant,
> Shall then be his, and like a vine grow to him."

For the other sense of *grow*, see *A. W.* ii. 3. 163:

> "It is in us to plant thine honour where
> We please to have it grow;"

also B. and F., *The Island Princess*, iii. 1: "So is my study still to plant thy person."

33–35. Malone cites Lucan, *Phars.* ix. 1038:

> "lacrymas non sponte cadentes
> Effudit, gemitusque expressit pectore laeto;
> Non aliter manifesta potens abscondere mentis
> Gaudia, quam lacrymis."

Cf. also *R. and J.* iii. 2. 102:

> "Back, foolish tears, back to your native spring;
> Your tributary drops belong to woe,
> Which you, mistaking, offer up to joy;"

and *W. T.* v. 2. 47: "There might you have beheld one joy crown another, so and in such manner that it seemed sorrow wept to take leave of them, for their joy waded in tears."

37. The throne of Scotland was originally not hereditary.

39. *Cumberland.* See extract from Holinshed (p. 142). "When the successor to the throne was designated in the lifetime of the king, the title of Prince of Cumberland was bestowed upon him. Cumberland was at that time held by Scotland of the crown of England as a fief". (Steevens).

44. *The rest,* etc. "The rest which is not spent in the king's service is like severe labour" (Hunter).

45. *Harbinger.* Used here in its original sense (see Wb.) of an officer whose duty it was to ride in advance of the king and secure lodgings for the royal retinue. Nares cites the old play of *Albumaz,* vii. 137:

> "I have no reason, nor spare room for any.
> Love's harbinger hath chalk'd upon my heart,
> And with a coal writ on my brain, *for Flavia,*
> This house is wholly taken up *for Flavia.*"

It appears that the custom was kept up as late as the time of Charles II. Hawkins, in his *Life of Bishop Ken,* says: "On the removal of the court to pass the summer at Winchester, Bishop Ken's house, which he held in the right of his prebend, was marked by the harbinger for the use of Mrs. Eleanor Gwyn; but he refused to grant her admittance, and she was forced to seek for lodgings in another place."

50. "Macbeth apparently appeals to the stars because he is contemplating night as the time for the perpetration of the deed. There is nothing to indicate that this scene took place at night" (C. P. ed.).

52. *The eye,* etc. "Let the eye not see what the hand does" (Moberly).

Let that be. Let that take place. Delius makes "the eye" the subject of "let;" that is, "the eye, in silent collusion with the executing hand, is to let that take place which it fears to see after the hand has executed it."

54. *Full so valiant.* Quite as brave as you say. While Macbeth has been soliloquizing, Duncan and Banquo have been talking about his recent deeds.

56. *Banquet.* Feast. It sometimes meant merely the *dessert.* See *Hen. VIII.* p. 204, note on *A running banquet.* Cf. *T. of S.* v. 2. 9:

> "My banquet is to close our stomachs up
> After our great good cheer."

58. *It is.* "A touch of affectionate familiarity" (C. P. ed.).

Scene V.—2. *By the perfectest report.* By the best intelligence—that of experience.

4. *They made themselves air.* Sheridan Knowles remarks that in the look and tone with which Mrs. Siddons delivered the word *air* "you

recognized ten times the wonder with which Macbeth and Banquo actually beheld the vanishing of the witches."

5. *Whiles.* See Gr. 137. Cf. *Matt.* v. 25.

Missives. Messengers; as in the only other instance in which S. uses the word (*A. and C.* ii. 2. 74).

6. *All-hailed.* The folio has the hyphen. Cf. Florio (*Ital. Dict.* quoted in C. P. ed.): "Salutare, to salute, to greet, to alhaile."

9. *Deliver thee.* Report to thee. Cf. *Temp.* v. 1. 313: "I'll deliver all," etc. See *Temp.* p. 144.

15. *It is too full o' the milk of human kindness.* Delius remarks that S. elsewhere uses this metaphor; as in iv. 3. 98 below, and in *R. and J.* iii. 3. 55. Cf. also *Lear*, i. 4. 364.

Bodenstedt (quoted by Furness) comments on the passage thus: "We are somewhat astonished to learn this about Macbeth, for throughout the drama we find no trace of this 'milk of human kindness.' We must presume that the lady has too high an opinion of her husband. . . . We already know him as a quickly determined murderer in thought, and as an accomplished hypocrite; and this nature of his is not belied by the present letter; it appears only thinly disguised. The lady knows at once what he is after; she knows and openly acknowledges that his 'milk of human kindness' will not deter him from attempting the life of old King Duncan, but only from 'catching the nearest way;' that is, from laying his own hand to it."

Ulrici remarks: "Macbeth's is a lofty, glorious, and highly gifted nature. He strives for what is highest and greatest, from an internal sympathy for all that is great. But in endeavouring to acquire it he, at the same time, has the wish to satisfy his own self, to possess what is highest, not only because it is high, but in order thereby to raise himself. . . . Up to the commencement of the drama he has kept this desire, this ambition, under the discipline of the law; as yet he has nowhere gone beyond the lawful limit, that delicate line which preserves honour from becoming ambition, and distinguishes it from vice. Thus, at least, he is described by his own wife, who must surely be the best judge."

16. *Wouldst.* See Gr. 329.

18. *The illness should.* The evil which should. See Gr. 244. The C. P. ed. remarks that *illness* "is not used elsewhere by S. in this sense." He does not use it elsewhere in any sense. The word does not occur at all in Milton's poems.

20–23. The general meaning seems to be: "You want to have what can only be obtained on conditions which it proclaims of itself; you wish also to have what you rather fear to do than wish not to be done" (Moberly).

Seymour (quoted by Furness) says: "The difficulty here arises from the accumulative conjunction, which leads us to expect new matter, whereas that which follows [line 23] is only amplification. 'Thou wouldst have the crown; which cries, *Thou must* kill Duncan, if thou have it.' This is an act which thou *must* do, if thou have the crown. 'And,' adds the lady, 'what thou art not disinclined to do, but art rather fearful to *perform* than unwilling to have executed.'"

Malone wished to include in the "cry" all from "Thus thou must do" to "should be undone;" Hunter, only the words "Thus thou must do." Johnson thought it necessary to read "if thou have *me;*" but such "confusions of construction" are not uncommon in S. See Gr. 415.

23. *Hie thee.* Here, as in "Look thee" (*W. T.* iii. 3. 116), "Hark thee" (*Cymb.* i. 5. 32), etc., *thee* seems to be used for *thou.* See Gr. 212.

25. *Chastise.* Accented by S. on the first syllable. Cf. *Rich. II.* ii. 3. 104. Gr. 491.

26. *The golden round.* Cf. iv. 1. 88:

> "And wears upon his baby brow the round
> And top of sovereignty."

Dyce remarks that the phrase had been previously applied to a ring by Abraham Faunce, *Countesse of Pembrokes Yuychurch*, 1591: "Wedding ring, farewell! . . . full well did I cause to be grauen In thy golden round those words," etc.

27. *Metaphysical.* Supernatural (to which word it is etymologically analogous). S. uses the word nowhere else. The C. P. ed. cites Minsheu's *Spanish Dict.*, 1599: "Metafisica, things supernaturall, the metaphisickes," and Florio's *World of Wordes*, 1598: "Metafisico, one that professeth things supernaturall." Delius quotes *The Puritan* (1607), ii. 1: "Metaphysically and by a supernatural intelligence."

Seem. Cf. i. 2. 47 above; also *A. W.* iii. 6. 94: "that so confidently seems to undertake this business;" *Per.* i. 1. 121: "How courtesy would seem to cover sin!" As Schmidt remarks, in these instances, like the present, the word seems to be "almost periphrastical." *Doth seem to have* is nearly equivalent to *would have.*

28. *Tidings.* Like *news*, used by S. both as singular and plural. See *Rich. II.* pp. 177, 198.

29. *Thou 'rt mad*, etc. "The lady's self-control breaks down for a moment at hearing that Duncan is rushing into the toils; and is only by a powerful effort regained in the next words" (Moberly).

33. *Had the speed of him.* Has outstripped him.

35. *Tending.* Attendance; or *tendance*, which S. uses instead. Cf. *T. of A.* i. 1. 57; *Hen. VIII.* iii. 2. 149; *Cymb.* v. 5. 53, etc. *Tending* occurs as a noun only here.

36. *The raven.* Delius, Moberly, the C. P. editors, and some other critics understand this to refer to the messenger, who is hoarse from lack of breath; but the simpler and more obvious sense seems to be that the ill-boding raven is hoarse with proclaiming the fate of Duncan. Johnson, Hunter, Collier, and others so explain it.

37. *Entrance.* A trisyllable here. Gr. 477.

38. *My battlements.* Hunter remarks: "The word *my* is purposely used by S. to let the audience into the spirit of the character intended for the wife of the thane; *nihil non arrogat;* the castle is *hers*—not Macbeth's, not theirs jointly. It prepares for that overbearing of the milder and gentler spirit of the thane which follows." This seems making overmuch of the *my*, which is natural enough in the lady's present mood. Cf. Weiss: "*Mine*, for this night only; Macbeth's at every other time, but mine this once, to hold out with against my husband's mood."

"If there be any one who does not feel the sublimity of the pause after *battlements*, we can only say that he has yet to study Shakespeare" (K.). Yet Pope wanted to read "all you spirits," and Steevens, "Come, come."

39. *Mortal.* Deadly; as very often in S. and other writers. See *Rich. II.* p. 189. On *tend*, see on i. 2. 25.

40. *Top-full.* Used again in *K. John*, iii. 4. 180.

42. *Access.* Accented as here by S. except in *Ham.* ii. 1. 110. See Gr. 490.

Remorse. Relenting, pity. Cf. *V. and A.* 257: "'Pity,' she cries, 'some favour, some remorse!'" See also *Temp.* v. 1. 76; *M. of V.* iv. 1. 20; *K. John*, ii. 1. 478, etc. So S. uses *remorseful*=pitiful (*T. G. of V.* iv. 3. 13; *A. W.* v. 3. 58, etc.) and *remorseless*=pitiless (*R. of L.* 562; *Ham.* ii. 2. 609, etc.). This last word is still used in the same sense.

43–45. "That no natural feelings of pity may intervene between my cruel purpose and its effect, may stop the meditated blow" (C. P. ed.). The meaning seems clear enough, but "keep *peace*" has worried some of the critics. Johnson suggested "keep *pace*," and Bailey "keep *space*." As K. remarks, anything that stands between a purpose and its accomplishment may be said to keep peace between them, "as one who interferes between a violent man and the object of his wrath keeps peace."

46. *Take my milk for gall.* Johnson says: "Take *away* my milk, and put *gall* into the place;" but the simpler meaning is, turn it to gall.

47. *Sightless substances.* Invisible forms. See on *careless*, i. 4. 11, and cf. i. 7. 23 below. Gr. 3.

48. *Mischief.* "This expresses both *injury engendered in human nature* and *done to it*" (Elwin).

49. *Pall.* Wrap (Latin *pallire*, from *pallium*). Used by S. only here, and perhaps by no other writer as a verb. Of course, *pall*=become vapid (*Ham.* v. 2. 9; *A. and C.* ii. 7. 88) is an entirely different word.

Dunnest. Steevens notes that a writer in the *Rambler* (No. 168) criticises the epithet *dun* as mean. Milton, however, uses it (*P. L.* iii. 72; *Comus*, 127), and, as the C. P. ed. remarks, to our ears it no longer sounds mean. As Horace says (*Ars Poet.* 70),

> "Multa renascentur quae jam cecidere, cadentque
> Quae nunc sunt in honore vocabula, si volet usus."

50. *See not.* Elwin says, rather fancifully, "that the wound may not be reflected in the brightness of the blade."

51. *Blanket.* This word has sorely troubled the critics. Coleridge was driven to the fearful suggestion of "blank height," but omitted it in the 2d ed. of his *Table Talk* ("on my urging its absurdity," Dyce says). *Blackness* and *blankest* are other attempts at emendation where none is needed. Malone compares Drayton's *Mortimeriados*, 1596: "The sullen night in mistie rugge is wrapp'd," and adds: "*Blanket* was perhaps suggested by the coarse woollen curtain of S.'s own theatre, through which, probably, while the house was but yet half-lighted, he had himself often peeped." Whiter (quoted by Furness) says: "Nothing is more certain than that all the images in this passage are borrowed from the

stage. The peculiar and appropriate dress of *Tragedy* is a *pall** and a *knife.* When tragedies were represented, the stage was hung with black. . . . In *R. of L.* (764–770) there is a wonderful coincidence with this passage, in which we have not only '*Black stage* for *tragedies* and *murders fell,*' but also '*comfort-killing Night, image of Hell,*' corresponding with *thick Night* and the dunnest smoke of hell. Again, in line 788, we have 'Through *Night's black* bosom should not *peep* again.'"

But whatever may have suggested it, *blanket*, though homely, is Shakespearian; and, as W. suggests, "the man who does not apprehend the meaning and the pertinence of the figure had better shut his Shakespeare, and give his days and nights to the perusal of—some more correct and classical writer."

53. *Hereafter.* Mrs. Jameson remarks: "This is surely the very rapture of ambition! and those who have heard Mrs. Siddons pronounce the word *hereafter* cannot forget the look, the tone, which seemed to give her auditors a glimpse of the awful *future*, which she, in her prophetic fury, beholds upon the instant."

55. *Ignorant.* "Unknowing; I feel by anticipation those future honours, of which, according to the process of nature, the *present time* would be *ignorant*" (Johnson). Delius takes it to mean "our unknown, obscure, inglorious present," and cites *W. T.* i. 2. 397: "ignorant concealment."

Feel. Metrically a dissyllable. Gr. 484.

59. On the measure, see Gr. 511.

61. *To beguile the time.* That is (as Delius and Schmidt explain), to *deceive* men; not "to wile away the time," as in *T. N.* iii. 3. 41. The same expression occurs in Daniel's *Civil Wars*, book viii. (1609):

> "He drawes a Trauerse 'twixt his greeuances:
> Lookes like the time: his eye made not report
> Of what he felt within."

Perhaps Daniel borrowed it from S.

63. Cf. *Rich. II.* iii. 2. 19:

> "And when they from thy bosom pluck a flower,
> Guard it, I pray thee, with a lurking adder;"

and 2 *Hen. VI.* iii. 1. 228: "The snake roll'd in a flowering bank."

70. *To alter favour*, etc. "To bear an altered face marks fear in you and creates it in others" (Moberly). On *favour*=face, cf. *J. C.* i. 2. 91: "Your outward favour," etc. See also *Prov.* xxxi. 30.

Scene VI.—Sir Joshua Reynolds remarks: "This short dialogue between Duncan and Banquo has always appeared to me a striking instance of what in painting is termed *repose.* Their conversation very naturally turns upon the beauty of the situation, and the pleasantness of the air; and Banquo, observing the martlets' nests in every recess of the cornice, remarks that where those birds most breed and haunt the air is delicate.

---

* Cf. Milton, *Il Pens.* 97:

> "Sometime let gorgeous Tragedy
> In sceptred pall come sweeping by."—(*Ed.*)

The subject of this quiet and easy conversation gives that repose so necessary to the mind after the tumultuous bustle of the preceding scenes, and perfectly contrasts the scene of horror that immediately succeeds."

Franz Horn (*Shakespeare's Schauspiele Erläutert*, translated by Furness) says:

"A very remarkable passage is found in act i. scene 6. Duncan has, in a pleasant way, invited himself to sup and pass the night in Macbeth's castle, and every reader and spectator anticipates that he is here delivered to his murderers. Duncan now actually appears before the castle in company with his faithful Banquo, and the question presses upon us: How would a hundred and again a hundred of our European poets have made Duncan talk?

"Most of them would have made him express himself thoughtfully, gravely, ominously, after the manner, doubtless, of Henry IV. of France, who hears 'in his presaging ear the footfall of the murderer seeking him through the streets of Paris; feeling the spectral knife long ere Ravaillac had armed himself therewith.' Or, if the king were represented as unaware of coming evil, some friend, at least, would warn him, and upon being questioned whence came his forebodings, would say no more than that a mysterious voice within prompted him thus to speak. It is not to be denied that in many tragedies such a treatment might be proper. But here it would disturb the effect; for into the calm, soft spirit of Duncan, and into the bold heart of Banquo, no mystic voices can penetrate.

"Other poets might perhaps have hoped to produce an exhilarating effect by sharp contrasts, and even to have put the king in a light-hearted, merry mood, which would have been sufficiently out of place.

"Our poet, in his wisdom and clear insight into human nature, has struck the right point, and is thoroughly human and humane in introducing the repose which he here opens before us, in order to deepen the tragic pathos that follows."

Moberly comments on the passage as follows: "Perfect peace seems to welcome the doomed king to his kinsman's house. No startling omens; a light and cheerful air; martins building as on a temple, and 'securely hatching their young.' The poetic instinct is the same as that which makes Homer, in *Il.* xxii. 126, introduce into Hector's bitter farewell to life the soft image of the 'youth and maiden conversing near some oak-tree or by some shadowy rock.'"

Compare what Sheridan Knowles says in his *Lectures on Dramatic Literature:*

"We come to the sixth scene, which has been instanced by a celebrated artist and critic—Sir Joshua Reynolds—as an example of relief, analogous to what is technically called repose in painting. The artist and critic I allude to considers this to be the effect of design on the part of Shakespeare—that it is intended by him to relax the tension, the extreme tension of that interest which has been hitherto excited in the audience, and kept constantly upon the strain. Notwithstanding the eloquence of the remark, and the ingenuity with which it is enforced, I am inclined to take a different view of the subject, and to consider this scene as another and a higher step in the climax of the action. That Duncan should contemplate with satisfaction the pleasant seat of Macbeth's castle, and that Banquo should participate in the feelings of the king, are perfectly natural; but that the audience should partake this view is as preposterous as to suppose that we could see a man about to step into a cavern which we know to be the den of a wild beast, and participate in his admiration of the foliage which might happen to adorn its entrance. So far, if I mistake not, from there being any relaxing of the interest here, there is an absolute straining of it. The unconsciousness of the destined victim to the fate that awaited it, the smiling flowers that dressed it, and its playful motions as it walked to the altar of sacrifice, must have served, not to assuage, but to aggravate in the beholder the feeling of its predicament. There is no relief, no repose here. How often in witnessing this scene have I felt a wish that some suspicion of foul play would flash across the mind of Banquo, and that he would hang upon the robes of the king and implore him not to enter."

1. *Seat.* Reed quotes Bacon, *Essay* 45: "Hee that builds a faire House, upon an ill Seat, committeth himself to Prison."

3. *Senses.* "*Senses* are nothing more than *each man's sense. Gentle sense* means *placid*, *calm*, *composed*, and intimates the peaceable delight of a fine day" (Johnson). It may be considered an instance of prolepsis. Cf. i. 3. 84 and iii. 4. 76.

4. *Martlet.* The folios have "Barlet." The emendation is Rowe's, and is adopted by all the editors. It is supported by *M. of V.* ii. 9. 28: "Like the martlet, Builds in the weather on the outward wall." Cf. *T. of A.* iii. 6. 31.

Approve=prove; as often in S. Cf. *M. of V.* iii. 2. 79; 2 *Hen. IV.* i. 2. 180; *A. W.* iii. 7. 13, etc.

5. *Mansionry.* Theobald's emendation for the "Mansonry" of the folios. Perhaps *masonry*, adopted by Pope (2d ed.), was S.'s word. He uses it in *Sonn.* 55. 6 and *A. W.* ii. 1. 31. *Mansionry* is found nowhere else.

6. *Jutty.* The same word as *jetty* (see Wb.). The C. P. ed. cites Cotgrave (*Fr. Dict.*): "Soupenduë, f. A penthouse; iuttie, or part of a building that iuttieth beyond, or leaneth ouer, the rest." The folios read "jutty frieze" without a comma between, as if *jutty* were an adjective. It is not, however, found as an adjective, though it occurs both as a substantive and as a verb. For the latter, see the passage just quoted from Cotgrave, and *Hen. V.* iii. 1. 13:

> "O'erhang and jutty his confounded base."

S. uses the word only twice.

7. *Coign of vantage.* "Convenient corner" (Johnson). Hunter thinks it means *projecting* corner. Dyce remarks that *coign* is a word of rare occurrence, and cites Sylvester's *Du Bartas:* "Cape of Hope, last coign of Africa;" where the original has, not *coin*, but "*angle* dernier d'Afrique." S. uses the word only here and in *Cor.* v. 4. 1, unless *Per.* iii prol. 17 is to be added.

9. *Most.* The folios have "must," out of which Coll. says "sense might be made." His MS. corrector has "much." *Most* is Rowe's emendation.

11–14. *The love,* etc. "Duncan says that even love sometimes occasions him trouble, but that he thanks it as love, notwithstanding; and that thus he teaches Lady Macbeth, while she takes trouble on his account, to 'bid God yield,' or reward, him for giving that trouble" (Coll.). S. uses *sometime* and *sometimes* indifferently, both in this sense and as an adjective=former. See *Mer.* p. 130.

God 'ield is a corruption of "God yield." The folios have "God-eyld." "God ild" and "God dild" are common forms of it in the old writers. Cf. *A. Y. L.* iii. 3. 76 and v. 4. 56; *A. and C.* iv. 2. 33; *Ham.* iv. 5. 41, etc. For the colloquial contraction, cf. "God gi' good-den" ("Godgigoden" in the folio)=God give you good-evening, in *R. and J.* i. 2. 58.

15. *Twice done,* etc. Moberly remarks that the division into two processes intensifies the idea; as in Milton, *P. L.* i. 742:

> "from morn
> To noon he fell, from noon to dewy eve,
> A summer's day." *

16. *Single business.* "That is, small business. . . . There is a whimsical likeness and logical connection between this phrase and one which has lately come into vulgar vogue, 'a *one-horse* affair,' 'a *one-horse* town,' etc." (W.) Cf. i. 3. 140 above. *To contend against*=to vie with.

17. *Deep and broad.* On the transposition of adjectives, see Gr. 419.

19. *To them.* See Gr. 185, and cf. iii. 1. 51 below.

20. *Hermits.* "We as hermits, or *beadsmen,* shall always pray for you" (Steevens). See *Rich. II.* p. 190, note on *Beadsmen.*

21. *Cours'd.* Chased. Cf. *Lear,* iii. 4. 58: "to course his own shadow," etc.

22. *Purveyor.* An officer sent forward to provide food for the king and his retinue, as the *harbinger* to obtain lodging. On the accent, see Gr. 492.

23. *Holp.* Cf. *Rich. II.* v. 5. 62 (see note in our ed. p. 218), *Temp.* i. 2. 63, etc. Gr. 343.

26. *In compt.* In account, accountable. Cf. *T. of A.* ii. 1. 35; *A. W.* v. 3. 57, etc.

30. For the measure, see Gr. 492.

31. *By your leave.* "Here Duncan gives his hand to Lady Macbeth, and leads her into the castle" (C. P. ed.).

SCENE VII.—On *sewer* in the stage direction, see Wb. and Nares. Cf. also *Rich. II.* p. 216, foot-note.

1, 2. The punctuation given is essentially that of the folios, and is followed by most of the editors. W. points it thus:

> "If it were done when 't is done, then 't were well.
> It were done quickly if th' assassination
> Could trammel," etc.

---

* Moberly (probably quoting from memory) gives the passage thus:

> "From eve to morn, from morn to dewy eve,
> From eve to morn he fell."

This reading was suggested by G. Blink (*Notes and Queries*, May 25, 1850), and was ably defended by a writer in the *Boston Courier*, April 25, 1857, as the following extracts from his article (quoted by Furness) will show:

"The 'if' means, if, when the murder is committed, there were the end of it. So Schiller, in his admirable translation of the play, clearly discerns it: 'Wär' es auch *abgethan*, wenn es *gethan* ist, Dann wär' es gut, es würde rasch gethan!' . . . The words 'It were done quickly' sound supernumerary and out of place, as they are generally recited. They hang like an encumbrance. They clog the movement of the verse. Above all, they drag in a new and inferior thought, after the great argument has been sufficiently pronounced. Cut them off, then, from their connection with the preceding line, which they do but cumber, and see what new force you will give to the whole soliloquy:

> 'If it were done when 'tis done, then 'twere well.'

There is the full theme and true key-note of the piece. It is complete in itself. It prepares the way for all that follows. It announces the terrible problem with which Macbeth's unsteady purpose was wrestling. It reminds us of the first line of Hamlet's bewildered self-confidence: 'To be, or not to be; that is the question.' The speaker may well pause, in both cases, when he comes to that point of the awful debate. And there the rather, because by such a course the sentence that follows will be as much enriched by what it gains as the sentence that precedes is relieved by what it surrenders. The clause, that seemed almost impertinent where it stood, becomes a reinforcement in its new relation:

> 'It were done quickly, if the assassination
> Could trammel up the consequence,' etc.

Observe how much clearer and more compact the rest of the period becomes by beginning it in this new way.

"Macbeth professes to defy religion, and to care nothing for the threatened retributions of another world; but he dreads the avenging of his crimes 'here:' 'But here, upon this bank and shoal of Time.' This description, by the way, of the guilty thane, thinking only of the earth, with its shattering fortunes, and of the present life with its 'petty space' and its 'brief candle,' its creeping to-morrows and its yesterdays, that do nothing but light fools to their death, is wondrously sustained in every part of the play, till at last he cries out in despair:

> 'I 'gin to grow aweary of the sun,
> And wish the estate o' the world were now undone.'"

If we retain the old pointing—which seems best, on the whole—the meaning is: "If the act were really over when done, then the sooner we accomplish it the better." The sentences which follow are thus paraphrased by Moberly: "If the murder could be like a net, taking in all consequences at a single haul, and bringing up, as the haul ceases, a conclusive and final success; if only the blow could end all apprehensions here in this life, shallow as it is, we might risk the life to come. But it is not so; besides the great future, there is a nearer future of temporal retribution, which we teach others to execute on ourselves."

3. *Trammel up.* Entangle as in a net. A *trammel* was a kind of net. Cf. Quarles, *Emblems:* "Nay, Cupid, pitch thy trammel where thou please." In Spenser it is a net for the hair; as in *F. Q.* ii. 2, 15:

> "Her golden lockes she roundly did uptye
> In breaded tramels" (that is, braided nets);

and *Id.* iii. 9, 20:

> "Her golden locks, that were in trammells gay
> Upbounden, did them selves adowne display
> And raught unto her heeles."

4. *His surcease.* Its conclusion, or cessation. On *his*=its, see Gr. 228, and cf. *Temp.* p. 120, note on *With it's sweet air. Surcease* (see Wb.) has no etymological connection with *cease*, being derived from the Fr. *surseoir* (Lat. *supersedere*). S. uses it as a noun only here; but as a verb in *R. of L.* 1766, *Cor.* iii. 2. 121, and *R. and J.* iv. 1. 97.

Success. Used in its ordinary sense; as in i. 3. 90, 132, and i. 5. 1 above. St. takes it here as="sequel, what follows," making "to *catch*, with his surcease, *success*," an "enforcement of 'trammel up the consequence.'" He paraphrases the passage thus: "If the assassination were an absolutely final act, and could shut up all consecution—'be the be-all and the end-all' even of this life only—we would run the hazard of a future state." On *success* in this sense, see *J. C.* p. 151, note on *Opinions of success;* and cf. *T. and C.* ii. 2. 117: "fear of bad success," etc.

6. *But here.* Only here, only in this life.

Shoal. The folios have "Schoole," which some critics would retain. Elwin says: "*Bank* is used for *bench*, and *time* for *mortal life;* which, qualified as a *bench and school of instruction*, is placed in antithesis to *the life to come.* Here the idea of calling this life *the school of eternity*, as preparing man for the part he is to perform there, is not only thoroughly in accordance with the truthful genius of Shakespeare, but it is beautifully sustained in the expressions that follow it, 'that we but *teach* bloody instruction.' The feeling expressed is this: If here only, upon this bench of instruction, in this school of eternity, I could do this without bringing these, my pupil days, under suffering, I would hazard its effect on the endless life to come."

Theo. first suggested *shoal*, explaining it: "This *Shallow*, this *narrow Ford* of humane Life, opposed to the *great Abyss* of Eternity."

7. *Jump.* For *jump*=risk, hazard, cf. *Cor.* iii. 1. 154: "To jump a body with a dangerous physic;" *Cymb.* v. 4. 188: "jump the after inquiry on your own peril."

8. *That.* So that; as in line 25 below. Gr. 283.

11. *Commends.* Offers, commits. Cf. *Rich. II.* iii. 3. 116: "His glittering arms he will commend to rust;" *A. and C.* iv. 8. 23: "Commend unto his lips thy favouring hand," etc. See also iii. 1. 38 below.

17. *Faculties.* Official powers or prerogatives. The C. P. ed. cites *Hen. VIII.* i. 2. 73, where Wolsey says:

> "If I am
> Traduced by ignorant tongues, which neither know
> My faculties nor person."

20. *Taking-off.* Delius cites *Lear*, v. 1. 65: "His speedy taking off." See also iii. 1. 104 below.

21. *A naked new-born babe.* "Either like a mortal babe terrible in helplessness; or like heaven's child-angels, mighty in love and compassion" (Moberly).

22. *Cherubin.* Cf. *Temp.* i. 2. 152: "a cherubin," and see note in our ed. p. 115. Some editors print "cherubim" here, but that form is found nowhere in the folio. Malone remarks that the thought seems to have been borrowed from *Psalms*, xviii. 10; and the C. P. ed. quotes *R. and J.* ii. 2. 28–31.

23. *Sightless.* See on i. 5. 47.

25. *That tears*, etc. See on 8 above. Cf. *T. and C.* iv. 4. 55: "Where are my tears? Rain, to lay this wind."

I have no spur, etc. Malone says: "There are two distinct metaphors. I have no spur to prick the sides of my intent: I have nothing to *stimulate* me to the execution of my purpose, but ambition, which is apt to overreach itself; this he expresses by the second image, of a person meaning to vault into his saddle, who, by taking too great a leap, will fall on the other side."

28. *On the other.* That is, the other *side;* but there is no necessity for supplying "side," as Hanmer, Keightley, and others have done. As H. remarks, "the sense *feels* better without it, as this shows the speaker to be in such an eagerly expectant state of mind as to break off the instant he had a prospect of any news."

32. *Bought.* "Acquired, gained" (Schmidt); a figurative use of the word natural enough, and common in S. Cf. *L. L. L.* i. 1. 5:

> "The endeavour of this present breath may buy
> That honour;"

Hen. VIII. i. 1. 65:

> "The force of his own merit makes his way;
> A gift that heaven gives for him, which buys
> A place next to the king," etc.

Cf. the use of *purchase* in *Rich. II.* i. 3. 282 and *M. of V.* ii. 9. 43.

34. *Would.* See Gr. 329.

35. *Was the hope drunk*, etc. "A somewhat violent mixture of metaphors; but the sense is clear. 'Were you drunk when you formed your bold plan, and are you now just awake from the debauch, to be crestfallen, shrinking, mean-spirited?'" (Moberly). Cf. Gr. 529 (4). For a similar figure, without the "mixture," see *K. John*, iv. 2. 116.

37. *Green and pale.* "This refers to the wretched appearance that Hope presents on awaking from her drunkenness, and in consequence of it" (Delius, quoted by Furness).

41. *Wouldst thou have*, etc. Do you desire the crown, yet resolve to live a coward because your daring will not second your desire? Moberly substitutes *leave* for *have*, explaining it: "Would you forsake that courage which you have always viewed as the ornament of life, and be like the cat who * longed for fish but would not wet her feet."

---

* This use of *who* in referring to irrational animals is not uncommon in good English writers of our day. Even Mr. Grant White has "a dog who" in one of his papers in the *Galaxy*. On the Shakespearian usage, see Gr. 259 (2) and 264.

45. *The poor cat*, etc. Johnson quotes the Low Latin form of the proverb: "Catus amat pisces, sed non vult tingere plantas." In French it is "Le chat aime le poisson, mais il n'aime pas à mouiller ses pattes" (Peck). Boswell finds it among Heywood's *Proverbs*, 1566: "The cate would eate fishe, and would not wet her feete."

47. *Do more.* Rowe's emendation for the "no more" of the folios. Hunter would retain the old reading, and give the line to Lady Macbeth.

What beast, etc. "If, as you imply, this enterprise be not the device of a *man*, what *beast* induced *you* to propose it?" (Elwin). The antithesis of *beast* and *man* seems natural enough, but Hunter would read "What was 't then," and the Coll. MS. has "What *boast* was 't," which is defended by a writer in *Blackwood's Magazine* (Oct. 1853) quoted by Furness.

Steevens cites *M. for M.* ii. 4. 134:

> "Be that you are,
> That is, a woman; if you be more, you're none."

48. *Break.* Here followed by *to*, as it would be now, but often in S. by *with*; as in *J. C.* ii. 1. 150; *Hen. VIII.* v. 1. 47 (see note in our ed. p. 197), etc.

50. *To be.* On the use of the infinitive, see Gr. 356.

52. *Adhere.* Cohere, "be in accordance" (Schmidt). Cf. *M. W.* ii. 1. 62 and *T. N.* iii. 4. 86.

53. *That their fitness.* Abbott (Gr. 239) commenting on "that mouth of thine" (*K. John*, iii. 1. 299), remarks: "'This your mouth' requiring a forced and unnatural pause after 'this,' was somewhat more objectionable to S. than to the Latin style of Milton and Addison;" and then adds, in a foot-note: "See, however, 'this our lofty scene,' *J. C.* ii. 1. 112." The present passage affords another example; and (if we adopt the reading of the 1st folio) yet another occurs in *A. and C.* ii. 3. 19: "that thy spirit which keeps thee."* See also ii. 2. 61 and iii. 6. 48 below.

58. *The brains.* As the C. P. ed. remarks, we should now say "its brains," but *the* is found not unfrequently for the possessive pronoun. Cf. the version of *Lev.* xxv. 5 in the Bishops' Bible: "That which groweth of the owne accord of thy harvest, thou shalt not reape;" and Bacon, *Adv. of L.* i. 4. 1.: "For we see that it is the manner of men to scandalize and deprave that which retaineth the state and virtue."

59. *We fail.* The folio prints "we faile?" Most eds. have "We fail!" but K., H., and Sr. (2d ed.), "We fail." K. says: "We prefer the quiet self-possession of the punctuation we have adopted." D. remarks: "Whether the words be pointed 'We fail!' or 'We fail?' (and I much prefer the former method), they can only be understood as an impatient and contemptuous repetition of Macbeth's 'we fail,—.' *Any kind of admission* on the part of Lady Macbeth that the attempt might prove unsuccessful appears to me quite inconsistent with all that she has previously said, and all that she afterwards says, in the present scene. She

---

* The 2d folio has "that's thy spirit," which is adopted by many editors, as the passage in North's *Plutarch* which S. evidently copied reads: "For thy demon, said he (that is to say, the good angel and spirit that keepeth thee), is afraid," etc.

hastily interrupts her husband, checking the very idea of failure as it rises in his mind."

Mrs. Jameson says: "In her impersonation of the part of Lady Macbeth, Mrs. Siddons adopted successively three different intonations in giving the words *we fail.* At first a quick contemptuous interrogation —'*we fail?*' Afterwards with the note of admiration—'*we fail!*' and an accent of indignant astonishment, laying the principal emphasis on the word *we*—*we* fail! Lastly, she fixed on what I am convinced is the true reading—'we fail.' with the simple period, modulating her voice to a deep, low, resolute tone, which settled the issue at once—as though she had said, 'if we fail, why then we fail, and all is over.' This is consistent with the dark fatalism of the character and the sense of the line following, and the effect was sublime, almost awful."

Compare what Fletcher (see p. 24) says: "Her quiet reply, 'We fail,' is every way most characteristic of the speaker—expressing that moral firmness in herself which makes her quite prepared to endure the consequences of failure—and, at the same time, conveying the most decisive rebuke of such moral cowardice in her husband as can make him recede from a purpose merely on account of the possibility of defeat—a possibility which, up to the very completion of their design, seems never absent from her own mind, though she finds it necessary to banish it from that of her husband."

60. *But screw your courage*, etc. "A metaphor perhaps taken from the *screwing up* the chords of stringed instruments" (Steevens). Cf. *Cor.* i. 8. 11: "Wrench up thy power to the highest;" *T. N.* v. 1. 125:

> "And that I partly know the instrument
> That screws me from my true place in your favour."

Cf. also *T. and C.* iii. 3. 22:

> "But this Antenor,
> I know, is such a wrest in their affairs
> That their negotiations all must slack,
> Wanting his manage."

The C. P. ed. remarks that, as a *wrest* is an instrument for tuning a harp, this last passage favours Steevens's interpretation of the metaphor.*

64. *Wassail.* Cf. *L. L. L.* v. 2. 318: "At wakes and wassails;" *Ham.* i. 4. 9: "keeps wassail," etc. For the origin of the word, see Wb. Milton has *wassailers* in *Comus*, 179: "such late wassailers."

Convince. Overcome (Lat. *convincere*); as in iv. 3. 142 below. See also *Oth.* iv. 1. 28. On the literal use of Greek and Latin derivatives in the Elizabethan writers, see Gr. p. 12.

65–67. The C. P. ed. remarks: "By the old anatomists (Vigo, fol. 6 *b.* ed. 1586) the brain was divided into three ventricles, in the hindermost of which they placed the memory. That this division was not unknown to Shakespeare we learn from *L. L. L.* iv. 2. 70: 'A foolish, extravagant

---

* Mr. Neil, in his ed. of *Macbeth* (Edinburgh, 1876), has the following curious note on this passage: "*sticking place*—fixed point, with a covert allusion to the death-dealing spot chosen by the butcher. So [*sic*] in the *Gorgious Gallery of Gallant Inventors*, 1578:

> 'Which flowre out of my hande shall never passe,
> But in my harte shall have a sticking place.'"

spirit, full of forms, figures, shapes, objects, ideas, apprehensions, motions, revolutions; these are begot in the ventricle of memory.' The third ventricle is the cerebellum, by which the brain is connected with the spinal marrow and the rest of the body; the memory is posted in the cerebellum like a warder or sentinel to warn the reason against attack, when the memory is converted by intoxication into a mere fume (cf. *Temp.* v. 1. 67:

> 'The ignorant fumes that mantle
> Their clearer reason'),

then it fills the brain itself, the receipt or receptacle of reason, which thus becomes like an alembic or cap of a still. For *fume*, cf. *Cymb.* iv. 2. 301:

> 'A bolt of nothing, shot at nothing,
> Which the brain makes of fumes.'

And Dryden's *Aurengzebe:*

> 'Power like new wine does your weak brain surprise,
> And its mad fumes in hot discourses rise.'

See also *A. and C.* ii. 1. 24:

> 'Tie up the libertine in a field of feasts,
> Keep his brain fuming.'"

66. *Receipt.* "Receptacle" (Schmidt); the only instance of this meaning in S. Cf. *Matt.* ix. 9: "the receipt of custom." The C. P. ed. quotes Bacon, *Essay* 46: "a faire receipt of water" (the basin of a fountain).

67. *Limbeck.* Alembic. See Wb. Cf. Milton, *P. L.* iii. 605: "Drain'd through a limbec."

68. *A death.* "The article may be used because it is only a kind of death, a sleep, which is meant" (C. P. ed.). Cf. *W. T.* iv. 2. 3.

71. *Spongy.* "Imbibing like a sponge" (Schmidt). Cf. *T. and C.* ii. 2. 12: "More spongy to suck in the sense of fear."

72. *Quell.* Murder; a euphemism, according to Schmidt. *Quell* in Old English = *kill*, which is originally the same word. See Wb. Cf. Spenser, *F. Q.* ii. 7, 40:

> "and well could weld
> That cursed weapon, when his cruell foes he queld;

and *Id.* v. 10, 36:

> "he did him quell,
> And, hewing off his head, he it presented
> Before the feete of the faire Pastorell."

Man-queller (= manslayer, murderer) occurs in 2 *Hen. IV.* ii. 1. 58. The C. P. ed. says that the same compound is used by Wiclif for "executioner" in translating *Mark*, vi. 27, and for "murderer," *Acts*, xxviii. 4. According to Nares, the redoubtable "Jack" was formerly called "the giant-queller," instead of the more modern "giant-killer."

73. *Mettle.* In the early eds. no distinction is made between *metal* and *mettle.* See *Rich. II.* p. 157, note on *That metal.*

74. *Receiv'd.* Accepted as true, believed. Cf. *M. for M.* i. 3. 16:

> "For so I have strew'd it in the common ear,
> And so it is receiv'd;"

T. G. of V. v. 4. 78: "And once again I do receive thee honest."

77. *Other.* Otherwise. See Gr. 12.

79. *Bend up.* Strain, like a bow. Cf. *Hen. V.* iii. 1. 16:

> "Hold hard the breath, and bend up every spirit
> To his full height."

80. *Each corporal agent.* All-my bodily powers.

8·. *Mock the time.* See on i. 5. 61.

ACT II.

SCENE I.—The old stage direction says nothing about "a *servant* with a torch," as in many modern eds.; though, as D. remarks, "a Torch" sometimes means a *torch-bearer*, as "a Trumpet" means a *trumpeter.*

4. *Hold, take my sword*, etc. Flathe, to whose opinion of the character of Banquo we have already referred (p. 165 above), comments on this speech as follows:

"Banquo enters with his son Fleance, who holds a torch. Will not the man do something at last for his king, take some measures to prevent a cruel crime? Everything combines to enjoin the most careful watchfulness upon him, if duty and honour are yet quick within his breast; and here we come to a speech of Banquo's to his son to which we must pay special heed, since upon it the earlier English commentators, Steevens among them, have based their ridiculous theory that in this tragedy Banquo, in contrast to Macbeth, who is led astray, represents the man unseduced by evil. Steevens says that this passage shows that Banquo too is tempted by the witches in his dreams to do something in aid of the fulfilment of his hopes, and that in his waking hours he holds himself aloof from all such suggestions, and hence his prayer to be spared the 'cursed thoughts that nature gives way to in repose.'

"A stranger or more forced explanation of this passage can hardly be imagined. . . . As he has already done, Banquo here endeavours as far as possible to assert his own innocence to himself, while, for the sake of his future advantage, he intends to oppose no obstacle to the sweep of Macbeth's sword. It is, therefore, necessary that he should pretend to himself that here in Macbeth's castle no danger can threaten Duncan nor any one else. Therefore his sword need not rest by his side this night, and he gives it to his son. He must be able to say to himself, in the event of any fearful catastrophe, 'I never thought of or imagined any danger, and so I laid aside my arms.'

"And yet, try as he may, he cannot away with the stifling sensation of a tempest in the air, a storm-cloud destined to burst over Duncan's head this very night. He cannot but acknowledge to himself that a certain restless anxiety in his brain is urging him, in spite of his weariness, to remain awake during the remaining hours of the night. But this mood, these sensations, must not last, or it might seem a sacred duty either to hasten to the chamber of King Duncan or to watch it closely, that its occupant may be shielded from murderous wiles. To avoid this, Banquo denounces the thoughts of Macbeth that arise in his mind as 'cursed thoughts.' So detestably false are they that a merciful Power must be entreated to restrain them during sleep, when the mind is not to be completely controlled.

"With every change in the aspect of affairs Banquo's self-deceit appears in some new form. Banquo here banishes his thoughts from his mind, or rather maintains to himself that he has banished them, or that he must banish them because they do injustice to noble Macbeth, whom, nevertheless, he has thought it necessary to warn against the devil."

Husbandry. Thrift, economy. Cf. *Ham*. i. 3. 77: "borrowing dulls the edge of husbandry."

5. *Their*. S. several times uses *heaven* as plural. Cf. *Rich. II*. i. 2. 7:

> "Put we our quarrel to the will of heaven:
> Who, when they see the hours ripe on earth,
> Will rain hot vengeance on offenders' heads;"

and see note in our ed. p. 157.

For the metaphor, cf. *M. of V*. v. 1. 220: "these blessed candles of the night;" *R. and J*. iii. 5. 9: "Night's candles are burnt out;" and *Sonn*. 21. 12: "those gold candles fix'd in heaven's air."

Take thee that too. Probably a dirk or dagger. Elwin says: "Banquo has put from him his several weapons of defence from horror at the particular use his dreams have prompted him to make of them." More likely, as the C. P. ed. suggests, it was because in a friend's house he felt perfectly secure.

Abbott (Gr. 212) considers that *thee* is a dative here.

6. *Heavy*. "Drowsy, sleepy" (Schmidt); as often. Cf. *R. of L*. 121,

163, 1574; *Temp.* i. 2. 189, 194, 198; *M. for M.* iv. 1. 35; *M. N. D.* v. 1. 380, etc.

14. *Offices.* The servants' quarters. Cf. *Rich. II.* i. 2. 69, and see note in our ed. p. 159. Rowe, D., St., and others read "officers" here.

16. *Shut up.* "That is, concluded" (Steevens). Malone quotes Stowe's *Annals*: "the king's majestie shut up all with a pithy exhortation." Schmidt explains the passage thus: "Summed up all that he had to say, in expressing his measureless content." The 2d folio has "shut it up;" and Hunter says that "it" is "undoubtedly the jewel in its case!"

18. *Our will*, etc. "Our entertainment was necessarily *defective*, and we only had it in our power to show the king our *willingness* to *serve* him. Had we received sufficient notice of his coming, our zeal should have been more clearly manifested by our *acts. Which* refers to *will*" (Malone).

In other words, our will had to submit to our deficient means instead of being free to carry out our wishes.

On the adverbial use of *free*, see Gr. 1; and on the metrical lengthening of *wrought*, Gr. 484. On *weird* in the next line, see Gr. 485.

22. *When*, etc. When we can ask you to put an hour at our service. "Now that the crown is within his grasp he seems to adopt the royal 'we' by anticipation" (C. P. ed.).

Sheridan Knowles comments on this speech of Macbeth's and the context as follows: "What is the meaning of this? A sudden thought of precaution that when the murder is discovered—as of course it must be —this mention of a consultation with reference to the third prophetic 'All Hail,'—the promise of royal having—this hint of some enterprise to be attempted with a view to the fulfilment of that promise (for it is nothing else but a hint to that effect) may help to keep him clear from suspicion on the part of Banquo that he has had any hand in letting out the blood that is destined to flow that night. Banquo's reply ('so I keep My bosom franchis'd,' etc.) clearly establishes the fact. It is a matter that may involve the question of honour and loyalty."

24. *Kind'st.* See Gr. 473, and cf. "stern'st" (ii. 2. 4), "near'st" (iii. 1. 118), and "secret'st" (iii. 4. 126) below.

25. *If you*, etc. If you adhere to my party whenever it is established. As Johnson says, "Macbeth expresses his thought with affected obscurity; he does not mention the royalty, though he apparently had it in his mind." W. remarks: "This may mean, to those who agree with me, to my party. But I think there is not improbably a misprint of 'consort.' As in *T. G. of V.* iv. 1. 64: 'Wilt thou be of our consort?' and in *Lear*, ii. 1. 99: 'He was of that consort.'"

In Davenant's version of *Macbeth*, this passage reads:

> "If when the Prophesie begins to look like truth
> You will adhere to me, it shall make honour for you."

28. *Franchis'd.* "Free, unstained, innocent" (Schmidt).

31. *My drink.* "This night-cup or posset was an habitual indulgence of the time" (Elwin). Cf. ii. 2. 6: "I have drugg'd their possets."

32. *She strike.* See Gr. 311, 369.

33. *Is this a dagger*, etc. "A delusion appearing after the manner of the Highland second sight; more substantial than the 'image of murder' which shakes his soul in i. 4, but not accepted and believed by him like the apparition of Banquo afterwards" (Moberly).

Sheridan Knowles remarks: "I have long entertained the opinion that this dagger is not, as Macbeth assumes it to be, simply

> 'A dagger of the mind. . . .
> Proceeding from the heat-oppressed brain;'

but on the contrary, an apparition coming and vanishing, as the witches themselves do, and that consequently it ought to be actually presented, as indeed it used to be. In my mind the whole thing is too circumstantial, bears too much upon the action, to justify the common interpretation which coincides with that of Macbeth. It is a phantom raised by the witches to draw Macbeth on to his conclusion. It is the supernatural coadjutor of Lady Macbeth, dumbly but irresistibly persuading him to the deed. He falters yet. Yes! upon the very threshold of guilt he is faltering. But the evil agency of which he is the victim is at hand with the dagger, shows him the instrument he was to use, presents it to him with its handle towards him, inviting him to clutch it as he attempts to do, marshals for him with it the way he was to go; nor withdraws it then, but while he is yet in doubt whether it is substance or shadow that he looks upon, ends the debate by exhibiting it to him stained with gouts of blood—

> 'Which was not so before.'

Macbeth's interpretation of the vision is not to be taken as the truth. It is not

> 'The bloody business which informs
> Thus to his eyes.'"

Compare what Roffe * says on this point:

"The Spiritualist, when contending for the absolute objectivity of Banquo's Ghost, may possibly be asked whether he also claims a *like* reality for 'the air-drawn dagger.' To this he would reply, that, to the best of his belief, a *like* reality was *not* to be affirmed of that dagger, which he conceives to have been a *representation*, in the spiritual world, of a dagger, not however being on that account less real (if by unreality we are to understand that it was, in some incomprehensible way, generated in the material brain), but only differing from what we should term a real *bonâ fide* dagger, as a painting of a dagger differs from a real one.

"That the spiritual world must have its *representations* as well as its *realities*, is a point which has already been touched upon, and this dagger, called by Lady Macbeth 'the air-drawn dagger,' we suppose to be one of those representations. Its objective reality, however, still remains untouched; for, once grant that the spiritual world is a real world—nay, the most real world—and it follows that whatsoever is represented in it

---

* *An Essay upon the Ghost Belief of Shakespeare*, by A. Roffe (Privately printed London, 1851), quoted by Furness.

has its basis in reality, as much as an imitative dagger in a painting has *its* basis in the colours and canvas, which are also realities. . . .

"Mr. Fletcher maintains that Banquo's Ghost should be no more visible on the stage than the air-drawn dagger. We fully believe that there is a most powerful stage-reason, namely, *intelligibility*, for making the Ghost of Banquo visible to the theatre; but that reason does *not* apply to the dagger—because what is spoken by Macbeth makes intelligible all that he experiences with respect to that dagger. Also, when we go on to perceive that the spiritual world has, and must have, not only its *realities*, but its *representations* likewise—of which last the dagger is apparently one—we have an additional argument still to show that the reasoning which may belong to Banquo's Ghost would not necessarily apply, in all its points, to this appearance of the dagger."

34. *Toward.* S. used *toward* and *towards* (see line 55 below) interchangeably, or as either suited his ear; at least, both are found in the early eds. Cf. i. 3. 152, i. 4. 27, i. 6. 30, v. 4. 21, etc.

36. *Sensible.* "Perceptible, tangible" (Schmidt). See Gr. 3. Cf. *M. of V.* ii. 9. 89: "sensible regreets;" and see note in our ed. p. 145.

41. Abbott remarks (Gr. 511) that Macbeth may be supposed to draw his dagger after this short line.

44, 45. Either my eyes are deceived while the other senses are not, or they are more trustworthy than the latter.

46. *Dudgeon.* This undoubtedly means here the handle of a dagger, but its derivation is disputed. According to several early authorities and Wedgwood, it originally meant "the root of the box-tree," and was then applied to dagger-handles made of that wood. E. Coles, Abr. Fleming, and the Cambridge Dict. of 1693 (cited by Nares) all explain "dudgeon-haft" as *manubrium apiatum* or *buxeum*. Bishop Wilkins, in the *Alphabetical Dict.* appended to his *Essay towards a Real Character*, 1668, gives "*Dudgeon*, root of box," and "*Dudgeon-dagger*, a small sword whose handle is of the *root of box*." Gerrard, in his *Herball*, under the article *Box-tree*, says: "The root is likewise yellow, and harder than the timber, but of greater beauty, and more fit for dagger-hafts, boxes, and such like uses. . . . Turners and cutlers, if I mistake not the matter, doe call this wood *dudgeon*, wherewith they make *dudgeon-hafted* daggers." Gifford (notes on Ben Jonson) thinks it means simply *wooden*, and that a "dudgeon-hafted dagger" was so called to distinguish it from those that had more costly handles; whence it became a term of contempt in other connections. Thus in B. and F. (*The Captain*, ii. 1) we find "I am plain and dudgeon;" that is, coarse, rude. Richardson (*Dict.* s. v.), on the other hand, denies that it primarily means either box-root or wooden, and cites Holland's *Pliny*, xvi. 16: "Now for the box-tree, the wood thereof is in as great request as the very best; seldom hath it any graine crisped damaske wise, and never but about the root, the which is dudgin and full of worke." Here it seems to mean tough, or strong; and Richardson thinks it may be derived from the Dutch *dooghen*, A. S. *dugan*, to be strong. For a different derivation, see Wb.

Gouts. Drops (Fr. *goutte*). Steevens quotes *The Art of Good Lyving and Good Deyng*, 1503: "Befor the jugement all herbys shal sweyt read goutys of water, as blood." Halliwell (*Archaic Dict.*) states that "*gowtyth* for *droppeth* occurs in an early English MS. mentioned in *Arch.* xxx. 408."

48. *Informs.* Schmidt and Moberly make this = creates forms; the C. P. ed., "gives information." Cf. i. 5. 31.

49. *The one half world.* Commonly printed "the one half-world," but the hyphen is not in the early eds., and without it as with it the meaning is evidently half the world. Cf. 1 *Hen. IV.* iv. 1. 136: "this one half year." On the pronunciation of *one* in the time of S., see Gr. 80.

50. *Abuse.* Deceive; though Schmidt thinks it may also mean to misuse, pervert. Cf. *Temp.* v. 1. 112: "some enchanted trifle to abuse me;" *Much Ado*, v. 2. 100: "the prince and Claudio mightily abused," etc. In iii. 4. 142, "self-abuse" means self-deception. Cf. *abusion* (= illusion) in Spenser, *F. Q.* ii. 11, 11:

> "For by those ugly formes weren pourtrayd
> Foolish delights and fond abusions,
> Which doe that sence besiege with light illusions."

51. *The curtain'd sleep.* To help out the metre Rowe (following Davenant) inserted "now" before "witchcraft;" and Steevens suggested "sleeper." But see Gr. 484.

52. *Hecate's.* A dissyllable. Cf. *Lear*, i. 1. 112: "The mysteries of Hecate and of night;" *Ham.* iii. 2. 269: "With Hecate's ban thrice blasted, thrice infected." See also iii. 2. 41 and iii. 5. 1 below.

53. *Alarum'd.* The same word as *alarmed.* See Wb. The derivation (Ital. *all' arme*) may be illustrated by Holland's *Livy*, p. 331: "This sayd, he runs downe with as great a noyse and showting as he could, crying, *al' arme*, help help citizens, the castle is taken by the enemie, come away to defense."

54. *Whose howl 's his watch.* "Who marks the periods of his night-watch by howling, as the sentinel by a cry" (C. P. ed.).

55. *Strides.* The folios have "sides," which K. in his 1st ed. retained, making it a verb = matches. Moberly, who also has "sides," thinks it possible that it may be "a form of the A. S. *sith*, a step." Johnson suggested "slides" as more in keeping with "stealthy pace." Steevens cites Spenser, *F. Q.* iv. 8, 37: "With easie steps so soft as foot could stryde;" and Harrington's *Ariosto*, 1591: "He takes a long and leisurable stride." Warb. quotes *Rich. II.* i. 3. 268, and J. Sylvester (in *England's Parnassus*, 1600):

> "Anon he stalketh with an easy stride,
> By some clear river's lillie-paved side."

57. *My steps, which way*, etc. See Gr. 414.

58. As Z. Grey suggests, an allusion probably to *Luke*, xix. 40. The C. P. ed. compares *R. of L.* 302–306.

Whereabout. Delius remarks that elsewhere S. uses *where* and *wherefore* as substantives. See *Lear*, i. 1. 264, and *C. of E.* ii. 2. 45. We may add *wherewith* in *P. P.* 408: "Whilst thou hast wherewith to spend." Cf. *wherewithal* in *Hen. VIII.* i. 3. 59.

59. *And take*, etc. That is, break the universal silence that added such a horror to the night as suited well with the bloody deed he was

about to perform (Steevens). Malone cites Virgil, *Æn.* ii. 755: "*Horror* ubique animos, simul ipsa *silentia* terrent." Delius thinks that *it* refers to "my whereabout."

60. *Whiles.* See on i. 5. 5. On *threat*, see *Rich. II.* p. 195.

61. The C. P. editors consider this line a "feeble tag" which S. could not have penned. On *gives*, see Gr. 333.

62. *The bell invites me.* A "pre-arranged summons." See extract from W. just below.

63. *Knell.* "Alluding to the passing bell which was formerly tolled when a person was dying" (Elwin).

SCENE II.—The folio has "Scena Secunda" here, but some editors (as Rowe, Theo., D., St., W., and J. Hunter) make no change of scene. W. remarks: "The apparent continuance of the action is vitally essential to the dramatic impression intended to be produced. The ringing of the bell by *Lady M.*, the exit of *Macbeth* upon that pre-arranged summons, the entrance of the lady to fill the stage and occupy the mind during her husband's brief absence upon his fearful errand, and to confess in soliloquy her active accession to the murder, the sudden knocking which is heard directly after she goes out to replace the daggers, and which recurs until she warily hurries her husband and herself away lest they should be found watchers, the entrance of the *Porter*, and finally of *Macduff* and *Lenox*,—all this action is contrived with consummate dramatic skill; and its unbroken continuity in one spot, and that a part of the castle common to all its inhabitants, is absolutely necessary to complete its purpose."

We adhere to the old division of scenes solely to avoid confusion in referring to this part of the play. The Globe ed. follows the folio here.

1. *That which hath made them drunk*, etc. The C. P. ed. says: "Lady Macbeth had had recourse to wine in order to support her courage." Moberly explains it: "'I am emboldened by the guard's intoxication;' not, surely, 'I have given myself courage with wine.' She had taunted Macbeth with a 'drunken hope;' and such a mode of raising her own spirit seems thoroughly alien from her character."

Mrs. Griffiths (*Morality of Shakespeare's Dramas*, p. 412, quoted by Furness) remarks: "Our sex is obliged to Shakespeare for this passage. He seems to think that a woman could not be rendered completely wicked without some degree of intoxication. It required two vices in her, one to intend and another to perpetrate the crime."

Moberly's explanation seems rather forced; and the other, we think, goes too far in assuming that the lady was intoxicated. In saying "That which hath made *them* drunk," she implies that she herself was *not* drunk. Is anything more meant than that she had taken her regular night-cup (see on ii. 1. 31 above), and that she felt the slightly stimulating effect of the "posset?" The grooms would not have been "drunk," or stupefied, if their possets had not been drugged.

3. *The owl.* "Tschischwitz, in his *Nachklänge germanischer Mythe*, ii. 30, points out that the superstitious associations connected with the owl

are common to both England and Germany; indeed, that some of them belong to the whole Indo-Germanic family. They were rife among the Romans. See Ovid, *Met.* v. 550. See also Harting, *Ornithology of Shakespeare*, p. 83" (Furness).

The fatal bellman, etc. The C. P. ed. remarks that the full significance of this passage may be best shown by comparing the following lines from Webster's *Duchess of Malfi*, iv. 2, where Bosola tells the Duchess:

> "I am the common bellman,
> That usually is sent to condemn'd persons
> The night before they suffer."

Here, of course, Duncan is the condemned person. Cf. also Spenser, *F. Q.* v. 6, 27, where the cock is called "the native belman of the night." The owl is again mentioned, line 15, and in 1 *Hen. VI.* iv. 2. 15:

> "Thou ominous and fearful owl of death."

We may add *R. of L.* 165: "No noise but owls' and wolves' death-boding cries;" *Rich. III.* iv. 4. 509: "Out on you, owls! nothing but songs of death;" and 3 *Hen. VI.* v. 6. 44: "The owl shriek'd at thy birth—an evil sign."

5. *Grooms.* Originally, servants of any kind. See Schmidt or Wb.

6. *Possets.* Malone quotes Randle Holmes, *Academy of Armourie*, 1688: "Posset is hot milk poured on ale or sack, having sugar, grated bisket, and eggs, with other ingredients, boiled in it, which goes all to a curd." This explains why the posset is often spoken of as "eaten." Cf. *M. W.* v. 5. 180: "Thou shalt eat a posset to-night at my house." S. uses *posset* as a verb in *Ham.* i. 5. 68:

> "And with a sudden vigour it doth posset
> And curd, like eager droppings into milk,
> The thin and wholesome blood."

See on ii. 1. 31 above.

7. *That.* So that. See Gr. 283, and cf. line 23 below.

8. "Macbeth fancies that he hears some noise (see line 14), and in his nervous excitement has not sufficient control over himself to keep silence. The word '*within*' was added by Steevens. The folios make Macbeth enter before speaking, but it is clear that Lady Macbeth is alone while speaking the following lines" (C. P. ed.).

But, as K. reminds us, the king does not sleep in the first, but in the second chamber, whence a call could not easily be heard in the courtyard below. He adds: "Macbeth lingers yet a moment within; his unquiet mind imagines it hears a noise in the court below, and thoughtlessly, bewildered and crazed, he rushes back to the *balcony*, and calls beneath, 'Who 's there?' In his agony, however, he waits for no answer, but rushes back into the chambers to execute the murder."

11. *Confounds.* Ruins, destroys; the most common meaning of the word in S. Cf. iv. 1. 54 and iv. 3. 99 below. See also *M. of V.* iii. 2. 78; *Rich. II.* iii. 4. 60, etc.

12. *Had he not*, etc. See Mrs. Jameson's comment on this passage (p. 19). Cf. what Campbell says in his *Life of Mrs. Siddons:* "She is amiably unable to murder the sleeping king, because, to use Mrs. Jame-

son's words, 'he brings to her the dear and venerable image of her father.' Yes; but she can send in her husband to do it for her. Did Shakespeare intend us to believe this murderess naturally compassionate?"

Friesen (quoted by Furness) remarks: "The confession of Lady Macbeth that she could not murder the king with her own hand because in his sleep he resembled her father, is, according to my idea of her, a proof that the strength of will on which she relied in her first conversation with her husband was by no means so entirely at her disposal as she imagined. She enters trembling, convulsed with the most terrible anguish; she starts at every noise, and even her first words, 'That which hath made them drunk hath made me bold: What hath quenched them hath given me fire,' are not justified by her behaviour. I am convinced that this expression has no other aim than to let us know that she is not what she imagines herself to be. Why, otherwise, is she immediately afterwards startled by the cry of the owl?"

16. Hunter suggested the following distribution of speeches here, which Furness adopts:

> "*Macbeth.* Did not you speak?
> *Lady Macbeth.* When? Now?
> *Macbeth.* As I descended."

As Hunter remarks, "the 'Ay' of the lady then possesses an effect, which as the scene stands at present it wants." We do not, however, feel quite justified in making the change.

20. *Sorry.* Sad. Often applied, as here, to inanimate things. The C. P. ed. cites 2 *Hen. VI.* i. 4. 79: "a sorry breakfast." Cf. also Spenser, *F. Q.* v. 1, 14:

> "To whom as they approched, they espide
> A sorie sight as ever seene with eye,
> An headlesse Ladie lying him beside
> In her own blood all wallow'd woefully."

The stage direction here was added by Pope.

23. *That.* See on line 7 above.

24. *Address'd them.* "Made themselves ready" (Schmidt). Cf. *M. W.* iii. 5. 135; *M. of V.* ii. 9. 19, etc. Gr. 223.

27. *As.* "The *if* is implied in the subjunctive" (Gr. 107).

Hangman. Executioner. Cf. *M. of V.* iv. 1. 125: "the hangman's axe." It is applied jocosely to Cupid in *Much Ado*, iii. 2. 11: "the little hangman dare not shoot at him."

28. *Listening.* Used transitively, as in *Much Ado*, iii. 1. 12; *J. C.* iv. 1. 41; and *Rich. II.* ii. 1. 9. See Gr. 199.

31. *But wherefore*, etc. Bodenstedt (quoted by Furness) remarks: "This is one of those traits in which Macbeth's egotistic hypocrisy is most clearly displayed. He speaks as if murder and praying could join hand in hand in friendly companionship, and is astonished that he could not say 'Amen' when the grooms, betrayed and menaced by himself, appealed to heaven for protection."

Was this the kind of piety that Lady Macbeth had in mind when she said,

"What thou wouldst highly
That wouldst thou holily?"

33. *Thought.* Hanmer added "on," which Keightley adopts, though, as he says, it "is not absolutely necessary."

34. *So.* If we so think of them.

35-40. We follow Johnson (as do Coll., D., St., H., W., and others) in limiting what the "voice" says to "Sleep no more! Macbeth does murther sleep!" Hanmer, with the earlier editors generally except Johnson, makes the "voice" continue to "feast;" so also Sr. and Moberly. As H. remarks, "all from 'the innocent sleep' is evidently his own conscience-stricken reflections on the imaginary utterances."

37. *Ravell'd.* Tangled. See Wb. Mason cites *T. G. of V.* iii. 2. 52: "Lest it should ravel," etc.

Sleave. Malone explains this as "coarse, soft, unwrought silk," and quotes Florio, *Ital. Dict.*, 1598: "*Sfilazza.* Any kind of ravelled stuffe, or sleave silk;" also "*Capitone*, a kind of coarse silk, called sleave silke." Cf. *T. and C.* v. 1. 35: "Thou idle immaterial skein of sleave-silk." See also Drayton, *Quest of Cynthia*:

"The bank, with daffidillies dight,
With grass, like sleave, was matted."

38. *Death.* Warb. wanted to read "birth;" whereupon W. remarks: "Warb., though a clergyman, forgot, what S. did not forget, that in death the wicked cease from troubling, and the weary are at rest."

40. *Nourisher.* Steevens quotes Chaucer, *C. T.* 10661: "The norice of digestion, the sleep." On the measure, see Gr. 467. Rushton (quoted by Furness) cites Ovid, *Met.* xi. 623:

"Somne, quies rerum, placidissime Somne deorum,
Pax animi, quem cura fugit, qui corda diurnis
Fessa ministeriis mulces, reparasque labori." *

Malone suggests that S. may have had in mind the following verses from Sir Philip Sidney's *Astrophel and Stella*, a poem from which he has quoted a line in *M. W.*:

"Come sleepe, O sleepe, the certain knot of peace,
The bathing place of wits, the balm of woe,
The poor man's wealth, the prisoner's release,
The indifferent judge between the high and low."

42. *Glamis hath murther'd sleep.* Johnson made the "cry" end with these words; but we prefer to follow Hanmer and let it include the two lines.

W. remarks: "These two lines, unless their detailing of Macbeth's titles is the utterance of a distempered fancy, sink into a mere conceit unworthy of the situation." Elwin says: "Having, under one designation, *murdered sleep*, it exists no more for him under any *title or name* he can assume."

---

* Cf. Golding's quaint translation (1587):

"O sleepe, quoth she, the rest of things, O gentlest of the goddes,
Sweet sleepe, the peace of mind, with whom crookt care is aye at odds;
Which cherishest men's weary limbs appall'd with toyling sore,
And makest them as fresh to worke, and lustie as before."

46. *Brainsickly.* "Madly" (Schmidt). The only instance of the adverb in S. The adjective *brainsick* occurs six times (including *R. of L.* 175).

Go get some water, etc. Cf. v. 1. 58.

47. *Witness.* "One who, or *a thing which*, bears testimony" (Schmidt).

55. *A painted devil.* Steevens quotes Webster, *White Devil:* "Terrify babes, my lord, with painted devils."

56. *I'll gild*, etc. Nares remarks that, though there is no real resemblance between the colour of blood and that of gold, to *gild with blood* was an expression not uncommon in the 16th century. Gold was popularly and very generally styled *red* [as it still is in poetry sometimes]. So we have "golden blood," ii. 3. 94 below. Cf. *K. John*, ii. 1. 316: "all gilt with Frenchmen's blood."

For the quibble on *gilt* and *guilt*, cf. 2 *Hen. IV.* iv. 5. 129, and *Hen. V.* ii. chorus, 26. See also Middleton, *A Mad World:* "Though guilt condemns, 't is gilt must make us glad;" Marlowe, *Hero and Leander:*

> "That, this word gilt including double sense,
> The double guilt of his incontinence
> Might be express'd," etc.

Many other instances of it might be cited from the old plays. Elwin remarks that here it "serves to exhibit most forcibly, in the ferocious levity of the expression, the strained and sanguinary excitement of Lady Macbeth's mind." The C. P. ed. says: "A play of fancy here is like a gleam of ghastly sunshine striking across a stormy landscape, as in some pictures of Ruysdael."

Coleridge has said that except in the soliloquy of the Porter (which he believed to be an interpolation), there is not a pun or play upon words in the whole drama; and Schlegel has made a similar statement. Both seem to have overlooked the present passage, and another (which Abbott points out) in v. 8. 48.

57. *That knocking.* Macduff and Lenox are knocking at the south gate, as the next scene shows.*

---

* Cf. what De Quincey says on this knocking. After remarking that its effect on his feelings was to "reflect back upon the murder a peculiar awfulness and a depth of solemnity" for which he was long perplexed to account, he gives this solution of the problem:

"Murder, in ordinary cases, where the sympathy is wholly directed to the case of the murdered person, is an incident of coarse and vulgar horror; and for this reason, that it flings the interest exclusively upon the natural but ignoble instinct by which we cleave to life; an instinct which, as being indispensable to the primal law of self-preservation, is the same in kind (though different in degree) among all living creatures; this instinct, therefore, because it annihilates all distinctions, and degrades the greatest of men to the level of the 'poor beetle that we tread on,' exhibits human nature in its most abject and humiliating attitude. Such an attitude would little suit the purposes of the poet. What then must he do? He must throw the interest on the murderer. Our sympathy must be with *him* (of course, I mean a sympathy of comprehension, a sympathy by which we enter into his feelings, and are made to understand them—not a sympathy of pity or approbation). In the murdered person, all strife of thought, all flux and reflux of passion and of purpose, are crushed by one overwhelming panic; the fear of instant death smites him 'with its petrific mace.' But in the murderer, such a murderer as a poet will condescend to, there must be raging some great storm of passion—jealousy, ambition, vengeance, hatred—which will create a hell within him; and into this hell we are to look.

60. *Will all great Neptune's ocean*, etc. Steevens quotes Catullus, *In Gellium*, 5:

> "Suscipit, o Gelli, quantum non ultima Tethys,
> Non genitor Nympharum abluat Oceanus;"

and Seneca, *Hippol.* ii. 715:

> "Quis eluet me Tanais? aut quae barbaris
> Maeotis undis Pontico incumbens mari?
> Non ipse toto magnus Oceano pater
> Tantum expiarit sceleris!"

Holt White compares Lucretius, vi. 1076:

> "Non, si Neptuni fluctu renovare operam des;
> Non, mare si totum velit eluere omnibus undis."

62. *The multitudinous seas.* As admirably descriptive as Homer's πολυφλοίσβοιο θαλάσσης. One can almost hear in it the sound of the sea with its numberless waves. And yet Malone thought it might mean "the seas which swarm with myriad inhabitants."

"In *Macbeth*, for the sake of gratifying his own enormous and teeming faculty of creation, Shakespeare has introduced two murderers, and, as usual in his hands, they are remarkably discriminated; but, though in Macbeth the strife of mind is greater than in his wife, the tiger spirit not so awake, and his feelings caught chiefly by contagion from her—yet, as both were finally involved in the guilt of murder, the murderous mind of necessity is finally to be presumed in both. This was to be expressed; and on its own account, as well as to make it a more proportionable antagonist to the unoffending nature of their victim, 'the gracious Duncan,' and adequately to expound the 'deep damnation of his taking off,' this was to be expressed with peculiar energy. We were to be made to feel that the human nature, i. e., the divine nature of love and mercy, spread through the hearts of all creatures, and seldom utterly withdrawn from man, was gone, vanished, extinct; and that the fiendish nature had taken its place. And, as this effect is marvellously accomplished in the *dialogues* and *soliloquies* themselves, so it is finally consummated by the expedient under consideration; and it is to this that I now solicit the reader's attention. If the reader has ever witnessed a wife, daughter, or sister in a fainting-fit, he may chance to have observed that the most affecting moment in such a spectacle is *that* in which a sigh or a stirring announces the recommencement of suspended life. . . . All action in any direction is best expounded, measured, and made apprehensible by reaction. Now apply this to the case of Macbeth. Here, as I have said, the retiring of the human heart, and the entrance of the fiendish heart, was to be expressed and made sensible. . . . In order that a new world may step in, this world must for a time disappear. The murderers, and the murder, must be insulated—cut off by an immeasurable gulf from the ordinary tide and succession of human affairs—locked up and sequestered in some deep recess; we must be made sensible that the world of ordinary life is suddenly arrested—laid asleep—tranced—racked into a dread armistice; time must be annihilated; relation to things without abolished; and all must pass self-withdrawn into a deep syncope and suspension of earthly passion. Hence it is that when the deed is done, when the work of darkness is perfect, then the world of darkness passes away like a pageantry in the clouds: the knocking at the gate is heard; and it makes known audibly that the reaction has commenced; the human has made its reflux upon the fiendish; the pulses of life are beginning to beat again; and the re-establishment of the goings-on of the world in which we live first makes us profoundly sensible of the awful parenthesis that had suspended them.

"O mighty poet! Thy works are not as those of other men, simply and merely great works of art; but are also like the phenomena of nature, like the sun and the sea, the stars and the flowers—like frost and snow, rain and dew, hail-storm and thunder, which are to be studied with entire submission of our own faculties, and in the perfect faith that in them there can be no too-much or too-little, nothing useless or inert—but that the further we press in our discoveries, the more we shall see proofs of design and self-supporting arrangement where the careless eye had seen nothing but accident!"

Incarnadine. Nares gives *carnadine*=carnation red, and cites *Anything for a Quiet Life:*

> "Grograms, sattins, velvet fine,
> The rosy-colour'd carnadine."

Incarnadine is found in Sylvester. Hunter cites his description of the Phœnix:

> "Her wings and train of feathers mixed fine
> Of orient azure and incarnadine."

Furness quotes Collier's reprint of *An Antidote against Melancholy*, 1661, where it is the name of a red wine:

> "In love? 't is true with Spanish wine,
> Or the French juice, Incarnadine."

Carew uses it as a verb in his *Obsequies to the Lady Anne Hay* ("Incarnadine Thy rosy cheek"), but he probably borrowed it from S.

63. *Making*, etc. The folio has "Making the Greene one, Red," and some of the earlier editors follow that pointing. Malone says: "*One red* does not sound to my ear as the phraseology of the age of Elizabeth; and *the green*, for the green *one*, or for the green *sea*, is, I am persuaded, unexampled." Nares, too, thinks the interpretation "making the green [sea] one entire red" is "ridiculously harsh and forced." Of course any other interpretation is absurd. As Elwin remarks, "the imagination of Macbeth dwells upon the conversion of the *universal green* into *one pervading red*." Steevens compares *Ham.* ii. 2. 479: "Now is he total gules;" and Milton, *Comus*, 133: "And makes one blot of all the air." St. suggests "green zone," referring to *Cymb.* iii. 1. 19, 20; *Id.* iii. 1. 81; *A. and C.* ii. 7. 74; *T. A.* iii. 1. 94; *K. John*, v. 2. 34, etc.

65. *A heart so white.* The C. P. ed. quotes iv. 1. 85: "pale-hearted fear;" and Malone compares Marlowe, *Lust's Dominion* (written before 1593): "Your cheeks are black, let not your soul look white."

68. *Your constancy*, etc. Your firmness has forsaken you. Cf. *A.W.* ii. 1. 87; *J. C.* ii. 1. 299, etc.

70. *Nightgown.* "A loose gown used for undress" (Schmidt), or, as we should say, a dressing-gown. Cf. v. 1. 4 below. See also *Much Ado*, iii. 4. 18; *Oth.* iv. 3. 34; and stage-direction in *J. C.* ii. 2. W. remarks: "In Macbeth's time, and for centuries later, it was customary for both sexes to sleep without any other covering than that belonging to the bed when a bed was occupied. But of this S. knew nothing, and if he had known, he would of course have disregarded it. Macbeth's nightgown . . . answered to our *robe de chambre*."

72. *Poorly.* "Without spirit, dejectedly" (Schmidt). Cf. *Rich. II.* iii. 3. 128: "To look so poorly and to speak so fair." Cf. *poor* in *R. of L.* 710.

73. *To know*, etc. "If I must forever know my own deed" (Moberly). Cf. *W. T.* i. 2. 356:

> "To do this deed,
> Promotion follows."

See Gr. 357. The C. P. ed. says: "An easier sense might be arrived at by a slight change in punctuation: 'To know my deed? 'T were best not know myself.'" But the question does not seem naturally to follow what precedes.

74. Rowe and Pope read, "Wake Duncan with this;" and Theo., "Wake, Duncan, with this." Pope, Theo., Johnson, and others omit "I;" Steevens, Sr. (2d ed.), and St. have "Ay, 'would."

SCENE III.—The Porter's part in this scene has been the subject of much discussion. Coleridge says of it: "This low soliloquy of the Porter and his few speeches afterwards I believe to have been written for the mob by some other hand, perhaps with Shakespeare's consent; and that finding it take, he with the remaining ink of a pen otherwise employed just interpolated the words—

'I 'll devil-porter it no further: I had thought to have let in some of all professions, that go the primrose way to the everlasting bonfire.'

Of the rest not one syllable has the ever-present being of Shakespeare."

The C. P. editors remark: "Probably Coleridge would not have made even this exception unless he had remembered *Ham.* i. 3. 50:

'The primrose path of dalliance.'

To us this comic scene, not of a high class of comedy at best, seems strangely out of place amid the tragic horrors which surround it, and is quite different in effect from the comic passages which Shakespeare has introduced into other tragedies."*

---

* Dowden (p. 372, foot-note) says that Fleay rejects the Porter's part altogether, but this is not now the case. On p. 246 of his *Shakespeare Manual* he states that he does not agree with Coleridge's view of the passage, and on p. 256 he puts ii. 3 (except "rhyme-tag") among the portions of the play written by Shakespeare.

Schiller, in his translation of the play, has completely "reconstructed" the Porter's part. Furness (who, though compelled *ex officio* to record many wofully dull things from other commentators, is never dull when he speaks for himself), in his genial account of the various German translations of *Macbeth*, refers to this portion of Schiller's as follows:

"The severest wrench, however, to which Schiller subjected this tragedy is to be found in the Porter's soliloquy, where, instead of a coarse, low, sensual hind, we have a lovely, lofty character, the very jingling of whose keys calls to prayer like Sabbath bells. Is it not surprising that the great German poet should have failed utterly in seeing the purpose of this rough jostling with the outer world after the secret horrors of that midnight murder? Can such things be, and overcome us like a summer's cloud, without our special wonder? Schiller's scene I have here translated:

ACT II. SCENE V.

Enter Porter, *with keys. Afterwards* MACDUFF *and* ROSS.

Porter (*Singing*). The gloomy night is past and gone,
The lark sings clear; I see the dawn
With heaven its splendour blending,
Behold the sun ascending:
His light, it shines in royal halls,
And shines alike through beggar's walls,
And what the shades of night concealed
By his bright ray is now revealed. [*Knocking.*

Knock! knock! have patience there, whoe'er it be,
And let the porter end his morning song.
'T is right God's praise should usher in the day;
No duty is more urgent than to pray.—

On the other hand, Wordsworth (*Shakespeare's Knowledge and Use of the Bible*, p. 298) says: "As I do not doubt the passage was written with earnestness, and with a wonderful knowledge of human nature, especially as put into the mouth of a drunken man, so I believe it may be read with edification."

Mr. J. W. Hales, in a paper read before the New Shakspere Society, May 22, 1874 (see the *Transactions*, 1874, p. 255 fol.), takes the ground:

"(i.) That a Porter's speech is an integral part of the play.
(ii.) That it is necessary as a relief to the surrounding horror.
(iii.) That it is necessary according to the law of contrast elsewhere obeyed.
(iv.) That the speech we have is dramatically relevant.
(v.) That its style and language are Shakespearian."

After the reading of this paper Mr. Tom Taylor remarked: "The reasons set forth by Mr. Hales appear to me so consonant with what we know of Shakespeare, the general character of his plays, his language, and the relation of serious and comic in his treatment of dramatic subjects, that to me they carry absolute conviction that the Porter's speech is an integral part of the play."

(*Singing.*) Let songs of praise and thanks be swelling
To God who watches o'er this dwelling,
And with his hosts of heavenly powers
Protects us in our careless hours.
Full many an eye has closed this night
Never again to see the light.
Let all rejoice who now can raise,
With strength renewed, to heaven their gaze.
[*He unbars the gate. Enter Macduff and Ross.*

Ross. Well, friend, forsooth, it needs must be you keep
A mighty organ in your bosom there
To wake all Scotland with such trumpetings.
Porter. I' faith, 't is true, my lord, for I 'm the man
That last night mounted guard around all Scotland.
Ross. How so, friend porter?
Porter. Why, you see, does not
The king's eye keep o'er all men watch and ward,
And all night long the porter guard the king?
And therefore I am he that watched last night
Over all Scotland for you.
Ross. You are right.
Macduff. His graciousness and mildness guard the king;
'T is he protects the house, not the house him;
God's holy hosts encamp round where he sleeps.
Ross. Say, porter, is thy master stirring yet?
Our knocking has awaked him. Lo! he comes," etc.

Verily this is "admirable fooling," and another German has seen the absurdity of it. Horn (also quoted by Furness) comments on it thus: "Our Schiller has annihilated the whole Shakespearian Porter, from top to toe, and created instead one entirely new. This new creation is quite a good fellow and pious; he sings a morning song whose noble seriousness makes it worthy of admission into the best hymn-books. The jest also, which he subsequently throws out to the lords as they enter, that he had kept watch over all Scotland through the night, is respectable and loyal, like the whole man. But how comes this preacher in the wilderness here? Does he fit the whole organism of the piece? Does it not appear as if he were all ready to afford the repose which the whole idea of the scene is to give? And might not one almost say that it was a little officious in him that he wants to do it? It is possible that this Porter may be thought excellent, provided Shakespeare is not known; but him we know, and how he knew how to make the Columbus egg stand up, so I imagine the choice will not be found difficult."

Mr. Furnivall says that he asked Dr. George Macdonald what he thought of the Porter's speech, and the reply was: "Look at the grim humour of it. I believe it's genuine." He put the same question to the poet Browning, who answered: "Certainly the speech is full of humour; and as certainly the humour and the words are Shakespeare's. I cannot understand Coleridge's objection to it. It's as bad as his wanting to emend *blanket* by *blank height* [see on i. 5. 51]. As to Lamb, I've no doubt that he held the speech genuine, for he said that on his pointing out to his friend Munden the quality of the Porter's speech, Munden was duly struck by it, and expressed his regret at never having played the part."*

Bodenstedt (quoted by Furness) remarks: "After all, his uncouth comicality has a tragic background; he never dreams, while imagining himself a porter of hell-gate, how near he comes to the truth. What are all these petty sinners who go the primrose way to the everlasting bonfire compared with those great criminals whose gates he guards?"

Mr. and Mrs. Cowden Clarke, in their Annotated Edition of Shakespeare, say of the scene: "Its repulsively coarse humour serves powerfully to contrast, yet harmonize, with the base and gory crime that has been perpetrated. Shakespeare's subtilties of harmony in contrast are among his most marvellous powers; and we venture to think that this Porter scene is one of these subtilties." Cf. Weiss, pp. 187–195.

1. *Porter of hell-gate.* Mr. Hales compares *Oth.* iv. 2. 90:

> "You, mistress,
> That have the office opposite to St. Peter,
> And keep the gate of hell."

2. *Old.* A "colloquial intensive" used several times by S.; as in *M. of V.* iv. 2. 16; 2 *Hen. IV.* ii. 4. 21; *M. W.* i. 4. 5; *Much Ado*, v. 2. 98. Mr. J. R. Wise (*Shakespeare: His Birthplace*, etc., p. 106) says: "Whenever there has been an unusual disturbance or ado . . . the lower orders round Stratford-on-Avon invariably characterize it by the phrase, 'There has been *old* work to-day.'" D. remarks that the Italians use (or formerly used) *vecchio* in the same sense.

4. *A farmer*, etc. Malone quotes Hall, *Satires*, iv. 6:

> "Ech Muck-worme will be rich with lawlesse gaine,
> Altho he smother vp mowes of seuen yeares graine,
> And hang'd himself when corne grows cheap again."

Malone also considers this (as well as the references to the "equivocator" and the "French hose" below) as helping to fix the date of the play in 1606. He says: "That in the summer and autumn of 1606 there was a prospect of plenty of corn appears from the audit-book of the College of Eton; for the price of wheat in that year was lower than it was for thirteen years afterwards, being thirty-three shillings the quarter. In the preceding year (1605) it was two shillings a quarter dearer, and in

* At the meeting of the *New Shakspere Society*, June 26, 1874, Mr. Furnivall stated that Mr. Hales's conclusions had been accepted by every critic in England whose opinion he had asked; among them Mr. Tennyson, Mr. J. Spedding, Mr. A. J. Ellis, Professor Dowden, and Professor H. Morley.

the subsequent year (1607) three shillings a quarter dearer. In 1608 wheat was sold at Windsor market for fifty-six shillings and eight pence a quarter; and in 1609 for fifty shillings. In 1606 barley and malt were considerably cheaper than in the two years subsequent."

5. *Come in time.* That is, you've come in time; probably alluding to his suicide. St. would punctuate it "Come in, Time," the "Time" being "a whimsical appellation" for the farmer! Clarke explains it as = "Be in time!"

Napkins. Handkerchiefs. Cf. *L. C.* 15: "Oft did she heave her napkin to her eyne;" also *Oth.* iii. 3. 287, 290, 321, etc.

Enow. The plural of *enough.* Cf. *M. of V.* iii. 5. 24: "Christians enow." See also *Id.* iv. 1. 29; *Hen. V.* iv. 1. 240, etc.

8. *An equivocator*, etc. Warb. believed this to be an allusion to the Jesuits, "the inventors of the execrable doctrine of equivocation;" and Malone thought that it had "direct reference to the doctrine of *equivocation* avowed by Henry Garnet, Superior of the order of Jesuits in England, on his trial for the Gunpowder Treason, on the 28th of March, 1606, and to his detestable *perjury* on that occasion, or, as Shakespeare expresses it, 'to his swearing in both scales against either scale;' that is, flatly and directly contradicting himself on oath."

13. *A French hose.* According to Warb. "the joke consists in this, that the French hose being then very short and strait, a tailor must be master of his trade who could steal anything from them." Malone remarks: "From a passage in *Henry V.*, and from other proofs, we know that about the year 1597 the French hose were very large and lusty; but doubtless between that year and 1600 they had adopted the fashion here alluded to; and we know that French fashions were very quickly adopted in England. The following passage occurs in *The Black Year*, by Anthony Nixon, 1606: 'Gentlemen this year shall be much wronged by their taylors, for their consciences are now much larger than ever they were, for where [whereas] they were wont to steale but half a yeard of brood cloth in making up a payre of breeches, now they do largely nicke their customers in the lace too,' etc."

In *M. of V.* i. 2. 80 there is another reference to the large "round hose" borrowed from France. Cf. also *Hen. V.* iii. 7. 56.

14. *Goose.* "So called from its handle, which resembles the neck of a goose" (Wb.).

15. *At quiet.* Mr. Furnivall remarks that "as S. uses both '*in* rest' and '*at* rest,' there is nothing strange in his using both '*in* quiet' and '*at* quiet.'" Cf. *Judges*, xviii. 27. On the peculiar uses of *at* in S., see Gr. 143, 144.

17. *The primrose way*, etc. Steevens cites *Ham.* i. 3. 50: "the primrose path of dalliance;" and *A. W.* iv. 5. 56: "the flowery way that leads to the broad gate and the great fire."

22. *The second cock.* The time meant, as Mason suggests, is shown by *R. and J.* iv. 4. 3:

> "The second cock hath crow'd,
> The curfew bell hath rung, 't is three o'clock."

Cf. *Lear*, iii. 4. 121, and *M. N. D.* ii. 1. 267.

27. *Timely.* S. often uses adjectives ending in *-ly* as adverbs. Cf. *unmannerly* in 98 below, etc. We have *timely* as an adjective in iii. 3. 7. See Gr. 1.

31. *Physics.* Cures. Cf. *Cymb.* iii. 2. 34: "For it doth physic love." Steevens cites *W. T.* i. 1. 43; and Malone, *Temp.* iii. 1. 1.

32. *So bold to call.* Cf. *M. of V.* iii. 3. 10: "So fond to come abroad," etc. Gr. 281.

33. *Limited.* Appointed. Cf. *M. for M.* iv. 2. 176: "having the hour limited;" *K. John*, v. 2. 123: "warrant limited;" *Rich. III.* v. 3. 25: "Limit each leader to his several charge;" that is, "appoint to every leader his command" (Schmidt).

38. *Prophesying.* Prophecy, prediction. On the measure, see Gr. 470.

39. *Combustion.* Used by S. only here and in *Hen. VIII.* v. 4. 51; in both instances figuratively. *Combustious* occurs in *V. and A.* 1162: "As dry combustious matter is to fire."

40. *Obscure.* Accent on the first syllable, as in *Rich. II.* iii. 3. 154, etc. See Gr. 492. The *obscure bird* is "the nightly owl" (*T. A.* ii. 3. 97). See on ii. 2. 3 above.

42. Steevens quotes *Cor.* i. 4. 61:

> "Thou madest thine enemies shake, as if the world
> Were feverous and did tremble."

The reference is to an ague fever, or "shaking fever," as it is called in *K. John*, ii. 1. 228.

43. *Parallel.* "Adduce as equal" (Schmidt). It means "equal" in *T. and C.* ii. 2. 162, and *A. W.* iv. 3. 281.

45. *Tongue nor heart*, etc. Cf. i. 3. 60 above. On the use of the negatives, cf. *Sonn.* 86. 9: "He *nor* that affable familiar ghost . . . *cannot* boast." See also Gr. 396.

47. *Confusion.* Destruction. Cf. iii. 5. 29 below; also *K. John*, iv. 3. 153.

49. Delius calls attention to the confusion of metaphors here. The C. P. ed. remarks: "Reference is made in the same clause to 1 *Sam.* xxiv. 10: 'I will not put forth mine hand against my lord, for he is the Lord's anointed;' and to 2 *Cor.* vi. 16: 'For ye are the temple of the living God.'"

53. *Gorgon.* As the C. P. ed. suggests, S. probably derived his knowledge of the Gorgon's head from Ovid's *Metamorphoses*, v. 189–210, where it is related how Perseus turned his enemies to stone by making them look on it. There is an allusion to it also in *T. and C.* v. 10. 18:

> "Go into Troy and say there Hector's dead:
> There is a word will Priam turn to stone."

57. *Death's counterfeit.* Cf. *R. of L.* 402: "the map of death" (that is, sleep); and *M. N. D.* iii. 2. 364: "death-counterfeiting sleep."

59. *The great doom's image.* "A sight as terrible as an image of the Last Judgment" (Delius). Cf. *Lear*, v. 3. 264.

61. *Countenance.* "Be in keeping with" (Schmidt).

63. *Parley.* Cf. *parle* in *Rich. II.* i. 1. 192, and 3 *Hen. VI.* v. 1. 16.

72. *Had I but died*, etc. Malone compares *W. T.* iv. 4. 472:

> "If I might die within this hour, I have liv'd
> To die when I desire."

74. *Mortality.* "Human life" (Schmidt). Cf. *R. of L.* 403: "life's mortality;" *K. John*, v. 7. 5: "the ending of mortality;" *M. for M.* iii. 2. 196: "No might nor greatness in mortality," etc.

75. *Is dead.* For the singular, see Gr. 336; and for *is left* just below, Gr. 333.

83. *Badg'd.* Not elsewhere used as a verb by S. Malone cites 2 *Hen. VI.* iii. 2. 200: "Murder's crimson badge."

92. *Expedition.* Haste. Cf. *T. G. of V.* i. 3. 37: "the speediest expedition," etc.

93. *Outrun.* Johnson (followed by many modern editors) changed this to "outran;" but these past indicative forms in *u* are very common in S. See Gr. 339; and on *pauser*, Gr. 443.

94. *Lac'd.* To *lace* was "to adorn with a texture sewed on" (Schmidt). S. uses it literally in *Much Ado*, iii. 4. 20: "cloth o' gold, and cuts, and laced with silver;" and figuratively, as here, in *R. and J.* iii. 5. 8:

> "What envious streaks
> Do lace the severing clouds in yonder east!"

and *Cymb.* ii. 2. 22:

> "White and azure lac'd
> With blue of heaven's own tinct."

See also *Sonn.* 67. 4.

Golden blood. Pope wanted to change this to "goary blood," but see on ii. 2. 56 above.

95. *A breach in nature.* Steevens cites Sidney, *Arcadia*: "battering down the wals of their armour, making breaches almost in every place, for troupes of wounds to enter;" and *A Herring's Tayle*, 1598: "A batter'd breach where troopes of wounds may enter in."

98. *Breech'd with gore.* Schmidt explains *breech*, "to cover as with breeches, to sheathe." So Douce, Dyce, Delius, and others. Nares takes it to mean, "having the very hilt, or breech, covered with blood." "Reech'd," "drench'd," "hatch'd," etc., have been suggested as emendations; but, as Warb. remarks, "the whole speech is an unnatural mixture of far-fetched and commonplace thoughts, that shows him to be acting a part." Cf. Gr. 529.

100. *Make's.* "The abbreviation *'s* for *his* is very common even in passages which are not colloquial or familiar" (C. P. ed.).

101. T. Whately (*Remarks on Char. of Shakes.*, 3d ed., p. 77, foot-note) says: "On Lady Macbeth's seeming to faint while Banquo and Macduff are solicitous about her, Macbeth, by his unconcern, betrays a consciousness that the fainting is feigned."

Flathe (quoted by Furness) remarks: "Any child could declare that this swoon was only feigned to avoid all further embarrassment. But it must not be imagined that there is any feigning here. The poet, in Lady Macbeth, gives another view of human nature steeped in sin from that portrayed in Macbeth himself. In her, as her former dreams prove mockeries and unreal, the whole mental organization receives an annihilating blow from that first deed of blood, beneath which it may stagger on for a while, but from which it can never entirely recover. For one moment, immediately after the deed, Lady Macbeth can overmaster her husband, and stand defiantly erect, as if to challenge hell to combat. But this was but a momentary intoxication; it is even now over. She is already conscious that she can never banish from her breast the consciousness of her crime; she has found out that her wisdom, which spurned at reflection, is naught. The deed she has done stands clear before her soul in unveiled, horrible distinctness, and therefore she swoons away."

Horn and Bodenstedt also believe that the swoon is real. The latter says: "Various causes have co-operated to beget in Lady Macbeth a revulsion of feeling, which, from henceforth constantly increasing, drives her at last to self-destruction. The first intimation we found in ii. 2. 33, 34. She finds herself mistaken in her husband; a gulf has opened between him and her which nothing can hereafter bridge over. At the same time we perceive here the intimation of that internal and natural reaction of her overtaxed powers. Womanhood reasserts its rights."

Fletcher (see above, p. 29), referring to the theory that the fainting is feigned, remarks: "We believe, however, that our previous examination of her character must already have prepared the reader to give to this circumstance quite a different interpretation. He will bear in mind the burst of anguish which had been forced from her by Macbeth's very first ruminations upon his act: 'These deeds must not be thought After these ways; *so, it will make us mad.*' Remembering this, he will see what a dreadful accumulation of suffering is inflicted upon her by her husband's own lips [ii. 3. 93–98], painting in stronger, blacker colours than ever the guilty horror of their common deed."

Compare what Weiss (p. 421) says: "She has had no chance to calculate what effect this murder will have upon human sensibilities when they are taken by it unawares. She sees the awfulness of it suddenly reflected from the faces and gestures of Macduff, Banquo, and the rest. It beats at the gate across which she has braced a woman's arm, and breaks it in; and a mob of reproaches rush over her. What have those delicate hands been doing? . . . Nature, in making her, was so little in the male mood, so intently following the woman's model, that it left out the element which carries Macbeth through this scene. To hear her husband describe his simulated rage in butchering the grooms, and draw that painting of Duncan in his blood—'And his gash'd stabs look'd like a breach in nature For ruin's wasteful entrance'—it is too much, and 't is plain she is not needed. 'Help me hence, ho!' her sex cries. It is the revulsion of nature in a feminine soul. Love has exhaled all its hardihood into the deed which is just now discovered. She, too, has only now really discovered it. The nerves part at the overstrain of seeing what the deed is like, and drop her helpless into a swoon."

102. *Argument.* Theme, subject. Cf. *Sonn.* 76. 10: "And you and love are still my argument," etc. See also Milton, *P. L.* i. 24: "the highth of this great argument."

104. *Hid in an auger-hole.* "Concealed in imperceptible or obscure places" (Elwin). Steevens quotes *Cor.* iv. 6. 87: "Confin'd Into an auger's bore." On the measure of the line, see Gr. 480.

106. *Brew'd.* Delius remarks that this metaphor is amplified in *T. A.* iii. 2. 38.

107. The C. P. ed. says: "Sorrow in its first strength is motionless, and cannot express itself in words or tears." Cf. iv. 3. 209, and 3 *Hen. VI.* iii. 3. 22:

"And give my tongue-tied sorrows leave to speak."

108. *When we have*, etc. "When we have clothed our half drest bodies, which may take cold from being exposed to the air" (Steevens). The Porter had observed that the place was "too cold for hell." Malone quotes *T. of A.* iv. 3. 228:

"Call the creatures
Whose naked natures live in all the spite
Of wreakful heaven."

113. *Pretence.* Intention, purpose. Cf. *W. T.* iii. 2. 18; *Cor.* i. 2. 20, etc. In ii. 4. 24 below we have *pretend*=intend, design.

Steevens explains the passage thus: "I here declare myself an eternal enemy to this treason, and to all its further designs that have not yet come to light."

115. *Put on manly readiness.* "That is, dress ourselves" (Schmidt). So *ready*=dressed. Cf. *Cymb.* ii. 3. 86:

"*Cloten.* Your lady's person: is she ready?
Lady. Ay,
To keep her chamber;"

and the stage direction in 1 *Hen. VI.* ii. 1. 38: "The French leap over the walls in their shirts. Enter, several ways, the Bastard of Orleans, Alençon, and Reignier, half ready and half unready."

119. *Easy.* Easily. See Gr. 1.

122. *There 's.* See Gr. 335; and on *near*=nearer, Gr. 478, and *Rich. II.* p. 190.

Steevens remarks: "He suspected Macbeth; for he was the *nearest in blood* to the two princes, being the cousin-german of Duncan." The C. P. ed. quotes Webster, *Appius and Virginia*, v. 2:

"Great men's misfortunes thus have ever stood—
They touch none nearly but their nearest blood."

124. *Hath not yet lighted.* Has not yet spent its force.

126. *Dainty of.* Particular about. Cf. *T. and C.* i. 3. 145: "grows dainty of his worth."

127. *There 's warrant*, etc. Delius compares *A. W.* ii. 1. 33:

"*Bertram.* I 'll steal away.
First Lord. There 's honour in that theft."

Scene IV.—Mr. Fleay (in his paper read before the *New Shaks. Soc.*, June 26, 1874) says: "The old man in ii. 4 is suspicious. . . . He is of no use; the preternatural phenomena had been already dwelt on sufficiently in ii. 3. 35–44 in Shakespeare's best manner, not in the prosy would-be poetry of this scene: I am not sure that the effect in ii. 4 is not even comic. 'Dark night strangling the travelling lamp' is certainly queer, and 'Duncan's horses' (from Kilkenny) 'eating each other' might well amaze Ross's eyes when he 'looked upon 't.' I reject lines 1–20, and 'strangle' the old man."

To which Mr. Hales replied: "Shakespeare brings in the old man as the 'oldest inhabitant' of the newspapers to tell us he does not remember any such dreadful convulsions in his time. . . . There is a passage exactly parallel to this in *Lear*, iii. 1, where to be sure we have not an old man, but we have 'a gentleman.' At the end of act ii. we are told of the storm to which Lear is exposed. This gentleman describes it more particularly. Mr. Fleay proposes to strangle the old man; but the old man is much more likely, I suspect, to strangle Mr. Fleay—of course I mean Mr. Fleay *quâ* Shakespeare critic."*

4. *Trifled.* Made trivial. See Gr. 290.

Knowings. Experiences. Schmidt refers to *Cymb.* i. 4. 30 and ii. 3. 102; but, as the C. P. ed. notes, the present passage is the only one in which the plural is used.

6. *Threaten his bloody stage.* "Frown upon the earth where such horrors are enacted" (Moberly).

7. *Strangles the travelling lamp.* Cf. the description of the sun in 1 *Hen. IV.* i. 2. 226:

> —"breaking through the foul and ugly mists
> Of vapours, that did seem to strangle him."

The folio has here "the trauailing Lampe." In the time of S. the present distinction between *travel* and *travail* was not recognized, the forms being used indiscriminately without regard to the meaning. See Schmidt s. v. Coll. prefers *travailing* here as "having reference to the struggle between the sun and night;" but D. reminds him that, as the sun has not been previously mentioned in the passage, "the word *lamp* ceases to signify the sun," if *travelling* is changed to *travailing.*

8. *Is 't night's predominance*, etc. "Is it that night is aggressive, or that the day is ashamed to appear?" (Moberly). *Predominant* and *predominance* were astrological terms. Cf. *Lear*, i. 2. 134: "Knaves, thieves, and treachers by spherical predominance;" *A. W.* i. 1. 211:

> "*Helena.* The wars have so kept you under that you must needs have been born under Mars.
> *Parolles.* When he was predominant?"

see also *W. T.* i. 2. 202.

10. On the description of prodigies that follows, cf. extract from Holinshed, p. 136 above.

12. *Towering* and *place* are terms of falconry. D. cites Donne, who in one of his poems says of a hawk: "Which when herself she lessens in the aire, You then first say that high enough she toweres;" and Turbervile, *Booke of Falconrie*, 1611: "Shee is of the number of those Hawkes that are hie flying and towre Hawks."† *Place* = "pitch, the

---

* This the old man, with Mr. Hales's help, appears to have done; for Mr. Fleay omits the passage in reprinting the paper in his *Shakespeare Manual.* The "horses," by the by, are not "from Kilkenny," but from Holinshed. See p. 136.

† Cf. Milton, *P. L.* xi. 185: "The bird of Jove, stooped from his aery tour;" where, as D. suggests, "tour" is probably="tower" in this technical sense.

highest elevation of the hawk" (Schmidt). For *pitch*, cf. *Rich. II.* i. 1. 109, and see note in our ed. p. 153.

13. *Mousing.* "A very effective epithet, as contrasting the falcon, in her pride of place, with a bird that is accustomed to seek its prey on the ground" (Talbot).

14. *Horses.* A monosyllable here. See Gr. 471; and cf. *sense* in v. 1. 22 below, and in *Sonn.* 112. 10. In *A. and C.* iii. 7. 7 we have "horse" = "horses;" and in *K. John*, ii. 1. 289, "horse back" for horse's back."

15. *Minions.* Darlings. See on i. 2. 19 above.

16. *In nature.* "Their wildness was no casual or passing fit, but their whole nature had become suddenly changed" (Delius, quoted by Furness).

17. *As.* See on i. 4. 11 and ii. 2. 27. Gr. 107.

18. *Eat.* Changed by many critics to *ate*, which is nowhere found in the early copies. The present is there more frequently printed "eate." For the participle S. uses both *eat* (as in *L. L. L.* iv. 2. 26, *Rich. II.* v. 5. 85, etc.) and *eaten* (see i. 3. 84 and iv. 1. 64 in the present play). Milton always uses *eat* for the past tense (as in *P. L.* ix. 781, *P. R.* i. 352, and *L'All.* 102, where it rhymes with *feat*), but never, we believe, for the participle.

24. *Pretend.* See on ii. 3. 113.

28. *Ravin up.* "Devour greedily" (Schmidt). Cf. *M. for M.* i. 2. 133: "Like rats that ravin down their proper bane." In iv. 1. 24 below we have "ravin'd" = ravenous. Cf. *A. W.* iii. 2. 120: "the ravin lion."

29. *Like.* Likely; as often in S. Cf. *M. of V.* ii. 7. 49: "Is 't like that lead contains her?"

31. *Scone.* Of this ancient town, which was situated about two miles and a half from Perth, few memorials now remain. Of Scone Abbey, founded by Alexander I. in 1107, in which the Scottish kings from that date down to the time of James II. were crowned, nothing is left but part of an aisle now used as a mausoleum by the Earl of Mansfield, on whose estate it stands. The old market-cross of Scone also remains in the pleasure-grounds of Scone Palace, as the seat of the earl is called. At the north side of the mansion is a tumulus, known as the Moat Hill, said to have been composed of earth from the estates of those who here attended on the kings.

The famous "stone of Scone," which served for many ages as the seat on which the kings were crowned, now forms part of the English coronation-chair in Westminster Abbey. The connection that the stone is supposed to have with the destinies of the Scots is commemorated in ancient verse,* which has been thus rendered:

> "Unless the Fates are faithless grown,
> And prophet's voice be vain,
> Where'er is found this sacred stone,
> The Scottish race shall reign."

According to national tradition, this stone was the pillow of Jacob at Bethel, and long served for the coronation-seat of the kings of Ireland.

* "Ni fallat fatum, Scoti quocumque locatum
Invenient lapidem regnare tenentur ibidem."

It is said to have been brought from Ireland to Iona by Fergus, the son of Erc, then to have been deposited in Dunstaffnage Castle (still standing near Oban), and to have been transported thence to Scone by Kenneth II. in the year 842. Its history from that date is well authenticated, but the rest is of course more or less mythical.

33. *Colme-kill.* "The cell (or chapel) of Columba," now known as Icolmkill, or Iona, a barren islet, about eight miles south of Staffa. Here St. Columba, an Irish Christian preacher, founded a monastery in A.D. 563, and here he died about A.D. 597, or at the time when Augustine landed in Kent to convert the English. From this monastery in Iona Christianity and civilization spread, not only through Scotland, but even to the Orkneys and Iceland. Hence the island came to be considered holy ground, and there was a traditionary belief that it was to be specially favoured at the dissolution of the world. According to the ancient prophecy,

> "Seven years before that awful day
> When time shall be no more,
> A watery deluge shall o'ersweep
> Hibernia's mossy shore;
> The green-clad Isla, too, shall sink,
> While with the great and good,
> Columba's happier isle shall rear
> Her towers above the flood."

It is not to be wondered at that monarchs desired to be buried in this sacred spot, and that thus it became the cemetery where, as Collins has sung,

> "The mighty kings of three fair realms are laid"—

Scotland, Ireland, and Norway. No trace of their tombs now remains, the oldest monuments left on the island being those of Irish ecclesiastics of the 12th century. Besides these there are the ruins of a chapel (of the 11th century), of a nunnery (founded about 1180), and of the cathedral church of St. Mary, built early in the 13th century. Of the three hundred and fifty sculptured stone crosses which formerly adorned the island, only two are still standing. One is called "Maclean's Cross," and is a beautifully carved monolith, eleven feet high; the other, "St. Martin's Cross," is about fourteen feet high. All the other crosses were thrown into the sea, about the year 1560, by order of the anti-Popish Synod of Argyll.

Dr. Johnson, who visited Iona during his Scottish tour, writes of it: "We were now treading that illustrious island which was once the luminary of the Caledonian regions, whence savage clans and roving barbarians derived the benefits of knowledge and the blessings of religion. Far from me and from my friends be such frigid philosophy as may conduct us indifferent and unmoved over any ground which has been dignified by wisdom, bravery, or virtue. That man is little to be envied whose patriotism would not gain force upon the plain of Marathon, or whose piety would not grow warmer among the ruins of Iona."

36. *Thither.* That is, to Scone.

40. *Benison.* Cf. *Lear*, i. 1. 268: "our grace, our love, our benison;" *Id.* iv. 6. 229: "The bounty and the benison of heaven."

FORRES—EMINENCE AT THE WESTERN EXTREMITY.

ACT III.

SCENE I.—7. *Shine.* "Appear with all the *lustre of conspicuous truth*" (Johnson).

10. *Hush, no more.* "These words are in perfect moral keeping with Banquo's previous resolute fightings against evil suggestions" (Clarke).

Sennet. Also written *sennit*, *senet*, *synnet*, *cynet*, *signet*, and *signate.* It occurs often in the old stage directions, and "seems to indicate a particular set of notes on the trumpet, or cornet, different from a flourish" (Nares). See *Hen. VIII.* p. 176.

13. *All-thing.* "Every way" (Schmidt). Cf. the adverbial use of *nothing* and *something.* The 2d folio has "all-things;" the 3d and 4th, "all things." See Gr. 12, and cf. 55 and 68.

14. *Solemn.* "Ceremonious, formal" (Schmidt). Cf. *T. A.* v. 2. 115: "Solemn feast" (also in *A. W.* ii. 3. 187); *T. of S.* iii. 2. 103: "our solemn festival," etc.

15. *Let*, etc. Rowe changed this to "Lay your Highness's;" Pope, to "Lay your highness'," which is also in the Coll. MS. "Command upon" is not found elsewhere in S., but in *Per.* iii. 1. 3 we have the *noun* similarly used:

"and thou, that hast
Upon the winds command, bind them in brass."

See Gr. 191, and cf. 139.

Flathe (see above, p. 165) remarks here: "And Banquo can declare firm, unalterable fealty to the very man whom to himself he has just accused, almost in so many words, of attaining the throne by the assassination of his royal master! Such a declaration could only have been made by one whose own heart is closely allied to evil. The emotion excited in Banquo's breast against Macbeth must become stronger. He feels obliged to invent fair words to conceal his secret. The hypocrite Macbeth is served with hypocrisy."

16. *The which.* See Gr. 270.

21. *Still.* Always, ever; as very often in S. Cf. *M. of V.* i. 1. 17, 136; *Temp.* i. 2. 229; *Rich. II.* ii. 1. 22, etc.

Grave. Weighty, of importance; like the Latin *gravis.* Schmidt compares *Rich. III.* ii. 3. 20: "politic grave counsel." *Prosperous* = to our advantage.

22. *Take.* Needlessly changed by Malone to "talk."

25. *Go not my horse*, etc. Cf. *Rich. II.* ii. 1. 300: "Hold out my horse, and I will first be there." See Gr. 361, 364.

The better. "The better, considering the distance he has to go" (C. P. ed.). See Gr. 94, 102.

29. *Are bestow'd.* Have betaken themselves. Cf. iii. 6. 24 below; also *Ham.* iii. 1. 33, 44; *Hen. V.* iv. 3. 68, etc.

33. *Therewithal*, etc. That is, we shall have other state matters to discuss along with it. Cf. *Henry V.* i. 1. 45: "any cause of policy."

38. *Commend.* See on i. 7. 11 above. "*Commend you to their backs* is said jestingly, with an affectation of formality" (C. P. ed.).

39. *Farewell.* For the short line, see Gr. 512.

41, 42. The folios have a comma after *night*, and a colon after *welcome*; which pointing is followed by Rowe, Pope, Delius, and others. Most editors adopt the punctuation in the text, which was first suggested by Theo.

Schmidt makes *welcome* a noun; the C. P. ed. is doubtful whether it is a noun or an adjective. In the latter case, *sweeter* is used adverbially. Cf. *T. of A.* i. 2. 135: "Music, make their welcome."

Ourself. S. uses both *ourself* and *ourselves* in this "regal" sense. Cf. *Rich. II.* i. 1. 16: "ourselves will hear;" *Id.* i. 4. 42: "We will ourself in person," etc.

43. *While then.* Till then. Cf. *Rich. II.* i. 3. 122, and see note in our ed. p. 163. Gr. 137.

God be with you = "God b' wi' you" (Walker). Gr. 461. Our *good-by* (cf. the Fr. *adieu*) is perhaps a contraction of this contraction. See Wb.

45. *Our pleasure.* Some of the early editors (so K. and St.) join these words to the preceding line. Abbott (512) thinks that S. "could not possibly make 'our pleasure' a detached foot."

47, 48. "To be thus (that is, to reign) is nothing; but to be safely thus is something" (Gr. 385).

49. *Royalty.* "Nobleness" (Schmidt).

50. *Would be fear'd.* Is to be feared, should be feared. Gr. 329.

51. *To.* In addition to. Gr. 185. Cf. i. 6. 19.

53. *But.* See Gr. 118.

55, 56. *My genius*, etc. Cf. *A. and C.* ii. 3. 19:

"Thy demon, that 's thy spirit * which keeps thee, is
Noble, courageous, high, unmatchable,
Where Cæsar's is not; but near him thy angel
Becomes a fear, as being o'erpower'd."

This is from North's *Plutarch:* "For thy demon, said he (that is to say, the good angel and spirit that keepeth thee), is afraid of his; and being courageous and high when he is alone, becometh fearful and timorous when he cometh near unto the other." On *Genius*, cf. *J. C.* ii. 1. 65.

62. *With.* By. See Gr. 193.

64. *Fil'd.* Defiled; but not that word contracted. It is used in prose; as in Holland's *Pliny*, xiv. 19: "If the grapes have been filed by any ordure or dung falne from above thereupon." Johnson says that *to file* is found in the Bishops' Bible. See Wb. also.

66. *Vessel.* Often used figuratively by S. Cf. 2 *Hen. IV.* iv. 4. 44; *J. C.* v. 5. 13; *W. T.* iii. 3. 21, etc.

67. *Eternal jewel.* "Immortal soul" (C. P. ed.). For the use of *eternal*, cf. *K. John*, iii. 4. 18: "the eternal spirit."

69. *Seed.* The folios have "seedes" or "seeds," which W. retains.

70. *The list.* Elsewhere S. has *lists* in this sense. Cf. *Rich. II.* i. 2. 52; *Id.* i. 3. 32, 38, 43; 1 *Hen. VI.* v. 5. 32, etc. He has *list* several times in the more general sense of boundary, limit; as in *A. W.* ii. 1. 53; 1 *Hen. IV.* iv. 1. 51; *Ham.* iv. 5. 99, etc.

71. *Champion me to the utterance.* Fight with me *à outrance.* "A challenge, or a combat *à l'outrance*, to extremity, was a fixed term in the law of arms, used when the combatants engaged with an *odium internecinum*, an intention to destroy each other, in opposition to trials of skill at festivals, or on other occasions, where the contest was only for reputation or a prize" (Johnson). Cf. *Cymb.* iii. 1. 73: "Behoves me keep at utterance" (that is, defend to the uttermost). Steevens quotes Golding's Ovid, *Met.* xiv.:

"To both the parties at the length from battell for to rest,
And not to fight to utterance."

79. *Conference.* Metrically a dissyllable. Gr. 468.

Pass'd in probation with you. Spent in proving to you. For *probation* =proof, cf. *Oth.* iii. 3. 365; *M. for M.* v. 1. 156; *Cymb.* v. 5. 362, etc.

80. *Borne in hand.* Kept in expectation, flattered with false hopes. Cf. *T. of S.* iv. 2. 3; *Cymb.* v. 5. 43; *Ham.* ii. 2. 67, etc. In 1572, an act was passed against "such as practise abused sciences, whereby they bear the people in hand that they can tell their destinies, deaths," etc.

82. *To a notion craz'd.* "Even to the most feeble apprehension" (Moberly). Cf. *Lear*, i. 4. 248: "His notion weakens;" *Cor.* v. 6. 107: "his own notion," etc.

87. *Gospell'd.* Governed by gospel precepts. See *Matt.* v. 44.

88. *To pray.* *As* to pray. Gr. 281.

91. *Ay, in the catalogue*, etc. Yes, in a mere list of men as male human beings you would be reckoned, just as the meanest cur is counted among dogs.

93. *Shoughs*=shocks (see Wb.). *Water-rugs* were "a kind of poodle"

* See above on i. 7. 53.

(Schmidt); and "*demi-wolves*, a cross between dogs and wolves, like the Latin *lycisci*" (Johnson).

Clept. Participle from *clepe*, to call. Cf. *Ham.* i. 4. 19: "They clepe us drunkards;" *L. L. L.* v. 1. 23: "he clepeth a calf cauf;" *V. and A.* 995: "She clepes him king of graves," etc. *Yclept* is the same participle with the old English prefix. S. uses it in *L. L. L.* i. 1. 42 and v. 2. 602.

94. *The valued file.* The classification according to value or quality, as distinguished from the "catalogue," or "the bill that writes them all alike." Schmidt makes it an adjective; some take it to be the passive participle used in an active sense (*valued* = valuing). Cf. Gr. 374.

96. *Housekeeper.* Watch-dog. The C. P. ed. says that in Topsell's *Hist. of Beasts* (1658) the "housekeeper" is enumerated among the kinds of dogs. Cf. οἰκουρός in Aristophanes, *Vespæ*, 970.

98. *Clos'd.* "Enclosed" (Schmidt). Cf. *R. and J.* i. 4. 110: "a despised life clos'd in my breast."

99. *Addition.* Cf. i. 3. 106. On *from* = apart from, see Gr. 158.

102. *Worst* is lengthened metrically into a "quasi-dissyllable" (Gr. 485), as *enemy*, two lines below, is contracted into one (Gr. 468).

105. *Grapples.* On the metaphor, cf. *Ham.* i. 3. 63: "Grapple them to thy soul with hoops of steel." See also *Hen. V.* iii. prol. 18.

106. *In.* "In the case of" (Gr. 162). Cf. *Rich. II.* ii. 2. 10: "In Ross and Willoughby," etc.

107. On the measure, see Gr. 497.

111. *Tugg'd with fortune.* Pulled about in wrestling with fortune. Cf. *W. T.* iv. 4. 508: "Let myself and fortune Tug for the time to come." See also *K. John*, iv. 3. 146; 2 *Hen. VI.* iii. 2. 173, etc.

113. *On 't.* Of it. Cf. line 130 below, and see on i. 3. 84 above. Gr. 182.

115. *Distance.* "Alienation" (Schmidt). It was a fencing term, denoting the space between antagonists (D.). Cf. *M. W.* ii. 1. 233: "In these times, you stand on distance, your passadoes, stoccadoes, and I know not what;" *Id.* ii. 3. 27: "thy punts, thy stock, thy reverse, thy distance," etc. See also *A. W.* v. 3. 212; *R. and J.* ii. 4. 22, etc.

117. *My near'st of life.* My inmost life. See on ii. 1. 24: "kind'st leisure." Gr. 473.

119. *Bid my will avouch it.* Let my will answer for it, own it as an arbitrary act. Cf. *M. N. D.* i. 1. 106; *Hen. V.* v. 1. 77, etc.

120. *For.* Because of. Gr. 150.

121. *Loves.* For the plural, cf. *Rich. II.* iv. 1. 314: "your sights;" and see note in our ed. p. 206. On *may*, see Gr. 310; and on *but*, Gr. 385.

122. *Who.* See Gr. 218, 274. Cf. iii. 4. 42 and iv. 3. 171 below.

128. *Advise.* Instruct. Cf. *Lear*, i. 3. 23; *Hen. VIII.* i. 2. 107, etc.

129. *The perfect spy o' the time.* The precise time when you may look for him. The Coll. MS. has "*a* perfect spy," which W. adopts, referring it to the man who joins the murderers in scene 3. Various emendations have been suggested, but they are not worth mentioning.

130. *On 't.* Of the time; or, perhaps, of the deed.

131. *Something from.* At some distance away from. See Gr. 68, 158.

Always thought, etc. It being kept in mind (Gr. 378) that I must be free from suspicion.

133. *Rubs.* Hindrances, impediments; a term in bowling. See *Rich. II.* iii. 4. 4, and note in our ed. p. 197.

136. *Embrace.* "Undergo, suffer" (Schmidt). Cf. *T. G. of V.* v. 4. 126: "Thurio, give back, or else embrace thy death."

137. *Resolve yourselves.* Come to a determination, make up your minds. Cf. *A. and C.* iii. 11. 9; 3 *Hen. VI.* i. 1. 49; *W. T.* v. 3. 86, etc.

140. Hunter remarks that such negotiations with assassins were not uncommon in the age of Elizabeth. An instance had recently occurred in the neighbourhood of Stratford. Lodowick Grevile, who dwelt at Sesoncote, in Gloucestershire, and at Milcote, in Warwickshire, coveting the estate of one Webb, his tenant, plotted to murder him and get the estate by a forged will. This was successfully accomplished by the aid of two servants whom Grevile engaged to do the deed. Fearing detection, one of the assassins afterwards murdered his comrade. The body was found, and the investigation led to the arrest and conviction of Grevile and his servant, the surviving murderer. Grevile stood mute, and was pressed to death on November 14, 1589. The circumstance must have been well known to S., as the Greviles were at this time patrons of the living of Stratford.

SCENE II.—5. *Content.* Satisfaction. Clarke remarks: "This brief soliloquy allows us to see the deep-seated misery of the murderess, the profound melancholy in which she is secretly steeped; while on the instant that she sees her husband she can rally her forces, assume exterior fortitude, and resume her accustomed hardness of manner, with which to stimulate him by remonstrance almost amounting to reproach."

Gericke (quoted by Furness) says: "This profound sigh from the depths of a deeply wounded soul is the key to all that we afterwards hear and learn of Lady Macbeth. A complaint has been urged that between her first and last appearance the connecting link, the bridge, is wanting: *here*, and *only* here, is this bridge supplied. Here for an instant we overhear her, and from her own lips learn what her pride, her love for Macbeth even, will not suffer to be uttered aloud; it is what she convulsively locks in her breast, and what at last breaks her heart. This short monologue is the sole preparation for the sleep-walking and the death of the woman; her death would be unintelligible did we not here see the beginning of the end."

9. *Sorriest.* See on ii. 2. 20 above.

10. *Using.* Cherishing. St. suggested "Nursing" as an emendation, but as Schmidt remarks, S. joins *use* "with the most different nouns almost periphrastically."

11. *Without all remedy.* Beyond all remedy; or *all* = any (Schmidt), as in *Hen. VIII.* iv. 1. 113: "without all doubt;" *Sonn.* 74. 2: "without all bail." See Gr. 12, 197; and for the measure, 468.

13. *Scotch'd.* The folios have "scorch'd." Theo. made the change. Cf. *Cor.* iv. 5. 198.

16. *Frame of things.* Cf. *Ham.* ii. 2. 310: "This goodly frame, the earth."

Both the worlds. Heaven and earth. Cf. *Ham.* iv. 5. 134, where it means "this world and the next."

20. *To gain our peace.* The later folios have "our place," which is adopted by Pope, Johnson, Steevens, Malone, Sr., Hudson, St., and D. As K. remarks, "the repetition of the word *peace* seems very much in S.'s manner; and . . . there is something much higher in the sentiment conveyed by the original word than in that of *place.* In the very contemplation of the murder of Banquo, Macbeth is vainly seeking for peace. Banquo is the object that makes him eat his meal in fear and sleep in terrible dreams."

21. *On the torture,* etc. "To lie upon the rack of our own thoughts, in a frenzy of restlessness" (Moberly). *Ecstasy* in S. means "any state of being beside one's self" (Schmidt). Cf. iv. 3. 170 below. See also *Temp.* iii. 3. 108; *Much Ado,* ii. 3. 157; *T. A.* iv. 1. 125, etc.

23. *Life's fitful fever.* Cf. *M. for M.* iii. 1. 75: "a feverous life."

27. *Gentle my lord.* Like "Good my lord," etc. See Gr. 13.

Sleek is not used elsewhere as a verb by S. Cf. Milton, *Comus,* 882: "Sleeking her soft alluring locks." "The word, verb or adjective, is almost always applied to the hair" (C. P. ed.).

30. *Let your remembrance,* etc. "Take care to do all honour to Banquo by looks and words of the deepest respect; though our royalty will never be safe, so long as it is necessary to keep our honours bright by steeping them in flattery" (Moberly).

Remembrance is here a quadrisyllable. See Gr. 477.

32. *That.* On the construction, see Gr. 284.

34. *Visards.* Masks. Cf. *M. W.* iv. 4. 70; *L. L. L.* v. 2. 242, 246, 271, 385, 404, etc.

35. *Leave.* Leave off. Cf. "Where did I leave?" in *V. and A.* 715 and *Rich. II.* v. 2. 4; and "Where left we last?" in *T. of S.* iii. 1. 26.

37. *Lives.* Cf. *runs* in i. 3. 147. Gr. 336.

38. *But in them,* etc. The C. P. ed. explains the passage thus: "The deed by which man holds life of Nature gives no right to perpetual tenure. Nature is here compared to a lord of the manor under whom men hold their lives by copyhold tenure. 'Copyhold, *Tenura per copiam rotuli curiæ,* is a tenure for which the tenant hath nothing to shew but the *copy* of the rolls made by the steward of his lord's court. . . . Some copyholds are fineable at will, and some certain: that which is fineable at will, the lord taketh at his pleasure' (Cowel's *Law Dictionary,* s. v.). Monck Mason takes 'Nature's copy' to mean the human form divine. Steevens and Elwin agree in this interpretation. The latter quotes *Oth.* v. 2. 11:

> 'Thou cunning'st pattern of excelling Nature.'

But from what follows in line 49 it would seem that Shakespeare made here, as in so many other passages, a reference to legal phraseology. Compare, for instance, *Sonn.* 13. 5:

> 'So should that beauty which you hold in lease
> Find no determination.'

And see also iv. 1. 99 of this play."

Note Fletcher's comments on this passage (p. 29 above).

41. *Cloister'd.* Steevens remarks: "The bats wheeling round the dim

cloisters of Queen's College, Cambridge, have frequently impressed on me the singular propriety of this original epithet."

42. *Shard-borne.* The old English name of the horny wing-cases of the beetle was *shards.* Cf. *A. and C.* iii. 2. 20: "They are his shards and he their beetle" (that is, they serve as wings for him); *Cymb.* iii. 3. 20: "the sharded beetle." Steevens cites Gower, *Conf. Am.*: "a dragon tho, Whose scherdes shinen as the sonne" (that is, his scales, or scaly wings). The 3d and 4th folios have "shard-born," and some have retained that reading, explaining the word as = "dung-born." For the various meanings of *shard,* and its derivation, see Wb.

44. *Note.* The word, as Schmidt says, is used for "any distinction or eminence." Cf. *A. W.* v. 3. 14: "Offence of mighty note;" *L. C.* 233: "of holiest note," etc.

45. *Chuck.* A term of endearment, corrupted from *chick.* Cf. *Oth.* iii. 4. 49: "What promise, chuck?" and see *Id.* iv. 2. 24; *A. and C.* iv. 4. 2; *Hen. V.* iii. 2. 26, etc.

R. H. Hiecke (*Shakespeare's Macbeth erläutert und gewürdigt,* quoted by Furness) remarks: "Must all the reiterated terms of endearment in this scene, these manifold inflections in ever softer modulations, be deemed meaningless in such a poet as Shakespeare? . . . Of all the deeply tragic passages of this drama, this is the deepest. *Unintentionally* and *unconsciously* there here breathes from Macbeth's soul an echo of that happier time when the mutual esteem of a heroic pair was accompanied by the delicate attentions of first love. And, moreover, this state of feeling (at such a moment as this) is psychologically true, when we see them, as in the days of first love, united by the possession of a common secret. But what a secret is it that they now share! This involuntary return to the tone of a happier time, now, alas! vanished—for that early love has been long since overgrown in each by ambition—becomes in the phrases with which he unfolds his present situation to his wife the most cutting irony. Just as ambition, at first not alien to either of the pair, but grown at last by degrees the complete master of all other sentiments, has caused their love for each other to cool, until we see them united solely by a fiendish alliance in pursuit of an ambitious end—so here this love, *grown cold,* was *murdered* in the murder of the king, and the tenderness in this scene is naught but a dirge, rising unconsciously from the soul, over the sentiments of an earlier time."

46. *Seeling.* Blinding; a term in falconry. "To *seel* is to close the eyelids partially or entirely, by passing a fine thread through them; this was done to hawks until they became tractable" (Nares). Cf. *Oth.* i. 3. 270 and iii. 3. 210; also *A. and C.* iii. 13. 112.

49. *Cancel,* etc. Cf. *Rich. III.* iv. 4. 77: "Cancel his bond of life, dear God, I pray;" and *Cymb.* v. 4. 27:

"take this life,
And cancel these cold bonds."

50. *Light thickens.* Cf. *A. and C.* ii. 3. 27:

"He beats thee 'gainst the odds; thy lustre thickens
When he shines by."

Steevens quotes Fletcher, *Faithful Shepherdess*: "Fold your flocks up, for the air Gins to thicken;" and Malone adds Spenser, *Shep. Kal.*: "But see, the welkin thicks apace."

51. *Rooky*. It would seem natural to interpret this as = rook-haunted, frequented by rooks or crows. Mitford says: "The passage simply means, 'the rook hastens its evening flight to the wood where its fellows are already assembled;'" and Clarke remarks: "The very epithet *rooky* appears to us to caw with the sound of many bed-ward rooks bustling and croaking to their several roosts." But this does not satisfy certain editors, who have found an old word *roky* meaning misty. So Edwards (*Canons of Criticism*, 1765), Steevens, and the C. P. ed. explain it as = damp, misty, foggy, gloomy, etc.

52. See extract from Dowden, p. 39 above. *Drowse* is used by S. only here and in 1 *Hen. IV.* iii. 2. 81.

53. *Whiles*. See on ii. 1. 60. For the plural *preys* (perhaps = "their several preys") cf. iii. 1. 121 and v. 8. 61. *Rouse* is used intransitively by S. only here and in v. 5. 12.

54, 55. The C. P. editors think that "this couplet reads like an interpolation."

56. *Go with me*. Delius takes this to mean "Aid me, or let me quietly carry out my plan," and compares *Lear*, i. 1. 107: "But goes thy heart with this?" Moberly explains it, "Understand what my meaning is." Schmidt gives examples of *go with* = agree, accord; as *Ham.* i. 2. 15, i. 3. 28, i. 5. 49; *Lear*, iv. 7. 5, etc.

Scene III.—Some critics have thought that the 3d Murderer was Macbeth himself in disguise. See Furness, p. 160, and *Notes and Queries* for Sept. 11, Oct. 2, Nov. 13, and Dec. 4, 1869.

2. *He needs not our mistrust*, etc. "We may trust him, for Macbeth has evidently told him all we have to do. Macbeth's uneasiness makes him reinforce the party with a cleverer hand" (Moberly). See Gr. 308; and on *to* in line 4, Gr. 187.

6. *Lated*. Belated. Used by S. only here and in *A. and C.* iii. 11. 3: "I am so lated in the world." Gr. 290.

7. *To gain the timely inn*. Probably, to gain the inn betimes. The C. P. ed. prefers to make *timely* = "welcome, opportune;" and Schmidt explains it, "early, soon attained."

10. *The note of expectation*. The list of expected guests. Under *note* = list, Schmidt cites also *M. W.* iv. 2. 64; *T. of S.* i. 2. 145, etc.

11. *His horses*. Horn (quoted by Furness) says: "S., who dared do all that poet ever dared, nevertheless did not dare to bring upon the stage—a *horse*. And very properly; for there where noble poets represent the world's history upon the 'boards that imitate the world,' there no brutes should be allowed. But in the present scene it is hard to avoid introducing a horse, and the poet has to obviate the difficulty in four almost insignificant lines, in order to account for the absence of the steeds. It is after all undoubtedly better not to shrink from two or three such trivial lines than to have a horse come clattering on the stage."

14. *Enter Fleance with a torch*. Here again, as Coll. notes, Fleance

carries the torch to light his father. The "Servant" of many modern eds. is an interpolation. See on ii. 1. 1.

SCENE IV.—1. *At first And last.* Probably = once for all. Schmidt explains it "from the beginning to the end," and compares 1 *Hen. VI.* v. 5. 102. Johnson would read "to first And last;" that is, to "all, of whatever degree, from the highest to the lowest."

3. *Ourself.* See on iii. 1. 42.

5. *Her state.* "Her chair of state at the head of the table" (Steevens). Cf. *T. N.* ii. 5. 50: "Sitting in our state;" 1 *Hen. IV.* ii. 4. 415: "This chair shall be my state;" *Cor.* v. 4. 22: "He sits in his state," etc.

In best time. Used by S. only here, though he often has "in good time."

6. *Require.* Request, ask; not in the stronger sense of "demand." Cf. *Hen. VIII.* ii. 4. 144: "In humblest manner I require your highness;" *A. and C.* iii. 12. 12:

> "Lord of his fortunes he salutes thee,
> And requires to live in Egypt," etc.

8. *Speaks.* Says. Cf. *Oth.* v. 2. 327, and iv. 3. 154 below.

11. *Large.* "Unrestrained" (Schmidt). Cf. *A. and C.* iii. 6. 93: "large In his abominations."

Anon. Macbeth has just caught sight of the murderer standing at the door, and wishes to dismiss him before pledging the measure (Delius). On *measure*, cf. *Oth.* ii. 3. 31.

14. *'T is better*, etc. 'T is better that the blood should be on thy face than in his body; or it may possibly mean, "it is better that his blood were on thy face than he in this room" (Johnson). Hunter believes that the words are uttered aside, and mean "that, horrible as it is, thus in the midst of the feast, to behold the assassin of his friend just without the door, it is still better than that Banquo himself should be alive and within the hall a guest at this entertainment." If we accept the first explanation, *he within* = within *him*. Cf. *A. and C.* iii. 13. 98: "So saucy with the hand of she here." See other examples in Gr. 206–214.

19. *Nonpareil.* S. always uses the definite article with this word, except in *Temp.* iii. 2. 108 (Delius).

20. *Scap'd.* Not "'scap'd," as often printed. The word is found in prose; as in Bacon, *Adv. of L.* ii. 14. 9: "such as had scaped shipwreck." S. uses it much oftener than *escape*. Cf. Wb.

23. *Casing.* Surrounding. Moberly quotes *Oth.* iii. 3. 464: "You elements that clip us round about."

25. *Saucy doubts and fears.* His fellow-prisoners in this confinement (Delius). Schmidt explains *saucy* here as "unbounded, extravagant," and considers the passage "a very expressive oxymoron." The C. P. ed. makes *saucy* = "insolent, importunate, like the Latin *improbus*." Cf. *Oth.* i. 1. 129; *J. C.* i. 3. 12, etc.

27. *Trenched gashes.* Cf. *V. and A.* 1052:

> "the wide wound that the boar had trench'd
> In his soft flank;"

and *T. G. of V.* iii. 2. 7:

> "This weak impress of love is as a figure
> Trenched in ice."

29. *Worm.* Frequently used by Elizabethan writers for a serpent (Nares). Cf. *M. for M.* iii. 1. 17; *M. N. D.* iii. 2. 71; *A. and C.* v. 2. 243, 256, 261, 268, etc.

32. *We 'll hear ourselves again.* We 'll talk the matter over again. Under "*ourselves* = each other," Schmidt cites, besides this passage. *T. and C.* iv. 4. 42:

> "We two, that with so many thousand sighs
> Did buy each other, must poorly sell ourselves;"

Id. iv. 4. 140:

> "Lady, give me your hand, and, as we walk,
> To our own selves bend we our needful talk;"

and *K. John*, ii. 1. 407: "Make work upon ourselves."

Some editors put a comma after hear, making *ourselves again* = when I am once more myself; others point it thus: "We 'll hear, ourselves, again." Theo., Warb., and Johnson read "We 'll hear 't ourselves again;" Hanmer and Capell, "We 'll hear thee ourselves again."

33. *The cheer.* Schmidt explains this, "the merry disposition which should attend a feast;" the C. P. ed. "the usual welcome." The latter seems more in keeping with the context.

The feast is sold, etc. It is like selling a feast, not giving it, if you do not often assure your guests that it is given gladly. On *a-making*, see Gr. 24, 140.

35. *To feed*, etc. "Mere feeding would be best done at home" (C. P. ed.).

36. *From thence.* Away from home. See Gr. 41; and on *to*, Gr. 185. As the C. P. ed. remarks, there is no play upon words in *meat* and *meeting*, as the former word was pronounced *mate* in S.'s time. See White's *Shakespeare*, vol. xii. p. 417; and cf. the rhyme of *sea* with *play* in *Hen. VIII.* iii. 1. 9, 10, etc. In *T. G. of V.* i. 2. 68, 69, there is a play upon "meat" and "maid."

37. On the measure, see Gr. 494.

38. Cf. *Hen. VIII.* i. 4. 92:

> "A good digestion to you all; and, once more,
> I shower a welcome on ye. Welcome, all."

Dr. Bucknill calls this "a somewhat physiological grace."

39. *May 't please your highness sit.* That is, *to* sit. Cf. *Hen. VIII.* i. 4. 19, and Gr. 349. We have the *to* inserted after *please* just below in line 45.

40. *Roof'd.* Under one roof. S. does not use the verb *roof* in its modern sense.

41. *Grac'd.* "Full of graces" (Schmidt). Cf. *Lear*, i. 4. 267: "a grac'd palace."

42. *Who.* See on iii. 1. 122. Gr. 274. Douce paraphrases the passage thus: "I have more cause to accuse him of unkindness for his absence than to pity him for any accident or mischance that may have occasioned

it;" but, as Sr. remarks, *May I* seems to imply here a wish ("I hope I may rather have to accuse him," etc.) than an assertion.

43-45. Hunter remarks that it is during this speech that the ghost first becomes visible to Macbeth. He had been about to take his seat according to the invitation of Lennox, but now, full of horror, instead of doing so, he starts back, which leads to the invitation of Ross.

Some critics have thought that it is Duncan's ghost, not Banquo's, that first appears. It is said that lines 71-73 cannot apply to Banquo, who had not been buried; but the same objection may be made to the words, "thy bones are marrowless" (94), addressed to the *second* ghost. These are simply Macbeth's vivid expression of the general idea of coming back from the dead, and must not be taken literally. Macbeth was thinking and speaking of Banquo, and it is both natural and dramatically proper that his ghost, if any, should rise at the mention of his name; and the second appearance is in response to Macbeth's renewed reference to him. This view is confirmed by Dr. Forman's testimony (see p. 10, foot-note).

For an abstract of the arguments on both sides of this question, see Furness's *Macbeth*, pp. 167-172.

Another question that has been much discussed is whether the ghost should be represented on the stage. Even if the ghost is an objective reality, and not a mere hallucination, like the "air-drawn dagger," it is evident that no one sees it but Macbeth;* and, as Fletcher remarks, it seems an outrage to our senses that the apparition should be visible "to us, the distant audience, when he is invisible to every one of the guests who crowd the table at which he seats himself in the only vacant chair."

But is the ghost objective or subjective? Here too the critics are at odds. Dr. Bucknill (*Mad Folk of S.* p. 27) says: "Macbeth at this juncture is in a state of mind closely bordering upon disease, if he have not actually passed the limit. He is hallucinated, and he believes in the hallucination. The reality of the air-drawn dagger he did not believe in, but referred its phenomena to their proper source. Between that time and the appearance of Banquo the stability of Macbeth's reason had undergone a fearful ordeal. . . . In the point of view of psychological criticism, the fear of his wife in ii. 2. 33, 34 appears on the eve of being fulfilled by the man, when to sleepless nights, and days of brooding melancholy, is added that undeniable indication of insanity, a credited hallucination . . . Macbeth, however, saved himself from actual insanity by rushing from the maddening horrors of meditation into a course of decisive, resolute action. From henceforth he gave himself no time to reflect; he made the firstlings of his heart the firstlings of his hand; he became a fearful tyrant; but he escaped madness."

Rötscher (*Die Kunst der dramatischen Darstellung*, quoted by Furness) remarks: "The appearance of Banquo's ghost is the direct result of Macbeth's state of mind; the ghost is therefore visible only to him. Everything around and about Macbeth is, for Macbeth, as though it were

* Mrs. Siddons had an idea that Lady Macbeth beheld the spectre, and that her self-control and presence of mind enabled her to appear unconscious of the ghostly presence; but, as Mrs. Jameson remarks, this would be superhuman, and neither the character not the text bears out the supposition.

not; the instant that Banquo's ghost rises, he is completely transported out of himself, and is engrossed solely with the creatures of his brain. The difficult task which the actor has before him, when portraying the effect upon Macbeth of this apparition, is to make us feel in every speech addressed to the ghost that mental horror of the soul, that demoniacal terror of the mind, which communicates itself with irresistible power to every expression of the face and voice. The more conscious Macbeth becomes of this irresistible power, by the reappearance of the ghost, the more horror-stricken does he grow, until at last he is completely unmanned. The gradually increasing effect of this apparition depends, therefore, upon the power the actor has of unfolding the mental distraction, the growing discord, in the soul of Macbeth. Most actors endeavour to portray this climax by mere physical strength of voice, by struggling as it were to make a more powerful impression upon the ghost, whereas the mental horror at the sight of an apparition can only be made truly manifest by the intense strength of a terror which one strives to repress. It is not the heightened voice of passion, growing ever louder and louder, but the trembling tones almost sinking to a whisper, that can give us the true picture of the power of the apparition in this scene. It is Macbeth's vain struggle to command himself, and the dark forces constantly bursting forth with increasing power from his internal consciousness, that we want to see portrayed by the revelation of his mental exhaustion, and by his control over face and voice, weakened by mental terror. Thus alone can this scene be produced as it was in the mind of the poet; assuredly one of the greatest tasks ever set before an actor."

A. Mézières (*Shakespeare, ses Œuvres et ses Critiques*, also quoted by Furness) says on this point: "If the contemporaries of Shakespeare believed in witches, they also believed in spectres, and ghosts permitted to quit their abode of darkness to revisit this upper world. But the poet introduces spirits of a different sort in *Hamlet* and *Macbeth*, when he resuscitates Banquo and the King of Denmark. Are we to believe, as has been asserted, that these shadows are mere phantoms of the brain, appearing only to men of vivid imagination? Undoubtedly Banquo shows himself only to Macbeth, and remains invisible to the guests at table; and Gertrude does not see the spirit of her dead husband at the moment he is visible to their son. But the king's ghost walked in sight of the sentries on the ramparts of Elsinore, before accosting Hamlet. So far is it from the poet's intention to leave in the vague realm of dreams the phantoms he evokes that he is careful to clothe them with garments and with all the external peculiarities of life; he gives gashes to one, and to the other his very armour, his sable-silvered beard, his majesty and measured speech. Herein lies the originality of these apparitions. Possessing in truth only a conventional existence, the magic wand of the poet that invoked them has bestowed on them an appearance of living reality. They play the same part that the traditional dream filled in our classic tragedy, but they play it with all the advantage of action over recital. Instead, like Athalie, of beholding an imaginary vision, Macbeth and Hamlet see with their bodily eyes, the one his victims, the other his father, and these ghosts act more powerfully upon them than any mere dream possibly could. Shakespeare, far bolder than our poets, brings before the very eyes of the spectator those supernatural figures which our stage contents itself with depicting only to the fancy, without producing them to the sight."

50. *Thou canst not say I did it.* This is cited by W. and others as proving that the ghost was Banquo's. K. remarks: "If it be Duncan's ghost, we must read: 'Thou canst not *say* I did it.'"

55. *Upon a thought.* Used by S. only here. It is = "with a thought," which occurs in *Temp.* iv. 1. 64, *J. C.* v. 3. 19, *A. and C.* iv. 14. 9, 1 *Hen. IV.* ii. 4. 241, etc. Cf. *K. John*, iv. 2. 175: "fly like thought;" *L. L. L.* iv. 3. 330: "as swift as thought," etc.

57. *Extend his passion.* Prolong the fit. *Passion* is used by S. of "any violent commotion of the mind" (Schmidt). Cf. iv. 3. 114. On *shall*, see Gr. 315; and on the measure of the next line, Gr. 453.

60. *O proper stuff.* Ironical and contemptuous. *Proper* (=fine, pretty, etc.) is often so used. Cf. 2 *Hen. VI.* i. 1. 132: "A proper jest, and never heard before;" *Hen. VIII.* i. 1. 98: "A proper title of a peace;" *Much Ado*, i. 3. 54: "A proper squire!" On *stuff*, cf. *Temp.* ii. 1. 254: "What stuff is this?" 2 *Hen. IV.* ii. 4. 214: "Here's goodly stuff toward!" etc.

63. *Flaws.* It is of course *flaw*=gust of wind, that is here used figuratively; as in *M. for M.* ii. 3. 11: "the flaws of her own youth," etc.

64. *Impostors to true fear.* "Impostors when compared with true fear" (Mason). See Gr. 187.

65. The C. P. ed. quotes *W. T.* ii. 1. 25:

> "A sad tale 's best for winter: I have one
> Of sprites and goblins."

66. *Authoriz'd by.* Given on the authority of. Cf. *L. C.* 104: "His rudeness so with his authoriz'd youth;" and *Sonn.* 35. 6: "Authorizing thy trespass with compare." S. uses the word in these three places only, and in all with the accent on the second syllable. See Gr. 491.

73. Steevens compares Spenser, *F. Q.* ii. 8, 16:

> "What herce or steed (said he) should he have dight,
> But be entombed in the raven or the kight?"

The stage direction, "Ghost vanishes," which is required by the context, was inserted by Rowe.

76. *Human.* It is "humane" in the folios, in which the modern "human" is nowhere found (Schmidt). The accent is always on the first syllable, not excepting (says Schmidt) *W. T.* iii. 2. 166. In Milton, the modern distinction, in meaning and accent, between *humane* and *human* is recognized. As the C. P. ed. remarks, there are some passages in S. where it is difficult to determine which of the two senses best fits the word; indeed both might be blended in the mind of the writer.

Gentle is proleptic. Cf. i. 6. 3.

80. *There an end.* Cf. *Rich. II.* v. 1. 69.

81. *Mortal.* See on i. 5. 39; and cf. iv. 3. 3.

84. *Lack.* Miss; as in *Cor.* iv. 1. 15, *A. Y. L.* iv. 1. 182, *A. and C.* ii. 2. 172, etc.

85. *Muse.* Wonder. Cf. *V. and A.* 866: "Musing the morning is so much o'erworn;" *T. G. of V.* i. 3. 64: "Muse not that I thus suddenly proceed," etc.

91. *To all and him*, etc. I long to drink his health and that of all; and to wish every one all good. The C. P. ed. quotes *J. C.* iv. 3. 160, *T. of A.* i. 2. 234, and *Hen. VIII.* i. 4. 38.

95. *Speculation.* Cf. *T. and C.* iii. 3. 109. In *Lear*, iii. 1. 24 ("spies and speculations Intelligent of our state"), it is used in a concrete sense = speculators, observers, watchers (Schmidt). The C. P. ed. remarks: "The eyes are called 'speculative instruments' in *Oth.* i. 3. 271. Johnson, quoting this passage, explains 'speculation' by 'the power of sight;' but it means more than this—the intelligence of which the eye is the medium, and which is perceived in the eye of a living man. So the eye is called 'that most pure spirit of sense,' in *T. and C.* iii. 3. 106; and we have the haste that looks through the eyes, i. 2. 46 of this play, and a similar thought, iii. 1. 127. See also 1 *Hen. VI.* ii. 4. 24, and *L. L. L.* v. 2. 848:

'The window of my heart, mine eye.'"

100. *Russian bear.* Cf. *Hen. V.* iii. 7. 154.

101. *Arm'd.* "Armoured;" to use a word applied nowadays to iron-clad ships of war.

For *the Hyrcan tiger*, cf. 3 *Hen. VI.* i. 4. 155: "tigers of Hyrcania," and *Ham.* ii. 2. 472: "the Hyrcanian beast." In *M. of V.* ii. 7. 41, we have "Hyrcanian deserts." Malone quotes Daniel, *Sonnets* (1594): "To Hyrcan tigers, and to ruthless beares;" and Reed adds Riche's *Simonides* (1584): "like to Hyrcan tigers." Hyrcania was a district south and south-east of the Caspian Sea. The C. P. ed. says that these English poets probably derived their ideas of Hyrcania and the tigers from Pliny's *Natural History*, but not through Holland's translation, which was not published till 1601. It seems to us quite as likely that they had in mind Virgil's mention of the beasts in *Æn.* iv. 367: "Hyrcanaeque admorunt ubera tigres."

104. *Dare me to the desert*, etc. Cf. *Rich. II.* i. 1. 62–66.

105. *If trembling I inhabit then.* This is the great *crux* of the play, and space would fail us for enumerating the various emendations and explanations that the critics have suggested. We give the reading and pointing of the 1st folio. The later folios have, "If trembling I inhabit, then protest," etc. Pope changed this to "inhibit, then," which Steevens modified to "inhibit thee." These are the most plausible of the many readings proposed, but on the whole we prefer to keep to the folio. W. explains the passage: "If I then am encompassed by trembling, and so, if I inhabit trembling—a use of *inhabit* highly figurative and exceedingly rare, but which is neither illogical nor without example." Cf. *Psalms*, xxii. 3: "O thou that inhabitest the praises of Israel." Schmidt makes *inhabit* = "to take as a habit (whether a costume or a custom), to do on." Moberly renders it, "If I keep house, shrink under shelter," but prefers "I inhibit thee." Henley and St. take it to be = "If I, through fear, remain trembling in my castle." Cf. Milton, *P. L.* vii. 163: "Meanwhile inhabit lax, ye powers of heaven" (that is, dwell at large—Cice-

ro's "habitare laxe"). Steevens thinks that *inhabit* may mean "stay within doors," and cites *A. Y. L.* iii. 3. 10: "O knowledge, ill-inhabited! worse than Jove in a thatched house!" (that is, ill-lodged).

106. *The baby of a girl.* Walker, D., W., Moberly, Schmidt, and others make *baby*=doll; the C. P. ed. explains it as "infant," the other meaning not being found elsewhere in S. It occurs, however, in Sidney, Jonson, and other writers of the time. Walker quotes Sidney, *Arcadia:* "young babes think babies of wondrous excellency, and yet the babies are but babies;" and *Astrophel and Stella:* "Sweet babes must babies have, but shrewd girls must be beaten."

107. *Mockery.* "Mimicry, delusive imitation" (Schmidt). Cf. *Rich. II.* iv. 1. 260, and *Hen. V.* iv. prol. 53.

109. *Displac'd.* "Banished" (Schmidt). On *broke*, see Gr. 343.

110. *Admir'd.* To be wondered at, strange; if it be not used ironically=admirable.

111. *Overcome.* Spread over, overshadow. Farmer quotes Spenser, *F. Q.* iii. 7, 4: "All coverd with thick woodes that quite it overcame."

112, 113. *You make me strange*, etc. "You render me a stranger to, or forgetful of, the brave disposition which I know I possess, and make me fancy myself a coward, when I perceive that I am terrified by a sight that has not in the least alarmed you" (Malone). So Schmidt makes *disposition* here="natural constitution of the mind." The C. P. ed. takes it to mean "temporary mood," as in *Lear*, i. 4. 241, and *Ham.* i. 5. 172, and adds: "The general sense of the present passage may therefore be thus expressed: 'You make me a stranger even to my own feelings, unable to comprehend the motive of my fear.' He is not addressing his wife alone, but the whole company. He is particularly staggered by the fact that every one except himself is unmoved."

For *owe*=own, possess, see i. 3. 76, i. 4. 10, etc.

116. *Mine.* Possibly, as some explain it, referring to *ruby*, not to *cheeks;* but S. did not always trouble himself to make his pronouns agree in number with their antecedents. He very often has a singular *relative* (or at least one used as the subject of a singular verb) with a plural antecedent; as in *Cymb.* i. 6. 117: "your graces that charms." See many other examples in Gr. 247. W., following Hanmer and Johnson, reads "cheek," because "S., when he makes the cheek a sign, or exponent, or type, uses the word in the singular number." But see v. 3. 16: "those linen cheeks of thine;" 1 *Hen. IV.* ii. 3. 47: "Why hast thou lost the fresh blood in thy cheeks?" *T. A.* iii. 2. 38: "her sorrow, mesh'd upon her cheeks;" *K. John*, ii. 1. 225: "To save unscratch'd your city's threaten'd cheeks;" *Rich. II.* iii. 3. 57: "the cloudy cheeks of heaven" (but in *Temp.* i. 2. 4: "the welkin's cheek"); and many similar passages in which W. himself has the plural.

119. *Stand not*, etc. That is, do not be particular about retiring in the order of your rank (as court etiquette required). Cf. the first line of this scene.

122. *It will have blood*, etc. The 1st folio reads:

"It will haue blood they say:
Blood will haue blood:"

and this pointing is followed by the later folios. The arrangement in the text was proposed by Theo., and adopted by Capell and Malone; also by Coll., St., W., and Delius in our day. Most of the other editors follow Whalley and Johnson in reading: "It will have blood; they say blood will have blood." Johnson observes: "Macbeth justly infers that the death of Duncan cannot go unpunished, 'It will have blood!' then after a short pause declares it as the general observation of mankind that murderers cannot escape." Capell thinks that the line is "injured in the solemnity of the movement" by the change in pointing, and that "the proverb's naked repeating, coming after words that insinuate it, has great effect." The question between the two readings is a very close one.

123. *Stones*, etc. Mr. Paton (*Notes and Queries*, Nov. 6, 1869, cited by Furness) suggests that there may be an allusion "to the rocking stones, or 'stones of judgment,' by which it was thought the Druids tested the guilt or innocence of accused persons." There was one of these stones near Glamis Castle, and if S. visited Scotland (see p. 15) he probably saw it.

Trees to speak may allude to the story of Polydorus in Virgil, *Æn.* iii. 22–68 (Steevens).

124. *Augurs*, etc. The folios have "Augures," retained by Rowe, Pope, Sr., and the Camb. and C. P. eds. Schmidt is doubtful whether the word means *augurs* or *auguries*. The C. P. ed. says: "In Florio's *Ital. Dict.* 1611, the word 'augure' is given as the equivalent both for *augurio*, soothsaying, and *auguro*, a soothsayer. In the edition of 1598 'augure' is only given as the translation of *augurio*, and it is in this sense that it is used here. The word occurs nowhere else in S. For 'augur' in our modern sense he uses 'augurer,' *J. C.* ii. 1. 200 and ii. 2. 37; *Cor.* ii. 1. 1; *A. and C.* iv. 12. 4 and v. 2. 337. We find 'augure' used in the sense of 'augur' or 'augurer,' in Holland's *Pliny*, viii. 28, which was published in 1601."

Augur is not found in the *plays* of S., but it occurs in *Sonn.* 107. 6: "And the sad augurs mock their own presage;" and in *The Phœnix and the Turtle*, 7: "Augur of the fever's end."

Delius remarks that S. sometimes uses *and* to connect words which are "subordinate, not co-ordinate," and that the meaning here is, "the relations understood by augurs." Moberly explains it, "augurs by the help of understood relations between omens and events." Rowe changed the text to "Augurs that understood;" and Warb. and Johnson to "Augurs that understand;" the latter explaining *relations* as "the connection of effects with causes."

125. *Magot-pies*, etc. Nares explains *magot-pie* as "the bird now called, by abbreviation, a *mag-pie*." Minsheu and Cotgrave both have *maggatapie*, and Middleton *magot o' pie*. See Wb.

Chough, according to Schmidt, is the *Corvus monedula*. Cf. *Temp.* ii. 1. 266: "I myself could make A chough of as deep chat," and see note in our ed. p. 127.

126. *Secret'st*. See on *kind'st*, ii. 1. 24. Gr. 473.

What="in what state, how far advanced" (Gr. 253).

127. *At odds.* At variance, contesting; as in *M. W.* iii. 1. 54; *Rich. III.* ii. 1. 70, etc.

The C. P. ed. remarks: "Lady Macbeth, worn out by the effort she has made to maintain her self-possession in the presence of her guests, answers briefly and mournfully to her husband's questions, adding no word of comment, much less of reproach. Thus the part was rendered by Miss Helen Faucit, one of the best of all modern interpreters of Shakespeare." Cf. what Mrs. Jameson says, p. 22 above.

128. *How say'st thou,* etc. "What do you think of this circumstance, that Macduff refuses to come," etc. (Mason). Schmidt compares *T. G. of V.* ii. 5. 43, and *M. of V.* i. 2. 58. On *deny*=refuse, cf. *Temp.* i. 2. 80, *M. of V.* iii. 3. 26, *Rich II.* ii. 1. 204, etc. See also iv. 1. 104 below.

130. *By the way.* Indirectly, casually.

131. *A one.* See Gr. 81. Theo. reads "a Thane," and W. "a man." In *T. of A.* v. 1. 96 we have "There 's never a one." Walker says that the old poets ordinarily write *an one*, not *a one*; but, as Schmidt notes, S. generally has *a one*.

136. *I am in blood,* etc. For the repetition of *in*, cf. *Cor.* ii. 1. 18. Gr. 407.

The C. P. ed. cites *M. N. D.* iii. 2. 47–49. Steevens remarks that Dryden borrows the figure in *Œdipus*, iv. 1:

> "I have already pass'd
> The middle of the stream; and to return
> Seems greater labour than to venture o'er."

138. *As go o'er.* On the construction, see Gr. 384.

140. *Scann'd.* "Examined nicely" (Steevens). Cf. *Ham.* iii. 3. 75, and *Oth.* iii. 3. 245.

141. *The season of all natures.* "That which keeps them fresh" (Schmidt).

142. *Self-abuse.* Self-deception. See on ii. 1. 50.

143. *The initiate fear.* The fear of a novice, or of one who has not had "hard use" (hardening experience) in crime.

144. *In deed.* The folios have "indeed." The correction is due to Theo.

SCENE V.—The C. P. editors believe that "if this scene had occurred in a drama not attributed to Shakespeare, no one would have discovered in it any trace of Shakespeare's manner." Fleay also rejects it. See p. 12 above. It is almost certainly an interpolation.

S. has been criticised for introducing the classical Hecate in connection with modern witches; but Scot (*Discovery of Witchcraft*) mentions it as the common opinion of all writers that witches were supposed to have nightly "meetings with Herodias and the Pagan gods," and that "in the night-times they ride abroad with *Diana*, the goddess of the Pagans," etc. *Hecate* is only another name for Diana. Cf. Virgil, *Æn.* iv. 511: "Tergeminamque Hecaten, tria virginis ora Dianae."

1. *Hecate.* For the pronunciation, see on ii. 1. 52. It is a trisyllable in 1 *Hen. VI.* iii. 2. 64. Milton makes it a dissyllable in *Comus*, 135, but

a trisyllable in *Comus*, 535, the only other instance in which he uses the word.

Angerly. Angrily. See Gr. 447, and cf. *K. John*, iv. 1. 82.

7. *Close.* Secret. Cf. *R. and J.* i. 1. 155; *Cymb.* iii. 5. 86, etc.

13. *Loves.* As the C. P. ed. remarks, there is no hint elsewhere in the play of Macbeth's pretending love to the witches. Halliwell is "inclined to think that *loves* is an error for *lives*;" and St. conjectures "loves *evil* for," which makes the measure the same as that of the other line in the couplet.

15. *Acheron.* "The witches are poetically made to give this name to some foul tarn or gloomy pool in the neighbourhood of Macbeth's castle, where they habitually assemble" (Clarke).

23. *The corner of the moon.* Cf. Milton, *Comus*, 1016:

> "And from thence can soar as soon
> To the corners of the moon."

24. *Profound.* "Having deep or hidden qualities" (Johnson). The C. P. ed. explains it, "deep, and therefore ready to fall." Steevens suggests that the *vaporous drop* is "meant for the same as the *virus lunare* of the ancients, being a foam which the moon was supposed to shed on particular herbs or other objects, when strongly solicited by enchantment." Lucan mentions it, *Pharsalia*, vi. 666:

> "Et virus large lunare ministrat."

26. *Sleights.* Artifices. S. uses the word only here and in 3 *Hen. VI.* iv. 2. 20.

27. *Artificial.* Produced by art, or made visible by art. The word means "artful" in *M. N. D.* iii. 2. 203: "like two artificial gods."

29. *Confusion.* Destruction. See on ii. 3. 47.

31. *'Bove.* See Gr. 460.

32. *Security.* Carelessness. Cf. *Rich. II.* iii. 2. 34, and see note in our ed. p. 189.

Moberly quotes Webster, *Duchess of Malfi*, v. 2:

> "Security some men call the suburbs of hell,
> Only a dead wall between."

33. The folio has the stage direction, "*Sing within. Come away, come away, &c.*" It undoubtedly refers to the following "Song" in *The Witch* of Middleton:

> "*Song above.*
> Come away, come away,
> Hecate, Hecate, come away!
> *Hec.* I come, I come, I come, I come,
> With all the speed I may,
> With all the speed I may.
> Where 's Stadlin?
> [*Voice above.*] Here.
> *Hec.* Where 's Puckle?
> [*Voice above.*] Here;
> And Hoppo too, and Hellwain too;
> We lack but you, we lack but you;
> Come away, make up the count.
> *Hec.* I will but 'noint, and then I mount.
> [*A Spirit like a cat descends.*

[*Voice above.*] There 's one comes down to fetch his dues,
A kiss, a coll, a sip of blood;
And why thou stay'st so long
I muse, I muse,
Since the air 's so sweet and good.
Hec. O, art thou come?
What news, what news?
Spirit. All goes still to our delight:
Either come, or else
Refuse, refuse.
Hec. Now I 'm furnish'd for the flight.
Fire. Hark, hark, the cat sings a brave treble in her own language;
Hec. [*going up.*] Now I go, now I fly,
Malkin my sweet spirit and I.
O what a dainty pleasure 't is
To ride in the air
When the moon shines fair,
And sing and dance, and toy and kiss!
Over woods, high rocks, and mountains,
Over seas, our mistress' fountains,
Over steep* towers and turrets,
We fly by night, 'mongst troops of spirits:
No ring of bells to our ears sounds,
No howls of wolves, no yelps of hounds;
No, not the noise of water's breach,
Or cannon's throat our height can reach.
[*Voices above.*] No ring of bells," etc.

In Davenant's version of *Macbeth*, this passage is inserted, with some variations, and until the MS. of *The Witch* was discovered it was supposed to be his composition. Dyce remarks: "It is so highly fanciful, and comes in so happily where Davenant has placed it, that one is almost tempted to believe it was written by Shakespeare, and had been omitted in the printed copies of his play."

The C. P. ed. suggests that "from what Hecate says, 'Hark, I am called,' it is probable that she took no part in the song, which perhaps consisted only of the two first lines of the passage from Middleton."

SCENE VI.—*Enter Lennox and another Lord.* As there seems to be no reason for introducing a nameless character here, Johnson conjectured that the original copy had "*Lennox and An.*," meant for "*Lennox and Angus*," but mistaken by the transcriber.

Flathe remarks: "It is not without significance that in this scene there is frequent mention of most pious men and holy angels. Such mention is meant to remind us that there is a moral force always present in the world, ready to come forth victorious in its time and place."

1. *Have but hit your thoughts.* "Were only intended to stir your thoughts" (Moberly); or, more likely, *hit*=agreed with.

2. *Only.* On the position of the word, see Gr. 420.

3. *Borne.* Managed, conducted. Cf. line 17 below; also 2 *Hen. IV.* iv. 4. 88; *Cor.* v. 3. 4, etc.

* Davenant gives "Over steeples, towers, and turrets," which is probably the true reading. In another part of the play, Hecate says "In moonlight nights, on steeple-tops," etc.

4. *Marry.* Probably a corruption of *Mary*, and originally a mode of swearing by the Virgin. It is often, as here, equivalent to a monosyllable. Gr. 463. On *of* = by, see Gr. 170.

8. *Who cannot want*, etc. A much controverted passage. The sense, as Malone pointed out, seems to require *can* instead of *cannot*. Coll. explains it, "Who cannot but think," etc. Delius (trans. by Furness) says: "As S. sometimes, in order to express a single negative, multiplies the negatives *not*, *nor*, *never*, etc., so on the other hand he sometimes adds them, as in this case, to negative verbs or particles without altering the sense. Thus in *W. T.* iii. 2. 55:

> "That any of these bolder vices wanted
> Less impudence;"

and in *Cymb.* i. 4. 23: 'a beggar without less quality,' the negative *less* merely strengthens the negative already included in *wanted* and *without*." If we do not adopt this explanation (cf. *A. Y. L.* p. 156, note on 12), we must consider it one of the accidental "confusions of construction" which are so common in S. Cf. Gr. 409–416.

White, who in his *Shakespeare's Scholar* (p. 403) suggested making the sentence declarative instead of interrogative, and joining it to the preceding one ("Men must not walk too late who cannot help thinking," etc.), afterwards in his ed. of S. returned to the original reading, a more careful consideration of the passage having led him "unwillingly" to the belief that Malone may have been right, and that "the disagreement between the words and the thought is due to a confusion of thought which S. may have sometimes shared with inferior intellects."

Monstrous (which Capell printed "monsterous") is metrically a trisyllable. Gr. 477.

10. *Fact.* Delius points out that S. uses this word only in a bad sense = an evil deed; never in the sense of reality as opposed to fiction. The only meaning Schmidt gives for the word is "evil deed, crime." It occurs in S. fourteen times: *R. of L.* 239, 349; *M. for M.* iv. 2. 141, v. 1. 439; *A. W.* iii. 7. 47; *W. T.* iii. 2. 86; 1 *Hen. VI.* iv. 1. 30; 2 *Hen. VI.* i. 3. 176, ii. 1. 173; *T. A.* iv. 1. 39; *T. of A.* iii. 5. 16; *Cymb.* iii. 2. 17; *Per.* iv. 3. 12, and the present passage. If it is a mere coincidence that the word always has this bad sense, it is curious enough to be worth noting.

13. *Thralls.* Slaves, bondmen. S. uses the noun six times, and always in this sense except in *P. P.* 266, where it means slavery. Cf. 1 *Hen. VI.* i. 2. 117, ii. 3. 36; *Rich. III.* iv. 1. 46; and *Sonn.* 154. 12.

19. *An 't.* The folios, as elsewhere, have "And 't." See Gr. 101, 102, 103.

21. *From.* In consequence of, on account of. Cf. *Hen. VIII.* i. 1. 152; *Ham.* ii. 2. 580, etc. (Schmidt).

Broad. Free, unrestrained. Cf. *Ham.* iii. 4. 2: "his pranks have been too broad to bear with;" *T. of A.* iii. 4. 64: "Who can speak broader than he that has no house to put his head in? Such may rail against great buildings." See also iii. 4. 23 above.

On *'cause*, see Gr. 460.

Fail'd His presence. Failed to be present. Cf. iii. 1. 27: "Fail not our feast;" *Lear*, ii. 4. 144: "Would fail her obligation," etc.

24. *Bestows himself.* See on iii. 1. 29.

25. *Tyrant.* Perhaps = usurper, like the Greek τύραννος (Schmidt). Cf. *A. Y. L.* ii. 1. 61:

> "Swearing that we
> Are mere usurpers, tyrants, and what 's worse;"

and 3 *Hen. VI.* iii. 3. 69:

> "For how can tyrants safely govern home,
> Unless abroad they purchase great alliance?
> To prove him tyrant this reason may suffice,
> That Henry liveth still."

Holds = withholds.

27. *The most pious Edward.* Edward the Confessor. On *of* = by, cf. line 4 above. Gr. 170.

30. On the measure, see Gr. 498; and on *upon* = "for the purpose of," Gr. 191. Cf. *Oth.* i. 1. 100.

35. *Free.* Schmidt makes it here = "remove, do away," and compares *Cymb.* iii. 6. 80: "Would I could free 't!" Malone made the plausible suggestion that the line originally stood, "Our feasts and banquets free from bloody knives."

36. *Free honours.* "Either honours *freely bestowed*, not purchased by crimes; or honours *without slavery*, without dread of a tyrant" (Johnson). The C. P. ed. explains it: "Honours such as freemen receive from a lawful king."

38. *Exasperate.* Cf. *T. and C.* v. 1. 34: "Why art thou then exasperate?" So "consecrate" (*T. A.* i. 1. 14; *M. N. D.* v. 1. 422), "create" (*M. N. D.* v. 1. 412), and sundry other words directly derived from Latin perfect participles. See Gr. 342. Cf. Milton, *P. L.* iii. 6: "Bright effluence of bright essence increate;" *Id.* iii. 208: "But to destruction sacred and devote," etc. Examples might be added from the poets of our own time.

41. *Cloudy.* Frowning. Delius explains it as "foreboding, ominous;" the C. P. ed., "gloomy, sullen." Cf. 2 *Hen. VI.* iii. 1. 155: "cloudy brow." Sometimes it means "under a cloud," sorrowing; as in *Rich. III.* ii. 2. 112: "You cloudy princes and heart-sorrowing peers;" *R. of L.* 1084: "But cloudy Lucrece shames herself to see," etc. On *me*, see Gr. 220.

42. *As who should say.* See Gr. 257. Cf. *M. of V.* i. 2. 45, *Rich. II.* v. 4. 8, etc.

48, 49. *Our suffering country*, etc. That is, our country suffering under, etc. Gr. 419*a*. Cf. *Hen. VIII.* iii. 1. 134: "a constant woman to her husband; *Rich. II.* iii. 1. 9: "A happy gentleman in blood and lineaments," etc. See also v. 8. 7 below:

> "thou bloodier villain
> Than terms can give thee out."

OAK IN BIRNAM WOOD.

ACT IV.

SCENE I.—The C. P. editors remark : "The rich vocabulary, prodigal fancy, and terse diction displayed in iv. 1. 1–38, show the hand of a master, and make us hesitate in ascribing the passage to any one but the master himself. There is, however, a conspicuous falling-off in lines 39–47, after the entrance of Hecate."

Fleay rejects 39–44 and 94–100 ("That will never be. . . . mortal custom"). The *Hecate* part is probably spurious, as in iii. 5 above.

1. *Brinded.* Meaning the same as *brindled*, which (see Wb.) is a "diminutive" of it. S. uses it only here. Milton has it twice (*P. L.* vii. 466 ; *Comus*, 443), in both cases applied to the lion.

2. *Thrice and once.* Theo. wished to read "Twice and once ;" because, "as Virgil has remarked, 'Numero Deus impare gaudet,' and three and nine are the numbers used in all enchantments." Many editors point it thus, "Thrice ; and once."

Hedge-pig. Krauth (quoted by Furness) remarks : "The urchin, or hedge-hog, is nocturnal in its habits, weird in its movements; plants wither where it works, for it cuts off their roots. Fairies of one class were supposed to assume its form. *Urchin* came to mean *fairy* without reference to the hedge-hog shape; hence, because fairies are little and mischievous, it came to be applied to a child."

3. *Harpier*. Some eds. have "Harper," others "Harpy." It may be a corruption of the latter word.

'T is time, etc. This is not what "Harpier cries," as some have understood it. Cf. the Hecate of Middleton:

> "*Hecate.* Heard you the owle yet?
> *Stadlin.* Briefely in the copps.
> *Hecate.* 'T is high time for us then."

Cries = "gives them the signal" (Steevens).

5. *In the poison'd entrails throw.* Guizot translates the line "Jetons *dans* ses entrailles empoisonnées," and adds the note: "Shakespeare met souvent ainsi dans la bouche de ses sorcières des phrases interrompues, auxquelles elles semblent attacher un sens complet."

6. *Cold* is a dissyllable (Gr. 484). There is a shiver in the prolongation of the word. Cf. 3 *Hen. VI.* iv. 3. 14: "While he himself keeps in the cold field." Many eds. read "the cold;" some, "coldest."

8. *Venom.* Cf. 3 *Hen. VI.* ii. 2. 138: "venom toads;" *A. Y. L.* ii. 1. 13: "the toad, ugly and venomous;" *Rich. III.* i. 2. 148: "Never hung poison on a fouler toad;" and many other passages in which the same idea occurs. Hunter says: "There is a paper by Dr. Davy in the *Philosophical Transactions* of 1826, in which it is shown that the toad *is* venomous, and moreover that 'sweltered venom' is peculiarly proper, the poison lying diffused over the body immediately under the skin. This is the second instance in this play of Shakespeare's minute exactness in his natural history." Whether Dr. Davy, in his dissection of the toad, found also the "precious jewel in his head," is not stated.

16. *Blind-worm.* The slow-worm. Cf. *M. N. D.* ii. 2. 11: "Newts and blind-worms." In *T. of A.* iv. 3. 182, it is called the "eyeless venom'd worm." Steevens cites Drayton, *Noah's Flood*, 481: "The small-eyed slow-worm held of many blind;" and the C. P. ed. quotes the Suffolk proverb:

> "If the viper could hear and the slow-worm could see,
> Then England from serpents would never be free."

17. *Howlet's.* The old spelling, altered in some eds. to "owlet's." Cf. Holland's *Pliny*, x. 17: "Of Owles, or Howlets."

22. *Mummy.* Cf. *Oth.* iii. 4. 74:

> "there 's magic in the web of it:
> . . . .
> The worms were hallow'd that did breed the silk;
> And it was dyed in mummy which the skilful
> Conserv'd of maidens' hearts."

The C. P. ed. remarks that mummy was used as a medicine both long before and long after the time of S. Sir Thomas Browne tells us that Francis I. always carried mummy with him as a panacea against all disorders. He adds: "The common opinion of the virtues of mummy bred great consumption thereof, and princes and great men contended for this strange panacea, wherein Jews dealt largely, manufacturing mummies from dead carcases, and giving them the names of kings, while specifics were compounded from crosses and gibbet leavings." The same author, in his *Hydriotaphia* (ch. v.), says: "The Egyptian mummies which Cambyses spared, avarice now consumeth. Mummy is become merchandize; Mizraim cures wounds, and Pharaoh is sold for balsams." Cf. Webster, *The White Devil*, i. 1:

> "Your followers
> Have swallowed you like mummia, and, being sick
> With such unnatural and horrid physic,
> Vomit you up i' the kennel."

Maw and gulf. On *maw*, cf. iii. 4. 73 above. *Gulf* = gullet. Schmidt compares *R. of L.* 557, and *Cor.* i. 1. 101.

24. *Ravin'd.* Ravenous; like *ravin* in *A. W.* iii. 2. 129: "the ravin lion." See on ii. 4. 28. Steevens quotes P. Fletcher, *Locusts*, iii. 18: "his raven'd prey."

25. *Digg'd.* The only form used by S. for the past tense and participle of *dig*. Cf. *Rich. II.* iii. 3. 169; *T. A.* v. 1. 135, etc. The same is true of Milton (see *P. L.* i. 690, vi. 516, etc.) and of the *A. V.* (*Gen.* xlix. 6, l. 5; *Exod.* vii. 24, etc.).

27. *Yew.* This tree was reckoned poisonous (Douce).

28. *Sliver'd.* This word, which is common in this country (at least in New England), must be less familiar in England, as D. and others think it necessary to explain it.

Eclipse. An unlucky time. Cf. *Sonn.* 107. 5:

> "The mortal moon hath her eclipse endur'd,
> And the sad augurs mock their own presage."

See also Milton, *Lycidas*, 101:

> "It was that fatal and perfidious bark,
> Built in the eclipse, and rigg'd with curses dark."

32. *Slab.* Viscous, glutinous. *Slabby* has the same meaning. Cf. Selden (quoted by Wb.): "you must drink of a slabby stuff."

33. *Chaudron.* Entrails. Steevens found in a cookery book, printed in 1597, a receipt "to make a pudding of a calf's chaldron." Cf. Decker, *H. W.*: "calves' chauldrons and chitterlings." At the coronation feast of Elizabeth of York, queen of Henry VII., one of the dishes was "a swan with chaudron," meaning sauce made with its entrails.

37. *Baboon's.* Accented here on the first syllable, but on the second in *T. of A.* i. 1. 260: "Into baboon and monkey," etc. Cf. Gr. 490.

38. The stage direction in the folios is "*Enter Hecat, and the other three Witches*;" but there is no good reason for supposing that there are any other witches in the scene than those already on the stage. Steevens suggested that others might be brought in to join in the coming dance. The Camb. ed. reads "Enter Hecate to the other three Witches."

43. The stage direction is from the 1st folio. The "Song" is found in *The Witch* of Middleton, where it begins thus:

> "Black spirits and white, red spirits and gray,
> Mingle, mingle, mingle, you that mingle may!"

Davenant introduced this much of it into his version, but did not change "Red" to "Blue," as the C. P. ed. states. That change was made by Rowe, who inserted the lines here in *Macbeth*, and was followed by Pope and other editors until Steevens restored "Red" in 1785.

44. *Pricking*, etc. "It is a very ancient superstition that all sudden pains of the body, which could not naturally be accounted for, were presages of somewhat that was shortly to happen. Hence Upton has explained a passage in the *Miles Gloriosus* of Plautus: 'Timeo quod rerum gesserim hic, ita *dorsus totus prurit*'" (Steevens).

50. *Conjure*. "Used by S. always with the accent on the first syllable, except in *R. and J.* ii. 1. 26, and *Oth.* i. 3. 105" (C. P. ed.). Add *Ham.* v. 1. 279: "Conjures the wandering stars, and makes them stand."

53. *Yesty*. Foamy. Cf. *Ham.* v. 2. 198, where it is used figuratively = light, frivolous (Schmidt).

55. *Bladed*. In the blade. Cf. *M. N. D.* i. 1. 211: "the bladed grass." As corn in the blade is not liable to be "lodged," Coll. follows his MS. corrector, who has "bleaded," a provincial word = ripe, ready for the sickle. On *lodg'd* (= thrown down, laid), cf. *Rich. II.* iii. 3. 162.

57. *Slope*. S. has the word nowhere else, either as verb or noun. Its transitive use here is peculiar. The Coll. MS. substitutes "stoop," which had been suggested by Capell.

59. *Germens*. Germs, seeds. The folios have "germaine" or "germain." Pope gave "germains," which he explained as "relations, or kindred elements." *Germens* (spelled by him "germins," as by most editors) was first suggested by Theo. Cf. *Lear*, iii. 2. 8: "Crack nature's moulds, all germens spill at once" ("germaines" or "germains" in the early eds.).

60. *Sicken*. Be surfeited. Cf. *T. N.* i. 1. 3.

Masters. The pointing of the folio. Pope gave "master's?" which is followed by many modern editors, though the interrogation point should not be used with *indirect* questions. Some eds. adopt Capell's "masters'?"

65. *Farrow*. A litter of pigs. Steevens cites the law of Kenneth II., of Scotland, given by Holinshed: "If a sowe eate hir pigges, let hyr be stoned to death and buried."

On *sweaten*, see Gr. 344.

68. As Upton remarks, the *armed head* represents symbolically Macbeth's head cut off and brought to Malcolm by Macduff (v. 8. 53). The *bloody child* is Macduff (v. 8. 15). The *child crowned, with a tree in his hand*, is the royal Malcolm (v. 4. 4).

78. *Had I three ears*, etc. H. compares the expression still in use, "I listened with all the ears I had." Whately (*Rhetoric*, iv. 2. 2), in illustrating the imperfection of any system of marks or signs to indicate tones in elocution, says of this passage: "No one would dispute that the stress is to be laid on the word *three*, and thus much might be indicated to the reader's eye; but if he had nothing else to trust to, he might chance to deliver the passage in such a manner as to be utterly absurd; for it is possible to pronounce the emphatic word *three* in such a tone as to indicate that 'since he has but *two* ears he cannot hear.'"

80. *For none*, etc. Simrock (*Die Quellen des Shakespeare*, quoted by Furness) remarks: "This prediction we can trace in '*Prince Wladimir and his Table-round*' (Leipzig, 1819), where the same prophecy is made over the cradle of the hero Tugarin, the son of a snake. In the *Sháh-náma* of Firdausi, Rustum* was born as was Macduff. And in many other instances heroes and demi-gods were similarly ushered into the world, and it always implied power and heroic strength. Such an one was Wölsung, Sigurd's ancestor. It was, however, not the case with the unborn Burkart, Burchardus ingenitus, whose skin remained always so tender that every gnat brought blood, and his tutor was therefore obliged to abolish the rod utterly, and after all he grew up a learned and virtuous man."

84. *And take a bond of fate*. The C. P. ed. remarks: "Macbeth has just been assured that Macduff, whom he supposes to be comprised among those 'of woman born,' shall not harm him. By slaying Macduff he will bind fate to perform the promise, he will put it out of fate's power to break the promise, 'referring,' says Mr. Rushton (*Shakespeare a Lawyer*, p. 20), 'not to a single, but to a conditional bond, under or by virtue of which, when forfeited, double the principal sum was recoverable.' In iii. 2. 49 the same figure is used with a different application."

85. *Pale-hearted fear*. See on ii. 2. 65.

88. *The round*, etc. On *round*, cf. i. 5. 26; and on *top* (which, as Schmidt points out, is used metaphorically, and not in the prosaic literal sense of "the ornament that rises above" the crown, as Johnson explains it), *Temp.* iii. 1. 38: "the top of admiration;" 2 *Hen. VI.* i. 2. 49: "the top of honour;" *M. for M.* ii. 2. 76: "the top of judgment," etc.

92. Simrock (see on line 80 above) remarks that the incident of the moving forest is found in various myths: "It corresponds closely to the story of King Grünewald, which Professor Schwarz has preserved in his Hessian *Notabilia* derived from oral tradition. 'A King had an only daughter, who possessed *wondrous gifts*. Now, once upon a time there came his enemy, a King named Grünewald, and besieged him in his castle, and, as the siege lasted long, the daughter kept continually encouraging her father in the castle. This lasted till May-day. Then all of a sudden the daughter saw the hostile army approach with green boughs: then fear and anguish fell on her, *for she knew that all was lost*, and said to her father—

> "Father, you must yield, or die,
> I see the green-wood drawing nigh."'

See Grimm's *German Popular Tales*, i. 148. Here the correspondence to the legend of Macbeth is not to be mistaken. The daughter plays the same part here as the witches there. She knows, by means of her miraculous gifts, that her father cannot be conquered till the green-wood moves upon them; but, as she considers this impossible, she incites him to confidence; but when the supposed impossible incident actually comes to pass, she counsels him to surrender. On the other

---

* The "Hercules of Persia," as he is termed by Mr. Fitzgerald in his exquisite rendering of the *Rubáiyát of Omar Khayyám* (Furness).

hand, no prophecy appears to have anticipated the cunning of Fredegunda, who hung bells on her horses, and ordered each of her warriors to take a bough in his hand, and thus to march against the enemy; whereby the sentinels of the hostile camp were deceived, believing their horses were browsing in the neighbouring forest, until the Franks let their boughs fall, and the forest stood leafless, but thick with the shafts of glancing spears. (See Grimm's *German Popular Tales*, ii. 91.) It was merely a military stratagem; just as Malcolm, when he commanded his soldiers, on their forward march, to conceal themselves with boughs. had no other end in view, for he knew not what had been prophesied to Macbeth. The following passage from Joh. Weyer, *De Præstigiis*, Frankfurt, 1586, p. 329, is noteworthy: 'Whoever wishes to give himself the appearance of having a thousand men or horse round him, let him have a year-old willow bough cut off at a single stroke, with certain conjurations, repetition of barbarous words, and rude characters.' A single man might really find some difficulty in giving himself, by the use of this boasted charm, the appearance of a whole army; but the inventor evidently founded his pretension upon a popular legend, according to which a bold army had, by this artifice, concealed its weakness from an enemy superior in numbers. According to Holinshed, however, Malcolm's army was superior in number to that of Macbeth, and the concealment with the boughs was only made use of in order that, when they were thrown away, sudden vision of the superiority of numbers might create more terror. In my *Manual of German Mythology*, p. 557, it is shown that the legend of the moving forest originated in the German religious custom of May-festivals, or Summer-welcomings, and that 'King Grünewald' is originally a Winter-giant, whose dominion ceases when the May-feast begins and the green-wood draws nigh. This is the mythical basis of the Macbeth legend."

Halliwell says: "The incident of cutting down the branches of trees is related in the old romance life of Alexander the Great, thus translated in the Thornton MS., in the library of Lincoln Cathedral: 'In the mene tyme, Kyng Alexander remowed his oste, and drew nere the citè of Susis, in the whilke Darius was lengand the same tyme, so that he mygte see alle the heghe hillez that ware abowune the citee. Than Alexander commanded alle his mene that ilkane of thame suld cutte downe a brawnche of a tree, and bere thame furth with thame, and dryfe bifore thame alle manere of bestez that thay mygte fynde in the way; and, when the Percyenes saw thame fra the heghe hillez, thay wondred thame gretly.'"

93. *Birnam wood*, etc. The village of Birnam is a modern suburb of the beautiful town of Dunkeld, which is about sixteen miles from Perth by road or railway. Birnam Hill (1580 feet high) rises in front of the village, at present almost bare of trees, though an attempt is being made to clothe it again with fir saplings taken from the original "Birnam Wood." In the rear of the hotel are two trees, an oak (see cut on p. 227) and a plane, which are believed to be a remnant of this famous forest. The Dunsinane hills, twelve miles distant, are visible from the northern side of Birnam Hill, which, as a recent writer remarks, "is pre-

cisely the point where a general, in full march towards Dunsinane, would be likely to pause to survey the plain which he must cross, and from this spot would the leafy screen devised by Malcolm become necessary to conceal the number of the advancing army."

Dunsinane is here accented on the second syllable; but elsewhere in the play on the last syllable, or the first and last. The C. P. ed. says that the former is the local pronunciation, and that the word is now spelt "Dunsinnan." The statement in regard to the pronunciation is confirmed by *Chambers's Encyclopædia* (though Lippincott's *Gazetteer* gives the other accent), but the spelling is "Dunsinnane" in both these authorities. In Black's *Picturesque Guide to Scotland* (Edinburgh, 1875), as in Murray's, it is "Dunsinane."

95. *Impress.* Press (as in *Rich. II.* iii. 2. 58, etc.), force into his service. Cf. 1 *Hen. IV.* i. 1. 21, etc.

96. *Bodements.* Prophecies. Used by S. only here and in *T. and C.* v. 3. 80.

97. *Rebellion's head.* The folio has "Rebellious dead," which is retained by Davenant, Rowe, Pope, and Halliwell. The last defends it on the ground that Macbeth, confiding in the prophecy that none of woman born could harm him, would fear nothing but the reappearance of the dead, as in the case of Banquo's ghost; and this fear would be relieved by the second prophecy. But the emendation in the text (due to Theo.) yields a simpler sense, and is adopted by most of the modern editors. Some prefer "Rebellious head."

98. *Our high-plac'd Macbeth.* This seems strange in Macbeth's mouth, and we have seen no satisfactory explanation of it. Moberly says: "He who is so called by his subjects. So a Greek master called himself *αὐτός* in addressing his slaves, and the driver of Italian galley-slaves was called the 'nostromo.'" Walker suggested "Your" for "Our," which does not help the case much. Fleay remarks: "'Our high-plac'd Macbeth' cannot be said by Macbeth himself; it must be part of a speech of a witch. 'Sweet bodements!' looks also like Middleton, and the whole bit is, in my opinion, a fragment of *Hecate's* inserted by him. 'Rebellious dead' seems to me an allusion to Banquo's ghost, misplaced by Middleton."

99. *Lease of nature.* "That is, lease for term of life" (Rushton).

106. *Noise.* Music (Schmidt). Cf. *Temp.* iii. 2. 144:

> "the isle is full of noises,
> Sounds and sweet airs, that give delight and hurt not."

See also *Cor.* iii. 1. 95; *Ham.* v. 2. 360, etc. Cf. too Spenser, *F. Q.* i. 12, 39: "During the which there was a heavenly noise;" Milton, *Hymn on Nativ.* 97: "the stringed noise;" *Ode at a Solemn Musick*, 18: "that melodious noise;" and Coleridge, *Ancient Mariner*:

> "It ceased; yet still the sails made on
> A pleasant noise till noon—
> A noise like of a hidden brook
> In the leafy month of June,
> That to the sleeping woods all night
> Singeth a quiet tune."

The word was also used in the sense of a company of musicians; as in 2 *Hen. IV.* ii. 4. 13.

111. The stage direction in the folio reads: "*A shew of eight Kings, and Banquo last, with a glasse in his hand;*" but this is inconsistent with what Macbeth says in line 119. "A *show*, in theatrical language, is a procession, or pantomime in which the actors remained silent, hence usually called 'a dumb show'" (Delius).

113. *Hair.* Johnson substituted "air," which D. thinks receives some support from *W. T.* v. 1. 127. Monck Mason says: "It means that the *hair* of both was of the same colour, which is a natural feature more likely to mark a family likeness than the *air*, which depends upon habit, and a dancing-master."

116. *Start, eyes!* "Start from your sockets, so that I may be spared the horror of the vision" (C. P. ed.).

117. *The crack of doom.* The "burst of sound" (Schmidt) at the day of doom; or the thunder announcing that day (C. P. ed.). Cf. *T. A.* ii. 1. 3: "thunder's crack;" and *Temp.* i. 2. 203: "cracks of sulphurous roaring." See also on i. 2. 37 above.

121. *Twofold balls.* Probably referring to the double coronation of James, at Scone and Westminster (C. P. ed.). See Introduction, p. 9.

123. *Blood-bolter'd.* Malone says that *boltered* is a provincial term in Warwickshire. "When a horse, sheep, or other animal, perspires much, and any of the hair, or wool . . . becomes matted in tufts with grime and sweat, he is said to be 'boltered;' and whenever the blood issues out and coagulates, forming the locks into hard clotted bunches, the beast is said to be 'blood-boltered.'" Banquo, therefore, both here and at the banquet, ought to be represented with his hair clotted with blood. Cf. what the murderer says, iii. 4. 27:

> "Safe in a ditch he bides,
> With twenty trenched gashes on his head;
> The least a death to nature;"

and the exclamation of Macbeth himself, iii. 4. 50:

> "Thou canst not say I did it; never shake
> Thy gory locks at me."

The word, with slight difference of spelling, is used by Holland, himself living at Coventry, in his translation of *Pliny*, xii. 17, speaking of a goat's beard: "Now by reason of dust getting among, it *baltereth* and cluttereth into knobs and bals." Halliwell states that, according to Sharp's MS. *Warwickshire Glossary*, snow is said to *balter* together, and Batchelor (*Orthoepical Analysis*, 1809) says that "hasty pudding is said to be *boltered* when much of the flower remains in lumps."

127. *Sprights.* This is the spelling of the folio, and is preferred by some editors when, as here, the word does not refer to apparitions. Cf. *V. and A.* 181: "And now Adonis, with a lazy spright;" *R. of L.* 121: "with heavy spright," etc. Even when the word is spelled "spirits" in the early eds. it is generally a monosyllable.

130. *Antic.* The folio has "Antique" here. We find "antick" and "antique" (the accent always on the first syllable) used promiscuously

in the early eds. without any regard to the meaning. For the relation of the various meanings, see Wb.

Round. Steevens suggests that the idea (as well as that in i. 3. 32) may have been adopted from *Churchyard's Dreame*, 1593:

> "All hand in hand they traced on
> A tricksie ancient round;
> And soone as shadowes were they gone,
> And might no more be found."

144. *Anticipat'st.* Dost prevent. Cf. *Sonn.* 118. 9: "to anticipate Th ills that were not," etc.

145. *Flighty.* Fleeting. Used by S. nowhere else. The C. P. ed. cites, for the general sense, *A. W.* v. 3. 40:

> "For we are old, and on our quick'st decrees
> The inaudible and noiseless foot of Time
> Steals ere we can effect them."

On *o'ertook*, see Gr. 343.

147. *Firstlings.* "First produce or offspring" (Schmidt). Cf. *T. and C.* prol. 27: "The vaunt and firstlings of those broils."

150. *The castle of Macduff.* Tradition makes this Dunnemarle Castle near Culross, on the Forth.

152. *All unfortunate souls*, etc. All who are so unlucky as to be of his lineage.

153. *Trace.* Follow. Cf. *Hen. VIII.* iii. 2. 45: "Now all my joy Trace the conjunction!" See also 1 *Hen. IV.* iii. 1. 47.

155. *Sights.* The Coll. MS. has "Flights," which Sr. adopts. W. reads "sprights," but no change seems called for.

SCENE II.—4. *Traitors.* The treason is the desertion of his family.

7. *Titles.* Claims, rights (Schmidt).

9. *Touch.* Sensibility (Johnson), or feeling. Cf. *T. G. of V.* ii. 7. 18; *A. W.* i. 3. 122; *A. and C.* i. 2. 187, etc.

The poor wren, etc. Harting (*Ornithology of S.* p. 143) remarks that the wren is not the smallest of birds, that it is doubtful whether it would fight against a bird of prey in defence of its young, and that the owl will not take young birds from the nest. See on iv. 1. 8 above.

12. *All is the fear.* The fear is all that can have influenced him.

15. *For.* As regards (Gr. 149). Cf. *Rich. II.* v. 3. 137: "But for our trusty brother-in-law," etc.

17. *The fits o' the season.* The caprices or uncertainties of the time. Cf. *Cor.* iii. 2. 33.

18. *When we are traitors*, etc. That is, are counted traitors, but are not conscious of being such.

19. *When we hold rumour*, etc. When we believe rumours because of our fears, yet know not why we should fear, being conscious of no fault. The C. P. ed. remarks: "It is uncertain whether this very difficult expression means 'when we interpret rumour in accordance with our fear,' or 'when our reputation is derived from actions which our fear dictates,' as Lady Macduff has said in lines 3, 4:

'When our actions do not,
Our fears do make us traitors.'

Others would give to 'hold' the sense of 'receive,' 'believe.' A somewhat similar passage is found in *K. John*, iv. 2. 145:

'I find the people strangely fantasied;
Possess'd with rumours, full of idle dreams,
Not knowing what they fear, but full of fear.'"

On *from*=because of, cf. iii. 6. 21 above.

22. *Each way and move.* Theobald conjectured that we should read, "Each way and wave;" Capell, "And move each way;" Johnson, "Each way, and move;" Steevens, "And each way move;" and Dr. Ingleby, "Which way we move." The C. P. ed. says: "The following, which we put forward with some confidence, yields, by the change of two letters only, a good and forcible sense: 'Each way, and none.' That is, we are floating in every direction upon a violent sea of uncertainty, and yet make no way. We have a similar antithesis, *M. of V.* i. 2. 65: 'He is every man in no man.'" Perhaps S. wrote "Each way we move."

If we retain the old reading, it seems best to make *move*=toss about, as Schmidt explains it. Cf. *Cymb.* iii. 1. 28:

"and his shipping—
Poor ignorant baubles!—on our terrible seas,
Like egg-shells moved upon their surges," etc.

H. (2d ed.) makes *move*="movement, or motion;" which we might prefer if S. anywhere else used *move* as a noun.

23. *Shall.* For the "ellipsis of the nominative," see Gr. 399.

29. *It would be my disgrace.* That is, I should give way to unmanly weeping. The C. P. ed. compares *Hen. V.* iv. 6. 30:

"But I had not so much of man in me,
And all my mother came into mine eyes,
And gave me up to tears."

30. *Sirrah.* Used playfully. It was ordinarily addressed to inferiors, and was considered disrespectful, or unduly familiar, if applied to a superior. Cf. *Much Ado*, iv. 2. 14:

"*Dogberry.* . . . Yours, sirrah?
Conrade. I am a gentleman, sir, and my name is Conrade."

It was also addressed to women. See *A. and C.* v. 2. 229: "sirrah Iras, go." Furness cites other instances from B. and F. and Webster.

32. *With worms.* On worms. Cf. *Rich. II.* iii. 2. 175: "I live with bread like you." Gr. 193.

34. *Lime.* Bird-lime. Cf. *Temp.* iv. 1. 246 and *T. G. of V.* ii. 2. 68.

35. *Gin.* Snare. Cf. *T. N.* ii. 5. 92; 2 *Hen. VI.* iii. 1. 262, etc. See also *Psalms*, cxl. 5.

36. *They.* It is a question whether this refers to the traps just mentioned or to *birds* (Gr. 243). Delius makes it the latter. In either case, as the C. P. ed. remarks, the emphasis is on *Poor*, and the meaning is that in life traps are not set for the poor but for the rich.

47. *Swears and lies.* That is, proves false to his oath, perjures himself.

56. *Enow.* See on ii. 3. 7.

65. *In your state*, etc. I am perfectly acquainted with your noble rank and character. Clarke remarks: "The man sees her in her own castle, and knows her to be its lady mistress; but he also seems to know that she is a virtuous, a kind, a good lady as well as a noble lady, and therefore comes to warn her of approaching danger." On *perfect*, cf. *W. T.* iii. 3. 1:

> "Thou art perfect then, our ship hath touch'd upon
> The deserts of Bohemia?"

and *Cymb.* iii. 1. 73:

> "I am perfect
> That the Pannonians and Dalmatians for
> Their liberties are now in arms."

66. *I doubt.* I suspect, fear. Cf. *M. W.* i. 4. 42, etc.

67. *Homely.* Plain, humble. S. also uses it in the other sense of plain-featured, ugly; as in *T. G. of V.* ii. 4. 98, *C. of E.* ii. 1. 89, etc.

69. *To fright*, etc. On the construction, see Gr. 356, 357.

70. *To do worse.* That is, to let her and her children be destroyed without warning (Johnson). Another explanation assumes that the messenger was one of the murderers who, actuated by pity and remorse, had outstripped his companions to give warning of their approach.

75. *Sometime.* See on i. 6. 11, or *Rich. II.* p. 158.

81. *Where.* On *where* following *so*, see Gr. 279; and for *mayst*, Gr. 412.

82. *Shag-hair'd.* The folios have "shagge-ear'd," "shag-eard," or "shag-ear'd," which some modern eds. retain. Steevens was the first to substitute "shag-hair'd," which he shows to be common in the old plays. Cf. 2 *Hen. VI.* iii. 1. 367: "a shag-hair'd crafty kern" (the "rough, rug-headed kerns" of *Rich. II.* ii. 1. 156). Malone notes that *hair* was sometimes written "heare," and cites Lodge, *Incarnate Devils*, etc., 1596: "shag-heard slave."

Egg. The C. P. ed. quotes *L. L. L.* v. 1. 78: "thou pigeon-egg of discretion;" and *T. and C.* v. 1. 41: "Finch-egg!"

83. *Fry.* Cf. *V. and A.* 526: "No fisher but the ungrown fry forbears."

SCENE III.—*Before the King's Palace.* Given by D. in place of "*A Room in the King's Palace*," found in most eds. The change is favoured by line 140: "Comes the king *forth*, I pray you?"

Cf. the extract from Holinshed, p. 145 above.

3. *Mortal.* Deadly. Cf. i. 5. 39.

4. *Bestride.* Stand over to defend. Cf. *C. of E.* v. 1. 192:

> "When I bestrid thee in the wars and took
> Deep scars to save thy life;"

and 2 *Hen. IV.* i. 1. 207:

> "Tells them he doth bestride a bleeding land,
> Gasping for life under great Bolingbroke."

Birthdom (used by S. nowhere else) = mother country. It is "Birthdome" in the folio.

6. *Strike heaven*, etc. The C. P. ed. notes the somewhat similar hyperbole in *Temp.* i. 2. 4:

> "But that the sea, mounting to the welkin's cheek,
> Dashes the fire out."

Cf. *M. of V.* ii. 7. 45:

> "The watery kingdom, whose ambitious head
> Spets in the face of heaven."

We have also "the face of heaven" in *Rich. III.* iv. 4. 239; "the cloudy cheeks of heaven" in *Rich. II.* iii. 3. 57. The sun is called "the eye of heaven" in i. 3. 275, and "the searching eye of heaven" in iii. 2. 37, of the same play.

For *that*=*so* that, see on i. 2. 58. Gr. 283.

8. *Syllable.* Expression, cry. Cf. the figurative use of the word in v. 5. 21.

10. *To friend.* On *to*=for, see Gr. 189. Cf. *J. C.* iii. 1. 143: "I know that we shall have him well to friend;" *Rich. II.* iv. 1. 307: "I have a king here to my flatterer," etc. See also *Matt.* iii. 9, *Luke*, iii. 8, etc.

11. *It.* On the redundant use of pronouns, see Gr. 242, 243.

12. *Sole name.* Mere name, very name.

Blisters our tongues. We have the same figure in *R. and J.* iii. 2. 90, *L. L. L.* v. 2. 335, and *W. T.* ii. 2. 33.

14. *Touch'd.* Cf. iii. 2. 26.

15. *Deserve.* The folios have "discerne" or "discern." The correction, like so many others, is due to Theo.

And wisdom. And it is wisdom. See examples of similar ellipsis in Gr. 403. Various emendations have been suggested; as "'t is wisdom," "and wisdom 't were," "and wisdom bids," "and wisdom is it," etc.

19. *Recoil.* "Fall off, degenerate" (Schmidt). Cf. *Cymb.* i. 6. 128: "Recoil from your great stock." *In an imperial charge*="when acting by a king's command" (Moberly). J. Hunter explains it, "when invested with sovereignty," apparently referring it to Macbeth.

21. *Transpose.* Change, transform. It has the same meaning in the only other passage where S. uses it, *M. N. D.* i. 1. 233:

> "Things base and vile, holding no quality,
> Love can transpose to form and dignity."

23. *Would.* Apparently=*should;* but cf. Gr. 331.

24. *Look so.* That is, look like grace. Cf. *M. for M.* ii. 1. 297: "Mercy is not itself that oft looks so."

I have lost my hopes. That is, because they depended upon his being trusted by Malcolm.

25. *Perchance*, etc. Perhaps because your own course (in leaving your family as you did) compels me to distrust you.

26. *Rawness.* "Want of due preparation and provision" (Schmidt). S. uses the word only here, but the adverb *rawly* (also used but once) has a similar sense in *Hen. V.* iv. 1. 147: "children rawly left." The C. P. ed. quotes Tennyson: "Raw haste, half-sister to delay."

27. *Motives.* Often applied by S. to persons (Delius). Cf. *T. of A* v. 4. 27; *Oth.* iv. 2. 43; *A. and C* ii. 2. 96, etc.

29. *Jealousies.* "The plural indicates the repeated occasions for his suspicion to which the arrival of messengers from Scotland gives rise, not merely his present feelings towards Macduff; and this plural occasioned the two others, *dishonours* and *safeties*" (Delius).

30. On the measure, see Gr. 454.

34. *Affeer'd.* "Confirmed, sanctioned" (Schmidt). It is a law term, applied to the fixing of a fine in cases where it is not fixed by the statute. Toilet explains the passage thus: "Poor country, wear thou thy wrongs; the title to them is legally settled by those who had the final adjudication of it."

37. *To boot.* In addition; still in colloquial use, at least in New England.

39. *I think.* I think on the fact that, bear in mind that. Cf. iii. 1. 131: "always thought," etc.

43. *England.* The king of England. Cf. line 189 below. See also *K. John*, iii. 4. 8: "And bloody England into England gone;" *Hen. V.* iii. 6. 131: "England shall repent his folly;" *Id.* iii. 6. 166: "Though France himself," etc.; *W. T.* i. 1. 23: "Sicilia cannot show himself over-kind to Bohemia," etc.

48. *More sundry.* In more various. For the omission of the preposition, see Gr. 202.

49. *What should he be?* See Gr. 254, 325.

52. *Open'd.* Unfolded, like buds or leaves; carrying out the metaphor in *grafted.* The Coll. MS. has "ripen'd."

55. *Confineless.* Boundless. Not found elsewhere in S., but we have "fineless" in the same sense in *Oth.* iii. 3. 173: "riches fineless."

57. *Top.* Overtop, surpass. Cf. *Cor.* ii. 1. 23: "topping all others in boasting," etc

58. *Luxurious.* Lustful, licentious; the only sense in which S. uses the word. Cf. *Much Ado*, iv. 1. 42, etc. *Luxury* is used in a kindred sense; as in *Rich. III.* iii. 5. 80, *Ham.* i. 5. 83, etc.

59. *Sudden.* Violent, impetuous, passionate (Schmidt). Cf. *A. Y. L.* ii. 7. 151: "Sudden and quick in quarrel;" *Oth.* ii. 1. 279: "he is rash and very sudden in choler," etc.

64. *Continent.* Restraining. Cf. *Lear*, i. 2. 182: "a continent forbearance." Cf. also the use of the noun in *Lear*, iii. 2. 58, *A. and C.* iv. 14. 40, etc.

66. *Such an one.* Cf. 101 below, where we have "such a one." Both forms are found in the early eds.

67. *In nature.* Delius connects these words with tyranny = "organic intemperance," as contrasted with the "political tyranny" of Macbeth. It seems simpler to make it = in its nature. The C. P. ed. explains *tyranny* as "usurpation," and compares iii. 6. 25.

71. *Convey your pleasures.* "Indulge them secretly" (Schmidt). So in *Rich. III.* iv. 2. 96, "convey letters" = send them secretly. Cf. also *Lear*, i. 2. 109, and *Hen. V.* i. 2. 74. *Convey* was used as a cant term for *steal;* as in *M. W.* i. 3. 32, *Rich. II.* iv. 1. 317, etc. The Coll. MS. has "enjoy."

72. *The time you may so hoodwink.* "That no man shall be aware thereof" (Holinshed).

74. *That.* On the construction, see Gr. 277.

77. *Ill-composed.* Compounded of evil qualities. The C. P. ed. compares "well composed" in *T. and C.* iv. 4. 79. *Affection* = disposition.

78. *Stanchless.* Insatiate. Cf. *stanch* = satiate, in *T. A.* iii. 1. 15.

80. *His.* This one's. See Gr. 217.

82. *That.* So that. Gr. 283.

Forge. Frame, fabricate. Used by S. in both a good and a bad sense. Cf. *A. W.* i. 1. 85: "The best wishes that can be forged in your thoughts;" *Id.* iv. 1. 26: "the lies he forges," etc.

86. *Summer-seeming.* "Which appears to belong to the heyday of youth, and to pass with it" (Moberly). It is contrasted with *avarice*, which is lifelong. "Summer-teeming" and "summer-seeding" have been suggested as emendations. Malone notes that Donne has "winter-seeming" in *Love's Alchymy:*

> "So, lovers dreame a rich and long delight,
> But get a winter-seeming summers night."

88. *Foisons.* Rich harvests, plenty. Cf. *Sonn.* 53. 9:

> "Speak of the spring and foison of the year;
> The one doth shadow of your beauty show,
> The other as your bounty doth appear."

See also *Temp.* ii. 1. 163, iv. 1. 110, etc.

89. *Mere own.* Absolutely your own. Cf. line 152 below, and see *Temp.* p. 111, note on *We are merely cheated.* Gr. 15.

Portable. Endurable; as in *Lear*, iii. 6. 115: "How light and portable my pain seems now." In the only other instance of the word in S. it is used in the literal modern sense: "an engine not portable" (*T. and C.* ii. 3. 144). Holinshed has *importable* in this connection: "mine intemperancie should be more importable vnto you," etc. See p. 146 above.

90. *Weighed with.* Weighed against, counterbalanced by.

92. *Verity.* Truthfulness, honesty. Cf. *A. Y. L.* iii. 4. 25: "his verity in love."

Temperance. Self-restraint. Cf. *M. for M.* iii. 2. 251; *Hen. VIII.* i. 1. 124; *Cor.* iii. 3. 28; *Ham.* iii. 2. 8, etc.

93. *Perseverance.* Accented on the second syllable, as in *T. and C.* iii. 3. 150. S. uses the word nowhere else. *Persever* he always accents on the penult; as in *T. G. of V.* iii. 2. 25: "Ay, and perversely she persevers so." See also *C. of E.* ii. 2. 217; *M. N. D.* iii. 2. 237, etc. Gr. 492.

95. *Relish of.* Not = relish *for*, but smack or flavour of. Cf. 2 *Hen. IV.* i. 2. 111: "some smack of age, some relish of the saltness of time;" *Ham.* iii. 3. 92: "no relish of salvation."

98. *The sweet milk*, etc. Cf. i. 5. 15.

99. *Uproar.* "Stir up to tumult" (Schmidt). It is found nowhere else as a verb.

104. *Untitled.* Steevens quotes Chaucer, *C. T.* 17172: "a titleles tiraunt."

105. *Wholesome.* Healthy, prosperous. Cf. *M. W.* v. 5. 63: "In state as wholesome as in state 't is fit; *Lear*, i. 4. 230: "wholesome weal," etc.

106. *Since that.* See Gr. 287.

108. *Breed.* Parentage. Cf. *Rich. II.* ii. 1. 45: "This happy breed (race) of men;" and *Id.* ii. 1. 52: "royal kings, Fear'd by their breed" (on account of their birth), etc.

111. *Died every day she liv'd.* Lived a life of daily mortification (Delius). Malone cites 1 *Cor.* xv. 31: "I die daily."

The folio has "liv'd," which is retained by Sr., St., W., and others. *Fare* is then a dissyllable. Gr. 480. Pope has "Oh fare."

118. *Trains.* Artifices, lures. Cf. the use of the verb (= entice, allure) in *C. of E.* iii. 2. 45; *L. L. L.* i. 1. 71; 1 *Hen. IV.* v. 2. 21, etc.

119. *Modest wisdom*, etc. Cautious wisdom holds me back.

123. *Unspeak.* Cf. "unsay" in *Rich. II.* iv. 1. 9; *M. N. D.* i. 1. 181; *Hen. VIII.* v. 1. 177, etc.

125. *For.* As. See Gr. 148.

133. *Here-approach.* Cf. "here-remain" in line 148. Gr. 429.

134. *Old Siward.* As the C. P. ed. remarks, he was the son of Beorn, Earl of Northumberland, and rendered great service to King Edward in the suppression of the rebellion of Earl Godwin and his sons, 1053. According to Holinshed, who follows Boethius, Duncan married a daughter of Siward. It is remarkable that S., who seems to have had no other guide than Holinshed, on this point deserts him, for in v. 2. 2 he calls Siward Malcolm's uncle. It is true that "nephew" was often used like "nepos," in the sense of grandson, but we know of no instance in which "uncle" is used for "grandfather."

135. *Already.* The folio reading. Some editors adopt Rowe's "All ready."

At a point, like *at point* = completely, prepared for any emergency (Schmidt). Cf. *Ham.* i. 2. 200: "Arm'd at point;" *Lear*, i. 4. 347: "keep At point a hundred knights," etc. The C. P. ed. compares Foxe's *Acts and Monuments*, ed. 1570: "The Register there sittyng by, beying weery, belyke, of tarying, or els perceauyng the constant Martyrs *to be at a point*, called vpon the chauncelour in hast to rid them out of the way, and to make an end." So also in Bunyan's *Life*: "When they saw that I was *at a point* and would not be moved nor persuaded, Mr. Foster told the justice that then he must send me to prison." Florio (*Ital. Dict.*) gives, "Essere in punto, to be in a readinesse, to be at a point." Cf. Holinshed's "fallen at a point," p. 139 above.

136. *The chance*, etc. "May the chance of success be as certain as the justice of our quarrel" (C. P. ed.). Delius explains *chance of goodness* as "successful issue," and *warranted quarrel* as "our righteous cause." On *quarrel*, cf. i. 2. 14. Hanmer gave "our chance, in goodness," and Johnson suggested "the chance, O goodness." St. has "belike" = approve or favour.

140–159. The C. P. editors express the opinion that these lines "were probably interpolated previous to a representation at Court." Fleay ascribes them to Middleton. Mr. Hales suggests that, if they are an interpolation, S. may himself have inserted them for the Court performance.

142. *Stay his cure.* Wait to be healed by him. Cf. *T. G. of V.* ii. 2.

13: "My father stays my coming;" *M. of V.* ii. 8. 40: "But stay the very riping of the time," etc.

Convinces, etc. Overpowers the utmost efforts of medical skill. On *convinces*, cf. i. 7. 64.

145. *Presently.* Immediately. See *Mer.* p. 131, or *Rich. II.* p. 182.

146. *The evil.* The scrofula, or "the king's evil," as it was long called. The C. P. ed. remarks: "Edward's miraculous powers were believed in by his contemporaries, or at least soon after his death, and expressly recognized by Pope Alexander III., who canonized him. The power of healing was claimed for his successors early in the twelfth century, for it is controverted by William of Malmesbury, and asserted later in the same century by Peter of Blois, who held a high office in the Royal Household (see Freeman's *Norman Conquest*, vol. ii. pp. 527, 528). The same power was claimed for the kings of France, and was supposed to be conferred by the unction of the 'Sainte Ampoule' on their coronation. William Tooker, D.D., in his *Charisma seu Donum Sanationis*, 1597, while claiming the power for his own sovereign, Elizabeth, concedes it also to the Most Christian King; but André Laurent, physician to Henry IV. of France, taxes the English sovereigns with imposture. His book is entitled, 'De Mirabilis trumas sanandi vi solis Galliae Regibus Christianissimis divinitus concessa,' etc., 1609. The Roman Catholic subjects of Elizabeth, perhaps out of patriotism, conceded to her the possession of this one virtue, though they were somewhat staggered to find that she possessed it quite as much after the Papal excommunication as before. James the First's practice of touching for the evil is mentioned several times in Nichols's *Progresses*, e. g. vol. iii. pp. 264, 273. Charles I., when at York, touched seventy persons in one day. Charles II. also touched when an exile at Bruges, omitting perhaps, for sufficient reason, the gift of the coin. He practised with signal success after his restoration. One of Dr. Johnson's earliest recollections was the being taken to be touched by Queen Anne in 1712 (Boswell, vol. i. p. 38). Even Swift seems to have believed in the efficacy of the cure (*Works*, ed. Scott, vol. ii. p. 252). The Whigs did not claim the power for the Hanoverian sovereigns, though they highly resented Carte's claiming it for the Pretender in his History of England."

A form of prayer to be used at the ceremony was introduced into the Book of Common Prayer as early as 1684, and was retained up to 1719. As late as 1745 Prince Charles at Holyrood touched a child for the evil.

149. *Solicits.* Moves by his prayers. Cf. *Rich. II.* i. 2. 2: "Doth more solicit me than your exclaims."

152. *Mere.* See on line 89 above.

153. *A golden stamp.* As the C. P. ed. remarks, there is no warrant in Holinshed for the statement that the Confessor hung a golden coin or stamp about the necks of the patients. This was, however, a custom which prevailed in later days. Previously to Charles II.'s time some current coin, as an angel, was used for the purpose, but in his reign a special medal was struck and called a "touch-piece." The identical touch-piece which Queen Anne hung round the neck of Dr. Johnson is preserved in the British Museum.

On *stamp*=coin, cf. *M. W.* iii. 4. 16: "Stamps in gold or sums in sealed bags;" and *Cymb.* v. 4. 24: "they weigh not every stamp."

154. *Spoken.* Said. See on iii. 4. 8. Gr. 200.

160. *My countryman.* He recognizes him as such by his dress.

163. *Makes.* This may be viewed as the "3d person plural in *-s*" (Gr. 333), like "gives" in ii. 1. 61; but S. sometimes uses *means* as a singular. Cf. *M. of V.* ii. 1. 19: "that means;" *W. T.* iv. 4. 632: "this means;" *C. of E.* i. 1. 76: "Other means was none," etc. He also often uses the singular *mean;* as in *W. T.* iv. 4. 89, *Oth.* iii. 1. 39, *J. C.* iii. 1. 161, etc.

168. *Rent.* The folio reading, generally changed to the equivalent "rend." Cf. *M. N. D.* p. 166.

170. *Modern.* Ordinary, common; as in *R. and J.* iii. 2. 120: "modern lamentation;" *A. W.* ii. 3. 2: "modern and familiar," etc.

For *ecstasy*, see on iii. 2. 21.

171. *Scarce ask'd for who.* See Gr. 274, 414.

172. *Flowers in their caps.* H. Rowe observes that it was customary with the Highlanders, when on a march, to stick sprigs of heath in their bonnets.

173. *Or ere.* Cf. *Temp.* i. 2. 11; *Ham.* i. 2. 147, etc. The *or*, like the *ere*, is the A. S. *ær*, which is found in Early English in the forms *er*, *air*, *ar*, *ear*, *or*, etc. *Ere* seems to have been added to *or* for emphasis when the meaning of the latter was coming to be forgotten. *Or* is still found in northern dialects (Halliwell's *Archaic Dict.*). Cf. Scott, *Rob Roy:* "Ther will be broken heads amang us or it's long." See Mätzner, iii. 446, or Gr. 131.

174. *Too nice.* Too precise (Schmidt) or minute; not "too fancifully minute," as the C. P. ed., H., and others explain it. "Notwithstanding the relation is so full of distressing particulars, it is yet too true" (Noble Butler).

175. *That of an hour's age*, etc. Moberly explains this: "If a man tells a crime that is an hour old, they say 'buzz' to him for stale news;" and compares *Ham.* ii. 2. 412:

> "*Polonius.* The actors are come hither, my lord.
> *Hamlet.* Buz, buz!"

Blackstone says, "*Buz* used to be an interjection at Oxford when any one began a story that was generally known before." Cf. *T. of S.* ii. 1. 207. But in the present passage *doth hiss the speaker* may mean nothing more than "exposes him to derision."

176. *Teems.* Brings forth. Cf. *T. of A.* iv. 3. 179, and *Hen. V.* v. 2. 51.

177. *Children.* A trisyllable here. Gr. 477.

179. *At peace.* Cf. *Rich. II.* iii. 2. 127:

> "*Richard.* I warrant they have made peace with Bolingbroke.
> *Scroop.* Peace have they made with him indeed, my lord."

183. *Were out.* "Had taken the field" (Schmidt). In *Lear*, i. 1. 33 ("He hath been out nine years") *out*=abroad, in foreign countries.

184. *Witness'd.* Made credible.

185. *For that.* See Gr. 287, 288. *Power* = army, forces; as often.

Cf. line 236 below. The plural was used in the same sense (so *force* and *forces* now). See *J. C.* p. 168, note on *Are levying powers.*

191. *None.* There is none. For the ellipsis, see Gr. 403.

On *give out* = show (Schmidt), cf. *W. T.* iv. 4. 149; *T. N.* iii. 4. 203; *Oth.* iii. 3. 209, etc.

194. *Would.* See Gr. 329.

195. *Latch.* Catch. Cf. *Sonn.* 113. 6:

> "For it no form delivers to the heart
> Of bird, or flower, or shape, which it doth latch."

Schmidt explains the verb similarly in *M. N. D.* iii. 2. 36, where some make it = smear; a meaning found nowhere else.

Spenser has *latched* = caught, in *Shep. Kal.* March, 94:

> "So long I shott, that al was spent;
> Tho pumie stones I hastly hent,
> And threw; but nought availed;
> He was so wimble and so wight,
> From bough to bough he lepped light,
> And oft the pumies latched."

Cf. Golding's Ovid, *Met.* i.: "As though he would, at everie stride, betweene his teeth hir latch;" and *Met.* viii.:

> "But that a bough of chesnut-tree, thick-leaved, by the way
> Did latch it," etc.

196. *A fee-grief.* "A grief that hath a single owner" (Johnson).

202. *Possess them with.* Fill them with. Cf. *K. John*, iv. 2. 203: "Why seek'st thou to possess me with these fears?" See also 1 *Hen. IV.* ii. 2. 112; *Hen. VIII.* ii. 1. 158; *M. W.* i. 3. 110, etc.

206. *Quarry.* Dead bodies; literally, the game killed in hunting. Cf. *Cor.* i. 1. 202, and *Ham.* v. 2. 375.

208. *Ne'er pull your hat*, etc. Steevens notes that the same expression occurs in the old ballad of "Northumberland betrayed by Douglas:"

> "He pulled his hatt down over his browe,
> And in his heart he was full woe," etc.

209. *The grief that does not speak*, etc. Steevens quotes Webster, *White Devil:*

> "Poor heart, break;
> These are the killing griefs which dare not speak;"

Seneca, *Hippolytus:* "Curae leves loquuntur, ingentes stupent;" and Greene, *Fair Bellora:*

> "Light sorrowes often speake,
> When great the heart in silence breake."

Cf. *V. and A.* 329:

> "the heart hath treble wrong
> When it is barr'd the aidance of the tongue."

210. *Whispers.* For the omission of the preposition, see Gr. 200.

212. *Must be.* Was destined to be (Gr. 314).

216. *He has no children.* The C. P. ed. takes this as referring to Macbeth: "therefore my utmost revenge must fall short of the injury he has

inflicted upon me." We prefer, with Malone, to apply it to Malcolm. Cf. *K. John*, iii. 1. 91 : "He talks to me that never had a son." Moberly refers it to Macbeth, but explains it thus: "Had he had children, he could not have done it." He cites 3 *Hen. VI.* v. 5. 63 :

> "You have no children, butchers; if you had,
> The thought of them would have stirr'd up remorse."

220. *Dispute it.* "Contend with your present sorrows" (Steevens), fight against it; or, perhaps, "reason upon it," as Schmidt explains it.

221. *But I must also feel it*, etc. On this passage Horn (quoted by Furness) remarks: "Put these lines before hundreds of French, English, and German tragedies, and they sound like scathing satire; put them before Egmont or William Tell, and they give us a hearty delight. Let them never again, ye dear poets, sound like irony, but give us human beings with hearts that can bleed and heal! Then you will never shrink from that motto."

223. *That.* On *that* following *such*, see Gr. 279.

225. *Naught.* Worthless thing. Cf. *Ham.* iii. 2. 157 : "You are naught," etc.

229. *Convert.* Change. Cf. *R. of L.* 592 : "For stones dissolv'd to water do convert;" *Id.* 691 : "This hot desire converts to cold disdain;" *Much Ado*, i. 1. 123 : 'Courtesy itself must convert to disdain," etc.

231. *But, gentle heavens*, etc. It is here, and not at line 216, that the possibility of revenge on Macbeth first occurs to Macduff (Delius).

232. *Intermission.* Delay. Cf. *M. of V.* iii. 2. 201 :

> "You lov'd, I lov'd; for intermission
> No more pertains to me, my lord, than you."

234. *Scape.* See on iii. 4. 20.

235. *Too.* "If I don't kill him, then I am worse than he, and I not only forgive him myself, but pray God to forgive him also; or perhaps it is, then I am as bad as he, and may God forgive us both. I cannot point to an instance, anywhere, of language more intensely charged with meaning" (H.).

Tune is Rowe's emendation for the "time" of the folios. On the adverbial use of *manly*, see Gr. 447. Cf. iii. 5. 1.

Coleridge observes: "How admirably Macduff's grief is in harmony with the whole play! It rends, not dissolves the heart. 'The tune of it goes manly.' Thus is S. always master of himself and of his subject—a genuine Proteus;—we see all things in him, as images in a calm lake, most distinct, most accurate—only more splendid, more glorified."

237. *Our lack*, etc. We need only the king's leave to set out; or, perhaps, to take our leave of the king. Schmidt makes it the latter.

239. *Put on.* "Set to work" (Schmidt). Cf. *Ham.* iv. 7. 132, v. 2. 408, etc. It often means to instigate, incite; as in *Lear*, i. 4. 227, *Oth.* ii 3. 357, etc.

For *instruments* applied to persons, cf. i. 3. 124 and iii. 1. 80 above.

SCENE I.—3. *Went into the field.* Steevens thinks S. forgot that he had shut up Macbeth in Dunsinane; but, as Boswell notes, Ross says (iv. 3. 185) that he had seen "the tyrant's power afoot." The strength of his adversaries, and the revolt of his own troops (v. 2. 18), had probably led him to retreat into his castle.

4. *Nightgown.* See on ii. 2. 70.

9. *Effects.* Actions. Cf. *Ham.* iii. 4. 129; *Lear*, i. 1. 188, ii. 4. 182, etc.

10. *Slumbery.* For other adjectives of similar formation, see Gr. 450.

11. *Actual.* "Consisting in doing anything, in contradistinction to thoughts or words" (Schmidt); as in *Oth.* iv. 2. 153, the only other instance of the word in S.

17. *Close.* Hidden; as in *J. C.* i. 3. 131, etc.

20. *'T is her command.* Dr. Bucknill asks: "Was this to avert the presence of those 'sightless substances' (i. 5. 47) once impiously invoked? She seems washing her hands, and 'continues in this a quarter of an hour.' What a comment on her former boast, 'A little water clears us of this deed!'"

22. *Is shut.* The folios have "their sense are shut." It may be an instance under Gr. 471, like *horse*, etc. See on ii. 4. 14. Cf. *Sonn.* 112. 10:

> "my adder's sense
> To critic and to flatterer stopped are."

32. *Hell is murky.* Steevens thinks that she imagines herself talking to Macbeth, and that these are his words which she repeats contemptuously; but it seems better (with Clarke and Noble Butler) to regard them as the expression of her own dread of hell.

40. *You mar all*, etc. "Alluding to the terrors of Macbeth, when the Ghost broke in on the festivity of the banquet" (Steevens).

42. *Go to.* Often used as an expression of exhortation or reproof (Schmidt). Cf. *Temp.* iv. 1. 253; *Oth.* iv. 2. 194, etc. See also *Genesis*, xi. 3, 4, 7 and xxxviii. 16; 2 *Kings*, v. 5, etc.

46. *Smell.* Verplanck, after remarking that "the more agreeable associations of this sense" are often used for poetic effect, adds: "But the smell has never been successfully used as a means of impressing the imagination with terror, pity, or any of the deeper emotions, except in this dreadful sleep-walking scene of the guilty Queen, and in one parallel scene of the Greek drama, as wildly terrible as this. It is that passage of the *Agamemnon* of Æschylus, where the captive prophetess, Cassandra, wrapt in visionary inspiration, scents first the smell of blood, and then the vapours of the tomb breathing from the palace of Atrides, as ominous of his approaching murder."

49. *Sorely charged.* Heavily laden. Cf. iv. 3. 210: "the o'erfraught heart."

52. *The dignity*, etc. "The queenly rank of the lady herself" (C. P. ed.).

56. *Which.* See Gr. 266.

60. *On 's.* Cf. "on 't," i. 3. 42, etc. See also *Lear*, i. 4. 114, iv. 5. 20, etc. Gr. 182.

72. *Remove*, etc. Lest the lady in her despair might commit suicide (Delius). On *annoyance*, cf. *K. John*, v. 2. 150; *T. and C.* i. 3. 48, etc.

74. *Mated.* Bewildered, paralyzed. Cf. *V. and A.* 909; *C. of E.* iii. 2. 54, v. 1. 281; and 2 *Hen. VI.* iii. 1. 265.

Scene II.—3. *Revenges.* For the plural, cf. *M. for M.* iv. 3. 140; *A. W.* v. 3. 10; *T. N.* v. 1. 385; *Cor.* iv. 5. 143, etc.

Dear causes. Cf. *Lear*, iv. 3. 53: "Some dear cause." On the peculiar uses of *dear* in S. see *Temp.* p. 124, note on *The dear'st o' th' loss.*

4. *Alarm.* Call to arms. See on "alarum'd," ii. 1. 53.

5. *The mortified man.* "The veriest ascetic" (Moberly). Cf. *L. L. L.* i. 1. 28. Schmidt explains *mortified* as "deprived of vital faculty, made apathetic and insensible." There is little to choose between the two. The C. P. ed. suggests that it may mean "dead, mortified in the literal sense;" as in *Hen. V.* i. 1. 26.

8. *File.* List. See on iii. 1. 94.

10. *Unrough.* Beardless. Cf. *Temp.* ii. 1. 250: "rough and razor-

able." See also *W. T.* i. 2. 128, iv. 4. 744. Malone cites *K. John*, v. 2. 133: "This unhair'd sauciness and boyish troops."

11. *Protest.* Proclaim. Cf. iii. 4. 105; and on *first of manhood*, iii. 1. 117.

13. *Lesser.* S. uses it several times as an adverb. See on i. 3. 65.

15. Steevens notes that we have the same metaphor in *T. and C.* ii. 2. 30:

> "And buckle in a waist most fathomless
> With spans and inches so diminutive
> As fears and reasons."

Sr., D., Coll., and H. (2d ed.) adopt Walker's "course" for *cause*. The C. P. ed. explains *distemper'd cause* as the disorganized party, the disordered body over which he rules. Instead of being like "a well-girt man," εὔζωνος ἀνήρ, full of vigour, his state is like one in dropsy. We have the same metaphor more elaborated in 2 *Hen. IV.* iii. 1. 38:

> "*King.* Then you perceive the body of our kingdom
> How foul it is; what rank diseases grow,
> And with what danger, near the heart of it.
> *Warwick.* It is but as a body yet distemper'd," etc.

18. *Minutely.* "Happening every minute, continual" (Schmidt). Used nowhere else by S.

20. *Nothing.* Adverbial, as in v. 4. 2. Gr. 55. For the figure that follows, cf. i. 3. 145.

23. *Pester'd.* Troubled, perplexed. Cf. *Ham.* i. 2. 22; *T. and C.* v. 1. 38, etc. On *to recoil*=for recoiling, see Gr. 356. Cf. iv. 3. 19.

27. *Medicine.* Some critics take this to mean physician (Fr. *médecin*), as in *A. W.* ii. 1. 75, and *W. T.* iv. 4. 598. Schmidt so explains it here. But the next line rather favours taking it in its ordinary sense. *Him* may refer to Malcolm, as Heath suggests, not to *medicine*. It is not easy to decide between the two interpretations. Cf. iii. 4. 76.

30. *Dew.* Also used as a verb in *V. and A.* 66; *M. N. D.* ii. 1. 9; *R. and J.* v. 3. 14, etc.

SCENE III.—1. *Them.* That is, the thanes.

3. *Taint.* Be infected. Cf. *Cymb.* i. 4. 148, and *T. N.* iii. 4. 145. Walker conjectured "faint."

5. On the measure, see Gr. 496. For *pronounce*, cf. *Hen. VIII.* i. 1. 196.

8. *English epicures.* The C. P. ed. observes that gluttony was a common charge brought by the Scotch against their wealthier neighbours. "The English pock-puddings" is a phrase of frequent occurrence in the Waverley Novels. The English too brought similar charges against their Continental neighbours. Delius quotes from the drama of *Edward III.*, falsely attributed to Shakespeare:

> "Those ever-bibbing epicures,
> Those frothy Dutchmen, puff'd with double beer."

9. *The mind I sway by.* That is, am directed by (Schmidt). Some explain it, "by which I bear rule."

10. *Sag.* Droop. We infer from the C. P. ed. that the word is only provincial in England. Like some other words we have noted in S., it

is still in common use in New England. See *Mer.* p. 139, note on *Fill-horse;* also on *Paddock,* i. 1. 10, and *Sliver'd,* iv. 1. 28 above.

13. *There is.* See Gr. 335.

15. *Lily-liver'd.* Cowardly. Cf. *Lear,* ii. 2. 18: "A lily-liver'd, action-taking knave;" *M. of V.* iii. 2. 86: "livers white as milk;" 2 *Hen. IV.* iv. 3. 113: "the liver white and pale," etc.

Patch. Clown, fool. See *Mer.* p. 142. Cf. *Temp.* iii. 2. 71; *C. of E.* iii. 1. 32, etc.

16. *Linen cheeks.* Steevens quotes *Hen. V.* ii. 2. 74: "Their cheeks are paper." See on iii. 4. 116.

20. *Push.* Attack, onset (Schmidt); as in *J. C.* v. 2. 5, etc.

21. *Will cheer me,* etc. The 1st folio has "Will cheere me euer, or dis-eate me now;" the other folios have "disease" for "dis-eate." Capell conjectured "disseat," which has been generally adopted by the editors, with Bishop Percy's suggestion of "chair" for "cheer." S. uses neither *disseat* nor the verb *chair* anywhere else. Furness suggests "dis-ease," which, as he remarks, "is the logical antithesis to *cheer,* and is used with no little force in the earlier versions of the New Testament." Cf. *Luke,* viii. 49 (both in Cranmer's Version, 1537, and in the version of 1581): "Thy daughter is dead, disease not the Master." Cotgrave gives "disease, trouble," etc., as translations of the Fr. *malaiser.* See also Spenser, *F. Q.* ii. 2, 12: "His double burden did him sore disease;" *Id.* ii. 2, 24: "Whom raging winds . . . doe diversely disease," etc. Furness might have added as a confirmation of his reading that in the only other instance in which S. uses *disease* as a verb it is in this sense. See *Cor.* i. 3. 117: "She will but disease our better mirth." He uses the noun *disease* several times in the sense of trouble, vexation. Cf. 1 *Hen. VI.* ii. 5. 44:

> "First, lean thine aged back against mine arm;
> And in that ease I 'll tell thee my disease."

See also *A. W.* v. 4. 68, and *T. of A.* iii. 1. 56.

22. *Way.* Johnson conjectured "May," which the C. P. editors think S. "very probably wrote." Malone quotes *Rich. II.* iii. 4. 48:

> "He that hath suffer'd this disorder'd spring
> Hath now himself met with the fall of leaf."

W. says: "Dr. Johnson's emendation is a step prose-ward, although speciously poetic."

23. *Sear.* Schmidt and Moberly take this to be a noun; Steevens, Halliwell, and D. explain it as an adjective, which seems to us better. S. uses the noun or adjective *sere* (the same word) elsewhere only in *Ham.* ii. 2. 337: "tickled o' the sere" (where the meaning is much disputed), and in *C. of E.* iv. 2. 19: "He is deformed, crooked, old and sere."

On *yellow leaf,* cf. *Sonn.* 73. 1:

> "The time of year thou mayst in me behold
> When yellow leaves, or none, or few, do hang
> Upon those boughs," etc.

24. *Old age.* Clarke suggests that Macbeth's mention of himself as in

the autumn of life is "one of those touches of long time systematically thrown in at intervals, to convey the effect of a sufficiently elapsed period for the reign of the usurper since his murder of the preceding king, Duncan." Furness asks: "May we not add as one of these 'touches' the tardy recognition of Ross by Malcolm in iv. 3. 160?"

35. *Moe.* More. Cf. *Much Ado*, ii. 3. 72: "Sing no more ditties, sing no moe" (where it rhymes with *so*, as it does in *R. of L.* 1479); *J. C.* ii. 1. 72: "there are moe with him," etc. The modern eds. generally change it to "more," unless the rhyme requires "moe."

Skirr. Scour. Used by S. only here and in *Hen. V.* iv. 7. 64, where it is intransitive.

40. *Thou.* On the use of the pronoun in the time of S., see Gr. 231.

42. Delius notes that we have the same figure in *Ham.* i. 5. 103: "Within the book and volume of my brain."

43. *Oblivious.* Causing forgetfulness (Schmidt). S. uses the word only here and in the compound "all-oblivious" (forgetful of all), *Sonn.* 55. 9.

44. *Stuff'd bosom of that perilous stuff.* There may be a corruption of the text here, as many critics have supposed, but similar repetitions are not uncommon in S. Cf. v. 2. 19 and v. 8. 72 in the present play. See also *A. and C.* i. 1. 44; *A. W.* ii. 1. 163, v. 1. 35; *R. and J.* iii. 2. 92; *K. John*, ii. 1. 471, etc. V. has "load" and Coll. "grief" for *stuff*.

48. *Staff.* Lance, according to Schmidt; as in *K. John*, ii. 1. 318; *Rich. III.* v. 3. 65, 341; *Much Ado*, v. 1. 138, etc. The C. P. ed. explains it as "the general's bâton."

50. *Come, sir, dispatch.* These words are addressed to the attendant who is buckling on the armour. The agitation of the speaker's mind is marked by his turning from one to the other. No sooner is the armour put on than he bids the man pull it off (line 54), and then (line 58) orders it to be brought after him (C. P. ed.).

Cast. This was the word in use for finding out disorders by inspection of the water (Steevens). See *T. N.* p. 153, note on 97.

52. *Purge*, etc. Cf. iii. 4. 76.

55. *Senna.* The reading of the 4th folio. The 1st has "Cyme;" the 2d and 3d, "Cæny." D. suggests that "cyme" was a misprint for "cynne," one of the many ways of spelling *senna*.

59. *Bane.* Ruin, destruction; as in *T. and C.* iv. 2. 98, *T. A.* v. 3. 73, etc.

61, 62. Fleay rejects this couplet as a "washy sentiment," and "out of place after Macbeth's emphatic declaration."

SCENE IV.—2. *That.* When. See Gr. 284; and on *nothing*, Gr. 55. H. thinks the allusion is to the spies mentioned at iii. 4. 131; Ritter refers it to the circumstances of Duncan's murder.

6. *Discovery.* This refers to Macbeth's spies (Delius).

8. *Other.* See Gr. 12 and cf. 123.

10. For *set down*=sit down, or begin a siege, cf. *Cor.* i. 2. 28, i. 3. 110; *T. of A.* v. 3. 9, etc.

11. *Given.* The sense seems to require "gain'd," "ta'en," or "got," all of which have been suggested as emendations. The Coll. MS. has "gotten." Some have explained *given* as = given them.

12. *More and less.* Great and small. Cf. 1 *Hen. IV.* iv. 3. 68: "More and less came in with cap and knee;" 2 *Hen. IV.* i. 1. 209: "And more and less do flock to follow him," etc. See also Gr. 17.

14. *Let our just censures*, etc. "Let our just decisions on the defection of Macbeth's followers attend upon the actual result of the battle, and let us meanwhile be industrious soldiers; that is, let us not be negligent through security" (Elwin). On *censure* = judgment, opinion, cf. *W. T.* ii. 1. 37; *Hen. VIII.* i. 1. 33 (see note in our ed. p. 157); *Rich. III.* ii. 2. 144, etc.

18. *Owe.* Here used in the modern sense, as in i. 4. 22 and v. 2. 26. For the other meaning (= have, possess) cf. i. 3. 76, i. 4. 10, and iii. 4. 113. "The decision of the battle will show us what we have, and at the same time what it is our duty yet to do" (Delius).

19. On the measure, see Gr. 468.

20. *Arbitrate.* Decide. Mere speculations are of no use; fighting must settle it.

SCENE V. — 5. *Forc'd.* Reinforced, strengthened (Schmidt). The Coll. MS. has "farc'd" = "stuffed or filled out." *Force* = farce occurs in *T. and C.* ii. 3. 232 and v. 1. 64, and perhaps also in *Hen. V.* ii. chor. 22 (Schmidt).

6. *Dareful.* Used nowhere else by S.

7. *Beat.* On the form (as on *forgot* in line 9), see Gr. 343.

10. *Cool'd.* Malone suggested "'coil'd" (= recoiled, shrunk back), and the Coll. MS. has "quail'd," which, as D. remarks, is plausible.

11. *Fell.* Literally, skin. Cf. *A. W.* iii. 2. 55, and *Lear*, v. 3. 24.

12. *Treatise.* Tale, story; as in *V. and A.* 774, and *Much Ado*, i. 3. 317, the only other instances in which S. uses the word. On *rouse*, cf. iii. 2. 53.

13. *As.* As if. Cf. i. 4. 11. Gr. 107. On the passage, cf. *Ham.* iii. 4. 121. For *with*, see on iv. 2. 32.

14. *Direness.* Horror. Not used elsewhere by S.

15. *Once.* Ever, at any time; as in iv. 3. 167. Cf. *Rich. II.* ii. 3. 91; *Ham.* i. 5. 121, etc. *Start* = startle; as in *T. and C.* v. 2. 101, etc.

18. *Word.* Johnson wanted to make it a "broken sentence," reading "a time for—such a world!" Steevens compares *Rich. II.* i. 3. 152: "The hopeless word of 'never to return.'"

21. *Last syllable.* Cf. *A. W.* iii. 6. 75: "even to the utmost syllable of your worthiness."

23. *Dusty.* The 2d folio has "study," probably the result of an accidental transposition of the types; and the later folios copy the error. Upton prefers it to *dusty.* Theo. conjectured "dusky." Coll. quotes Anthony Copley, *Fig for Fortune*, 1596: "Inviting it to dusty death's defeature."

24. For the reference to the stage, the C. P. ed. compares i. 3. 128 and ii. 4. 5. See also *T. and C.* i. 3. 153: "Like a strutting player."

30. *Gracious my lord.* See on iii. 2. 27.

37. *This three mile.* On *this*, cf. 1 *Hen. IV.* iii. 3. 54; and for *mile* in the plural, *M. W.* iii. 2. 33, *Much Ado*, ii. 3. 17, etc. See also *Rich. II.* p. 182, note on *A thousand pound.*

Delius remarks that "S. has here somewhat shortened the distance of twelve miles between Birnam and Dunsinane;" but all that the messenger says is that the "moving grove" is *now* three miles distant.

40. *Cling.* Shrink or shrivel up (Schmidt). The C. P. ed. quotes Miege (*Fr. Dict.*, 1688): "Clung with hunger, maigre, sec, elancé, comme une personne affamée;" and "To clung, as wood will do being laid up after it is cut, secher, devenir sec." Moor, in his *Suffolk Words*, gives: "*Clung:* shrunk, dried, shrivelled; said of apples, turnips, carrots," etc.

42. *Pull in.* Rein in, check. M. Mason quotes Fletcher, *Sea Voyage*, ii. 1:

> "All my spirits,
> As if they had heard my passing-bell go for me,
> Pull in their powers and give me up to destiny."

"Pall in" and "pale in" have been suggested as emendations.

49. *Gin.* See on i. 2. 25. On *aweary*, cf. *M. of V.* i. 2. 2; *M. N. D.* v. 1. 255, etc.

The C. P. editors say that lines 47–50 "are singularly weak, and read like an unskilful imitation of other passages where Macbeth's desperation is interrupted by fits of despondency." We are rather disposed to agree with Craik, who, commenting on *J. C.* iv. 3. 95 ("For Cassius is aweary of the world"), refers to the present as another of Shakespeare's "most pathetic lines."

50. *Estate.* "Settled order" (C. P. ed.). Pope changed it to "state." Cf. i. 3. 140.

51. *Alarum-bell.* W. has "alarum." See on ii. 1. 53. On *wrack*, cf. i. 3. 114.

52. *Harness.* Armour; as in *T. and C.* v. 3. 31, *A. and C.* iv. 8. 15, etc. See also 1 *Kings*, xxii. 34; 2 *Chron.* xviii. 33 and ix. 24.

SCENE VI.—1. *Leavy.* Cf. *Much Ado*, ii. 3. 75, and *Per.* v. 1. 51 (where most modern eds. have "leafy").

2. *Show.* See on i. 3. 54.

4. *Battle.* Battalion. Cf. *J. C.* v. 1. 4, v. 3. 108; *Hen. V.* iv. 3. 69, etc. Holinshed uses the word (see p. 139).

5. *To do.* See Gr. 359, 405. Cf. v. 7. 28 and v. 8. 64.

7. *Do we but find.* See Gr. 364.

10. *Harbingers.* See on i. 4. 45.

SCENE VII.—1. *They have tied*, etc. Delius cites *Lear*, iii. 7. 54: "I am tied to the stake, and I must stand the course." Bear-baiting was a favourite sport in the olden time. The bear was tied to a stake, and a certain number of dogs allowed to attack him at once. Each of these attacks was called a *course.* Steevens quotes Brome, *The Antipodes*, 1638: "You shall see two ten-dog courses at the great bear."

2. *What 's he.* For *what*, see Gr. 254.

4. *Young Siward.* His name was really Osbeorn; but his cousin Siward was slain in the same battle (Moberly).

7. *Than any is.* Any *which* is. See Gr. 244.

17. *Kerns.* See on i. 2. 13. Furness adds here the following (sent to him by Rushton) from Coke, 4 *Inst.* 358: "*Gallowglasses*, equites triarii qui securibus utuntur acutissimis. *Kernes* sunt pedites qui jaculis utuntur."

18. *Staves.* The word *staff* was applied both to the shaft of a lance and to the lance itself. See on v. 3. 48. On *either* as metrically a monosyllable, see Gr. 466. After *thou*, "must be encountered," or something equivalent, is understood.

20. *Undeeded.* Not used elsewhere by S.; and the same is true of *clatter* in the next line. As the C. P. ed. remarks, *Macbeth* is particularly remarkable for the number of these *ἅπαξ λεγόμενα*.

22. *Bruited.* "Announced with noise" (Schmidt); as in *Ham.* i. 2. 127.

24. *Gently.* Readily. Schmidt compares *Temp.* i. 2. 298: "And do my spiriting gently."

27. *Itself professes.* Declares itself.

29. *Strike beside us.* "Strike the air" (Schmidt), or "deliberately miss us" (C. P. ed.). Delius makes it refer to "Macbeth's people who had gone over to the enemy." Cf. 3 *Hen. VI.* ii. 1. 129:

> "Their weapons like to lightning came and went;
> Our soldiers', like the night-owl's lazy flight,
> Or like an idle thresher with a flail,
> Fell gently down, as if they struck their friends."

SCENE VIII.—There is no new scene in the folios.

1. *The Roman fool.* Steevens suggests that this alludes perhaps to Cato, whose suicide is mentioned in *J. C.* v. 1. 101; or it may refer more generally to "the high Roman fashion of self-destruction, as in Brutus, Cassius, Antony, etc." (Sr.).

2. *Whiles.* See on i. 5. 5.

4. *Of all men*, etc. For the "confusion of construction," see Gr. 409.

7. *Bloodier villain*, etc. For the transposition, see on iii. 6. 48.

9. *Easy.* For the adverbial use, see Gr. 1.

Intrenchant. That cannot be cut; the active word in a passive sense. *Trenchant*, as Steevens notes, is used actively in *T. of A.* iv. 3. 115. Upton quotes here *Ham.* i. 1. 146 and iv. 1. 44. Cf. Milton, *P. L.* vi. 348.

13. *Despair.* Not elsewhere used transitively by S. Abbott (Gr. 200) says it is perhaps a Latinism. The verb is similarly used in Ben Jonson's verses prefixed to the folio of 1623:

> "Shine forth, thou Starre of Poets, and with rage,
> Or influence, chide, or cheere the drooping Stage;
> Which, since thy flight frō hence, hath mourn'd like night,
> And despaires day, but for thy Volumes light."

14. *Angel.* Genius, demon (Schmidt); as in *A. and C.* ii. 3. 21. We have *angel* in a bad sense in 2 *Hen. IV.* i. 2. 186; *Lear*, iii. 6. 34; *C. of E.* iv. 3. 20, etc. *Still* = constantly; as often. See Gr. 69.

18. *My better part of man.* Cf. *A. and C.* iv. 6. 39: "my latter part of life," etc. Gr. 423.

20. *Palter.* Equivocate. Cf. *T. and C.* ii. 3. 244; *J. C.* ii. 1. 126, etc.

24. Thus Anthony threatens Cleopatra in *A. and C.* iv. 12. 36. (Delius.)

The time. Cf. i. 5. 61, i. 7. 81, and iv. 3. 72.

26. *Upon a pole.* That is, upon a cloth hung to a pole. No explanation would seem to be needed, but some critics have thought it necessary to change *pole* to "scroll" or "cloth." On *underwrit*, see Gr. 343.

34. *Him.* See Gr. 208.

The stage-direction in the folio here is "*Exeunt fighting. Alarums,*" and then in a new line "*Enter Fighting, and Macbeth slaine.*" This is inconsistent with the stage-direction at line 53: "*Enter Macduffe; with Macbeth's head.*" The C. P. editors think that "this points to some variation in the mode of concluding the play," and that "in all likelihood Shakespeare's part in the play ended here." Fleay believes this to be one of the scenes altered by Middleton.

36. *Go off.* Die; as "take off" = kill, in i. 7. 20 and iii. 1. 104.

40. On *only . . . but*, see Gr. 130.

41. *The which.* Gr. 270. On *prowess* as a monosyllable, see Gr. 470; and on *but* in next line, Gr. 127.

42. *Unshrinking station.* "Unshrinking attitude" (Moberly). Schmidt explains it in the same way. Cf. *Ham.* iii. 4. 58, and *A. and C.* iii. 3. 22, where *station* is similarly used.

48. For the pun on *hairs*, see on ii. 2. 56.

49. *Wish them to.* Wish to them; "the relation of the dative and accusative peculiarly inverted" (Schmidt). For *wish to* = invite, see *T. of S.* i. 1. 113, and cf. *Id.* i. 2. 60, 64. See Holinshed, p. 150 above.

52. *Parted.* Departed, died. Cf. *Hen. V.* ii. 3. 12; *Rich. III.* ii. 1. 5, etc. On *paid his score*, cf. line 39 above.

54. *Stands.* This is explained by Holinshed (see p. 149), who states that the tyrant's head was set upon a pole. The Coll. MS. adds to the stage-direction "on a pike—stick it in the ground."

56. *Pearl.* Rowe substituted "peers," which W. adopts. The C. P. ed. suggests that the word "may be used generically, as well as to express a single specimen," and cites *Hen. V.* iv. 1. 279: "The intertissued robe of gold and pearl." The simplest emendation would seem to be "pearls," suggested in the anonymous "Variorum" ed. of *Macbeth*, 1807.

60. *Expense.* No emendation seems called for, but "expanse," "extent," "excess," etc., have been suggested.

61. *Loves.* Cf. iii. 1. 121 above; also *L. L. L.* v. 2. 793, 798; *W. T* i. 1. 10; *J. C.* iii. 2. 241, etc.

63. *Be earls.* See extract from Holinshed, p. 149 above.

64. *To do.* See on v. 6. 5.

65. *Would.* See Gr. 329; and for *as* in next line, Gr. 113.

66. *Exil'd friends abroad.* See on iii. 6. 48.

68. *Producing forth.* Bringing forward; that is, in a court of justice. Cf. *J. C.* iii. 1. 228: "Produce his body to the market-place." See also *W. T.* iii. 2. 8; *A. W.* iv. 1. 6; *K. John*, i. 1. 46, etc.

70. *Self and violent hands.* Cf. *Rich. II.* iii. 2. 166: "self and vain conceit." Gr. 20.

72. *The grace of Grace.* Theo. remarks that this is a favourite repetition with S. Cf. *T. G. of V.* iii. 1. 146, and *A. W.* ii. 1. 163. See on v. 3. 44.

74. *One.* Rhyming with *Scone.* Cf. *V. and A.* 293, and *Sonn.* 39. 6. See on ii. 1. 49, or Gr. 80.

75. *Scone.* See on ii. 4. 31.

ADDENDA.

Note on INTRODUCTION, p. 12.—In an article in *The Galaxy* for January, 1877 (p. 76), White remarks that the opinion of the Cambridge editors seems to him "to a certain extent sound," though he "cannot go to the length which they do in rejecting parts of the play as not being Shakespeare's work." The passages which he does reject are the following: the speech of Hecate, iii. 5. 2–35, which is "little more than an unmeaning jingle of verses;" the Porter's speeches in ii. 3, which are "low-lived, thoughtless, without any other significance than that of the surface meaning of the poor, gross language in which they are written;" the speech of the First Witch, iv. 1. 125–132, which "seems to be manifestly from the same hand as Hecate's speech," iii. 5. 2–35; and the closing lines of the play, v. 8. 35–75. He adds: "The person who wrote these un-Shakespearian passages was probably Middleton. Shakespeare, writing the tragedy in haste for an occasion, received a little help, according to the fashion of the time, from another playwright; and the latter having imitated the supernatural parts of this play in one of his own, the players or managers afterward introduced from that play songs by him—'Music and a Song, Come away, come away,' iii. 5, and 'Music and a Song, Black Spirits,' etc., iv. 1. This was done to please the inferior part of the audience."

White does not reject i. 2 nor v. 2. The passage on "the evil," iv. 3. 140–159, he believes to have been an interpolation previous to a performance at court, and "probably not Shakespeare's." Of v. 5. 47–50, which the Cambridge editors call "singularly weak" lines (see note, p. 252 above), he says: "The first two have no particular character, nor need they have any, as they merely introduce the last two, which contain an utterance of blank despair and desolation which seems to me more expressive than any other that I ever read."

Note on Lady Macbeth's personal appearance (p. 35).—We may add what Weiss (p. 407) says of "the Mary Stuart of history and the Lady Macbeth of Shakespeare:"

"We know that the former had a delicate exterior, auburn hair, and beaming blue eyes: her tone of speaking was gentle and sweet, excellently soft and low. Mrs. Siddons, whose style and colour were altogether different, became so saturated with Lady Macbeth as to be convinced she must have been a blonde. We think that Shakespeare im plies and justifies this delicate perception, and turns it into history. Both the queens of Scotland represented the kind of blonde women who are fired by sunlight: it crisps the golden or the chestnut hair, becomes quicksilver in the veins, hits every brain-cell with its actinic ray, and chases over the yielding hair in ripples like a blown wheat-field." . . .

The raven himself is hoarse, etc. (p. 170). — Compare James Russell Lowell's remarks on the passage (*Among My Books*, p. 186):

"Here Shakespeare, with his wonted tact, makes use of a vulgar superstition, of a type in which mortal presentiment is already embodied, to make a common ground on which the hearer and Lady Macbeth may meet. After this prelude we are prepared to be possessed by her emotion more fully, to feel in her ears the dull tramp of the blood that seems to make the raven's croak yet hoarser than it is, and to betray the stealthy advance of the mind to its fell purpose. For Lady Macbeth hears not so much the voice of the bodeful bird as of her own premeditated murder, and we are thus made her shuddering accomplices before the fact. Every image receives the colour of the mind, every word throbs with the pulse of one controlling passion. The epithet *fatal* makes us feel the implacable resolve of the speaker, and shows us that she is tampering with her conscience by putting off the crime upon the prophecy of the Weird Sisters to which she alludes. In the word *battlements*, too, not only is the fancy led up to the perch of the raven, but a hostile image takes the place of a hospitable one; for men commonly speak of receiving a guest under their roof or within their doors. When Duncan and Banquo arrive at the castle, their fancies, free from all suggestion of evil, call up only gracious and amiable images. The raven was but the fantastical creation of Lady Macbeth's overwrought brain.

'This castle hath a pleasant seat; the air
Nimbly and sweetly doth commend itself
Unto our gentle senses.
This *guest* of summer,
The *temple-haunting* martlet, doth approve
By his *lov'd mansionry* that the heaven's breath
Smells *wooingly* here; no jutty, frieze,
Buttress, or coign of vantage, but this bird
Hath made his pendent bed and procreant cradle.'

"The contrast here cannot but be as intentional as it is marked. Every image is one of welcome, security, and confidence. The summer, one may well fancy, would be a very different hostess from her whom we have just seen expecting *them*. And why *temple-haunting*, unless because it suggests sanctuary? *O immaginativa, che si ne rubi delle cose di fuor*, how infinitely more precious are the inward ones thou givest in return! If all this be accident, it is at least one of those accidents of which only this man was ever capable."

The multitudinous seas incarnadine (p. 193). Lowell (*Among My Books*, p. 161) remarks that "the huddling epithet implies the tempest-tossed soul of the speaker, and at the same time pictures the wallowing waste of ocean more vividly than the famous phrase of Æschylus [*ἀνήριθμον γέλασμα*] does its rippling sunshine."

THE "TIME-ANALYSIS" OF THE PLAY.—This is summed up by Mr. P. A. Daniel, in his paper "On the Times or Durations of the Action of Shakspere's Plays" (*Transactions of New Shaks. Soc.* 1877–79, p. 207), as follows:

"Time of the Play nine days represented on the stage, and intervals.

Day 1. Act I. sc. i. to iii.
" 2. Act I. sc. iv. to vii.
" 3. Act II. sc. i. to iv.
An interval, say a couple of weeks.
" 4. Act III. sc. i. to v.
[Act III. sc. vi., an impossible time.]
" 5. Act IV. sc. i.
[Professor Wilson supposes an interval of certainly not more than two days between Days 5 and 6; Paton marks two days. The general breathless haste of the play is, I think, against any such interval between Macbeth's purpose and its execution.]
" 6. Act IV. sc. ii.
An interval. Ross's journey to England. Paton allows two weeks.
" 7. Act IV. sc. iii., Act V. sc. i.
An interval. Malcolm's return to Scotland. Three weeks, according to Paton.
" 8. Act V. sc. ii. and iii.
" 9. Act V. sc. iv. to viii."

On i. 3 Mr. Daniel comments as follows: "Ross and Angus come from the King. Ross describes how the news of Macbeth's success reached the King, by post after post. He appears to have entirely forgotten that he himself was the messenger; he however greets Macbeth with the title of Cawdor, and Angus informs Macbeth that Cawdor lies under sentence of death for 'treasons capital,' but whether he was in league with Norway, or with the rebel [Macdonwald], or with both, he knows not. Ross did know when, in the preceding scene, he took the news of the victory to the King; but he also appears to have forgotten it; at any rate he does not betray his knowledge. Macbeth's loss of memory is even more remarkable than Ross's. He doesn't recollect having himself defeated Cawdor but a few short hours—we might say minutes—ago; and the Witches' prophetic greeting of him by that title, and Ross's confirmation of it, fill him with surprise; for, so far as he knows (or *recollects*, shall we say?) the thane of Cawdor lives, a prosperous gentleman."

As to the interval between Days 3 and 4, Mr. Daniel says: "Between Acts II. and III. the long and dismal period of Macbeth's reign described or referred to in Act III. sc. vi., Act IV. sc. ii. and iii., and elsewhere in the play, must have elapsed. Macbeth himself refers to it where, in Act III. sc. iv., speaking of his Thanes, he says:

'There 's not a one of them but in his house
I keep a servant fee'd.'—

And again— 'I am in blood
Stepp'd in so far, that, should I wade no more,
Returning were as tedious as go o'er.'

Yet, almost in the same breath he says—

> 'My strange and self-abuse
> Is the initiate fear *that wants hard use:*
> *We are yet but young in deed.*'

And the first words with which Banquo opens this Act—'Thou hast it now,' etc.—would lead us to suppose that a few days at the utmost can have passed since the coronation at Scone; in the same scene, however, we learn that Malcolm and Donalbain are bestowed in England and in Ireland: some little time must have elapsed before this news could have reached Macbeth. Professor Wilson suggests a week or two for this interval. Mr. Paton would allow three weeks."

Of iii. 6, Mr. Daniel says: "It is impossible to fix the time of this scene. In it 'Lenox and another Lord' discuss the position of affairs. The murder of Banquo and the flight of Fleance are known to Lenox, and he knows that Macduff lives in disgrace because he was not at the feast, but that is the extent of his knowledge. The other Lord informs him that Macbeth did send to Macduff, and that Macduff has fled to England to join Malcolm. And that thereupon Macbeth 'prepares for some attempt of war.' All this supposes the lapse, at the very least, of a day or two since the night of Macbeth's banquet; but in the next scene to this we find we have only arrived at the early morning following the banquet, up to which time the murder of Banquo could not have been known; nor had Macbeth sent to Macduff, nor was the flight of the latter known. The scene in fact is an impossibility in any scheme of time, and I am compelled therefore to place it within brackets.—See Professor Wilson's amusing account of this 'miraculous' scene in the fifth part of *Dies Boreales* [reprinted in *New Shaks. Soc. Trans. for* 1875–76, pp. 351–58]."

INDEX OF WORDS EXPLAINED.

FINIS

From F. J. FURNIVALL, *Director of the New Shakspere Society, London.*

The merit I see in Mr. Rolfe's school editions of Shakspere's Plays over those most widely used in England is that Mr. Rolfe edits the plays as works of a poet, and not only as productions in Tudor English. Some editors think that all they have to do with a play is to state its source and explain its hard words and allusions; they treat it as they would a charter or a catalogue of household furniture, and then rest satisfied. But Mr. Rolfe, while clearing up all verbal difficulties as carefully as any Dryasdust, always adds the choicest extracts he can find, on the spirit and special "note" of each play, and on the leading characteristics of its chief personages. He does *not* leave the student without help in getting at Shakspere's chief attributes, his characterization and poetic power. And every practical teacher knows that while every boy can look out hard words in a lexicon for himself, not one in a score can, unhelped, catch points of and realize character, and feel and express the distinctive individuality of each play as a poetic creation.

From Prof. EDWARD DOWDEN, LL.D., *of the University of Dublin, Author of "Shakspere: His Mind and Art."*

I incline to think that no edition is likely to be so useful for school and home reading as yours. Your notes contain so much accurate instruction, with so little that is superfluous; you do not neglect the æsthetic study of the plays; and in externals, paper, type, binding, etc., you make a book "pleasant to the eye" (as well as "to be desired to make one wise")—no small matter, I think, with young readers and with old.

From EDWIN A. ABBOTT, M.A., *Author of "Shakespearian Grammar."*

I have not seen any edition that compresses so much necessary information into so small a space, nor any that so completely avoids the common faults of commentaries on Shakespeare—needless repetition, superfluous explanation, and unscholar-like ignoring of difficulties.

From HIRAM CORSON, M.A., *Professor of Anglo-Saxon and English Literature, Cornell University, Ithaca, N. Y.*

In the way of annotated editions of separate plays of Shakespeare for educational purposes, I know of none quite up to Rolfe's.

From Prof. F. J. CHILD, *of Harvard University.*

I read your "Merchant of Venice" with my class, and found it in every respect an excellent edition. I do not agree with my friend White in the opinion that Shakespeare requires but few notes—that is, if he is to be thoroughly understood. Doubtless he may be enjoyed, and many a hard place slid over. Your notes give all the help a young student requires, and yet the reader for pleasure will easily get at just what he wants. You have indeed been conscientiously concise.

Under date of July 25, 1879, Prof. CHILD *adds:* Mr. Rolfe's editions of plays of Shakespeare are very valuable and convenient books, whether for a college class or for private study. I have used them with my students, and I welcome every addition that is made to the series. They show care, research, and good judgment, and are fully up to the time in scholarship. I fully agree with the opinion that experienced teachers have expressed of the excellence of these books.

From Rev. A. P. PEABODY, D.D., *Professor in Harvard University.*

I regard your own work as of the highest merit, while you have turned the labors of others to the best possible account. I want to have the higher classes of our schools introduced to Shakespeare chief of all, and then to other standard English authors; but this cannot be done to advantage unless under a teacher of equally rare gifts and abundant leisure, or through editions specially prepared for such use. I trust that you will have the requisite encouragement to proceed with a work so happily begun.

From the Examiner and Chronicle, N. Y.

We repeat what we have often said, that there is no edition of Shakespeare which seems to us preferable to Mr. Rolfe's. As mere specimens of the printer's and binder's art they are unexcelled, and their other merits are equally high. Mr. Rolfe, having learned by the practical experience of the class-room what aid the average student really needs in order to read Shakespeare intelligently, has put just that amount of aid into his notes, and no more. Having said what needs to be said, he stops there. It is a rare virtue in the editor of a classic, and we are proportionately grateful for it.

From the N. Y. Times.

This work has been done so well that it could hardly have been done better. It shows throughout knowledge, taste, discriminating judgment, and, what is rarer and of yet higher value, a sympathetic appreciation of the poet's moods and purposes.

From the Pacific School Journal, San Francisco.

This edition of Shakespeare's plays bids fair to be the most valuable aid to the study of English literature yet published. For educational purposes it is beyond praise. Each of the plays is printed in large clear type and on excellent paper. Every difficulty of the text is clearly explained by copious notes. It is remarkable how many new beauties one may discern in Shakespeare with the aid of the glossaries attached to these books. . . . Teachers can do no higher, better work than to inculcate a love for the best literature, and such books as these will best aid them in cultivating a pure and refined taste.

From the Christian Union, N. Y.

Mr. W. J. Rolfe's capital edition of Shakespeare . . . by far the best edition for school and parlor use. We speak after some practical use of it in a village Shakespeare Club. The notes are brief but useful ; and the necessary expurgations are managed with discriminating skill.

From the Academy, London.

Mr. Rolfe's excellent series of school editions of the Plays of Shakespeare. . . . They differ from some of the English ones in looking on the plays as something more than word-puzzles. They give the student helps and hints on the characters and meanings of the plays, while the word-notes are also full and posted up to the latest date. . . . Mr. Rolfe also adds to each of his books a most useful "Index of Words and Phrases Explained."

THOMAS GRAY.

SELECT POEMS OF THOMAS GRAY. Edited, with Notes, by WILLIAM J. ROLFE, A.M., formerly Head Master of the High School, Cambridge, Mass. Illustrated. Square 16mo, Paper, 40 cents; Cloth, 56 cents (*Uniform with Rolfe's Shakespeare.*)

Mr. Rolfe has done his work in a manner that comes as near to perfection as man can approach. He knows his subject so well that he is competent to instruct all in it; and readers will find an immense amount of knowledge in his elegant volume, all set forth in the most admirable order, and breathing the most liberal and enlightened spirit, he being a warm appreciator of the divinity of genius.—*Boston Traveller.*

The great merit of these books lies in their carefully edited text, and in the fulness of their explanatory notes. Mr. Rolfe is not satisfied with simply expounding, but he explores the entire field of English literature, and therefrom gathers a multitude of illustrations that are interesting in themselves and valuable as a commentary on the text. He not only instructs, but stimulates his readers to fresh exertion; and it is this stimulation that makes his labor so productive in the school-room.—*Saturday Evening Gazette*, Boston.

Mr. William J. Rolfe, to whom English literature is largely indebted for annotated and richly illustrated editions of several of Shakespeare's Plays, has treated the "Select Poems of Thomas Gray" in the same way—just as he had previously dealt with the best of Goldsmith's poems.—*Philadelphia Press.*

Mr. Rolfe's edition of Thomas Gray's select poems is marked by the same discriminating taste as his other classics.—*Springfield Republican.*

Mr. Rolfe's rare abilities as a teacher and his fine scholarly tastes enable him to prepare a classic like this in the best manner for school use. There could be no better exercise for the advanced classes in our schools than the critical study of our best authors, and the volumes that Mr. Rolfe has prepared will hasten the time when the study of mere form will give place to the study of the spirit of our literature.—*Louisville Courier-Journal.*

An elegant and scholarly little volume.—*Christian Intelligencer*, N. Y

ROBERT BROWNING.

A BLOT IN THE 'SCUTCHEON AND OTHER DRAMAS. By ROBERT BROWNING. Edited, with notes, by WILLIAM J. ROLFE, A.M., and HELOISE E. HERSEY. With Portrait. 16mo, Paper, 40 cents; Cloth, 56 cents. *(Uniform with Rolfe's Shakespeare.)*

Prepared in the same thorough manner as the previous volume upon the Select Poems of the same author and the numerous manuals of Mr. Rolfe. No poet needs, for the average reader, such an interpretation as is here given more than Browning. Read carefully, with reference to the notes of the editors, the richness of the great poet's thoughts and fancies will be the better apprehended.—*Zion's Herald*, Boston.

Out of the eight dramas which the poet wrote between 1837 and 1845 the three most characteristic ones have been selected, and a full idea of his dramatic power may be gained from them. A synopsis of critical opinions of Mr. Browning's works is included in the volume. The same careful scholarship that marked Professor Rolfe's editions of Shakespeare is shown in this edition of Browning. The lovers of the poet will be pleased to have old favorites in this attractive form, while many new readers will be attracted to the author by it. Robert Browning will fill a larger space in the world's eye in the future than he has done already. —*Brooklyn Union.*

The introduction and notes are all that could be desired.—*N. Y. Sun.*

The book itself is not only a compact compilation of the three plays, but it is valuable for the commentatory notes. The editing work has been done in an able manner by Professor Rolfe and Miss Hersey, who has gained a high place among the modern Browning students.—*Philadelphia Bulletin.*

This dainty volume, with flexible covers and red edges, contains not merely Browning's dramas, with the author's latest emendations and corrections, but notes and estimates, critical and explanatory, in such volume, and from sources so exalted, that we have not the temerity to add one jot or tittle to the aggregate.—*N. Y. Commercial Advertiser.*
